# International and Comparative

# Human Resource Management

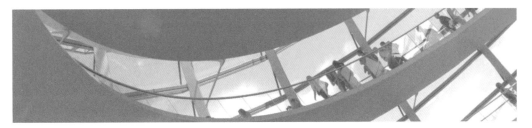

# International and Comparative Human Resource Management

Graham Hollinshead

## McGraw-Hill
## Higher Education

London    Boston    Burr Ridge, IL    Dubugue, WI    New York    San Francisco
St. Louis  Bangkok  Bogotá  Caracas  Kuala Lumpur  Lisbon  Madrid  Mexico City
Milan  Montreal  New Delhi  Santiago  Seoul  Singapore  Sydney  Taipei  Toronto

International and Comparative Human Resource Management
Graham Hollinshead
ISBN-13 978-0-07-712160-0
ISBN-10 0-07-712160-0

## McGraw-Hill
## Higher Education

Published by McGraw-Hill Education
Shoppenhangers Road
Maidenhead
Berkshire
SL6 2QL
Telephone: 44 (0) 1628 502 500
Fax: 44 (0) 1628 770 224
Website: *www.mcgraw-hill.co.uk*

British Library Cataloging in Publication Data
A catalogue record for this book is available from the British Library

Library of Congress Cataloging in Publication Data
The Library of Congress data for this book has been applied for from the Library of Congress

Senior Commissioning Editor: Rachel Gear
Head of Development: Caroline Prodger
Development Editor: Emma Gain
Marketing Director: Alice Duijser
Production Editor: Louise Caswell

Text Design by Ken Vail Design
Cover design by Adam Renvoize
Printed and bound in the UK by Bell and Bain Ltd, Glasgow

ISBN-13 978-0-07-712160-0
ISBN-10 0-07-712160-0

The McGraw-Hill Companies

# Brief Table of Contents

# Detailed Table of Contents

# Preface

Issues in the management of people across borders have become a central concern not only for students, but for practitioners in private and public concerns, for policy makers, and many other interested groupings in recent years. In an era of intensifying international business activity, it is evident that challenges confronting managers and employees engaged in many forms of enterprise emanate not only from the nation state, but also from well beyond it, frequently in an unpredictable fashion.

A starting proposition for this text is that the internationalization of management activity potentially carries with it considerable complexity, ambiguity and risk. Familiar practices and unquestioned assumptions may appear to be less reliable as organizations move into the international 'unknown'.

Two main analytical trajectories are therefore pursued in order to enhance understanding of managing human resources in an international context. The first, *international*, refers to the strategic and staffing dilemmas associated with managing the international enterprise. Here focus is placed on multinational corporations and optimal arrangements for deployment of staff in 'parent' and 'subsidiary' operations, embracing the exigencies for intercultural working. The second, *comparative*, relates to grounded institutional and cultural facets of national 'business systems' in which international business is increasingly occurring. A guiding premise for this text is that as globalization engenders more distant organizational interconnections, comparative insight becomes more indispensable.

The aim of this book is to convey in accessible form critical facts and arguments relating to the contemporary discourse of international human resource management (IHRM). Material is presented in a reader-friendly fashion and is suitable for undergraduate and postgraduate students. Features include learning objectives, summaries, suggested activities and recommended readings and websites for assimilation of further factual materials relating to major themes. Case studies and scenarios are also provided based on the author's original research. For more information see the **Guided Tour** to the main features of the book on page x.

**Part 1 – *Introduction and the Global Context*** – addresses key concepts underlying the study of IHRM, commencing with an analysis of its nature and significance. Reference is then made to the institutional and cultural bedrocks that promote international diversity in management and organizational practices. This part also explores the effects of globalization that serve to 'make the world smaller' and the pivotal role of multinational corporations as global players impacting on economy and employment.

**Part 2 – *International Themes*** – 'goes inside' the multinational corporation (MNC) to explore the critical strategic relationship between 'parent' and 'subsidiary' and consequent staffing decisions. The vital issue of corporate social responsibility (CSR) is also addressed. Subsequently, an in-depth analysis of the staffing the MNC is embarked on, encompassing the selection of international assignees, training, pay, performance management and repatriation. The policy areas associated with international staffing are tackled in a fashion that highlights 'real' as well as 'best' practice, and potential risks and pitfalls associated with expatriation are considered.

**Part 3** – *Comparative Themes and Regional Studies* – comprises an analysis of a range of regional and national contexts that may constitute the territory for international engagement. Although primary focus is on the leading global economic triad of Europe, North America and Japan, including an investigation of primary employment relations features of these regions, our cross-national overview also incorporates some perhaps under-explored settings, including Mexico, China, central and eastern Europe and India.

Graham Hollinshead
May 2009

# Guided Tour

## Learning Objectives and Introductions
Each chapter opens with a set of objectives to help you to navigate through the chapters, plus an overview which helps to introduce the key ideas you will learn about in the chapter.

## Boxed Examples and Case Studies
Short example boxes provide scenarios from real research or HRM practice, illustrating the concepts that are presented throughout the chapter. Two longer case studies take a closer look at a particular issue in IHRM, providing a real-life business case. Questions ask you to reflect on the ideas raised by the case.

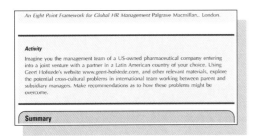

## Activities
Each chapter features a short activity. This poses a question on how you might tackle a particular issue as a practising manager, or how you could apply the theory explained in the chapter. This can be used in a classroom setting or as an exercise for reflection.

## Summaries and Further Reading
Each chapter concludes with a summary of key points, and an annotated list of further readings, references and websites for extra information and as a source for student research projects.

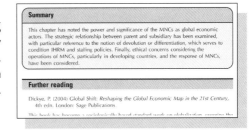

# For lecturers:
# Technology to enhance
# learning and teaching

*Visit* ***www.mcgraw-hill.co.uk/textbooks/hollinshead*** *today*

Online Learning Centre (OLC)

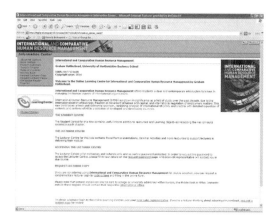

An Online Learning Centre website is available for lecturers who adopt this textbook for their teaching. The website offers lecturers the following useful resources to help them deliver an effective International Human Resource Management module:

- Seminar activities providing ideas, tips and resources for lecturers
- PowerPoint Slides for use in lecture presentations and as handouts
- Additional resources for teaching

The website also provides Learning Objectives and links to additional resources for students.

# Custom Publishing Solutions: Let us help make our content your solution

At McGraw-Hill Education our aim is to help lecturers to find the most suitable content for their needs delivered to their students in the most appropriate way. Our custom publishing solutions offer the ideal combination of content delivered in the way which best suits lecturer and students.

Our custom publishing programme offers lecturers the opportunity to select just the chapters or sections of material they wish to deliver to their students from a database called Primis at www.primisonline.com.

Primis contains over two million pages of content from:

- textbooks
- professional books
- case books – Harvard Articles, Insead, Ivey, Darden, Thunderbird and BusinessWeek
- Taking Sides – debate materials

Across the following imprints:

- McGraw-Hill Education
- Open University Press
- Harvard Business School Press
- US and European material

There is also the option to include additional material authored by lecturers in the custom product – this does not necessarily have to be in English.

We will take care of everything from start to finish in the process of developing and delivering a custom product to ensure that lecturers and students receive exactly the material needed in the most suitable way.

With a Custom Publishing Solution, students enjoy the best selection of material deemed to be the most suitable for learning everything they need for their courses – something of real value to support their learning. Teachers are able to use exactly the material they want, in the way they want, to support their teaching on the course.

Please contact your local McGraw-Hill representative with any questions or alternatively contact Warren Eels e: warren_eels@mcgraw-hill.com.

# Make the grade!

# 30% off any Study Skills book!

Our Study Skills books are packed with practical advice and tips that are easy to put into practice and will really improve the way you study. Topics include:

- Techniques to help you pass exams
- Advice to improve your essay writing
- Help in putting together the perfect seminar presentation
- Tips on how to balance studying and your personal life

## www.openup.co.uk/studyskills

Visit our website to read helpful hints about essays, exams, dissertations and much more.

**Special offer!** As a valued customer, buy online and receive 30% off any of our Study Skills books by entering the promo code **getahead**

# Acknowledgements

Thanks to the following reviewers for their invaluable comments on the manuscript:

Susan Shortland, London Metropolitan University
Brian Good, University of Surrey
Birgitta Fletcher-Tomenius, University of Birmingham
Dr Pauline Grace, Dublin City University
David Walsh, Nottingham Trent University
Charles Leatherbarrow, University of Wolverhampton
Dr Anita Hammer, De Montford University
Mike Leat, University of Plymouth
Pawan Budhwar, University of Aston
Damian Hodgson, Manchester Business School
Jakob Lauring, Aarhus School of Business
Linda Clarke, University of Westminster
Ulke Veersma, University of Greenwich
Aikaterini Koskina, University of Sunderland
Dr Alhajie Saidy-Khan, Keele University
Alison Moraes, Royal Holloway University of London
Dr Mathew Flynn, Middlesex University
Christine Porter, University of Westminster

The author also thanks the editorial team at McGraw-Hill for its effective and supportive contribution.

Every effort has been made to trace and acknowledge ownership of copyright and to clear permission for material reproduced in this book. The publishers will be pleased to make suitable arrangements to clear permission with any copyright holders whom it has not been possible to contact. We would like to thank the following for their permission to reproduce material in this textbook:
Pearson Education Ltd (p. 9), Ronald Inglehart (p. 36), Palgrave Macmillan (p. 40–1), Academy of Management Review (p. 81), Eurofound (pp. 110, 114, 116, 120–2, 130 and 169), Elsevier (p. 169–71) Ashgate (p. 201).

# About the Author

**Graham Hollinshead** is Reader in International Human Resource Management at the University of Hertfordshire Business School. He teaches International and Comparative Human Resource Management and related topics at postgraduate and undergraduate levels. He is a Chartered Fellow of the Institute of Personnel and Development. His major research interests relate to organizational transformation in post-socialist societies, power and politics in multinational corporations and cross-cultural issues in joint ventures. He has been engaged as a consultant by the German assistance agency, the GTZ, and the UN-sponsored European Center for Peace and Development (ECPD) in programmes designed to upgrade management capacities in Serbia.

Previous texts include Hollinshead, G., Nicholls, P. and Tailby, S. (eds) (2003) *Employee Relations*, FT Prentice Hall, 2nd edn. (first edition published in 1999), and Hollinshead, G. and Leat, M. (1995) *Human Resource Management: An International and Comparative Perspective*, FT Pearson.

# PART 01
# Introduction and the Global Context

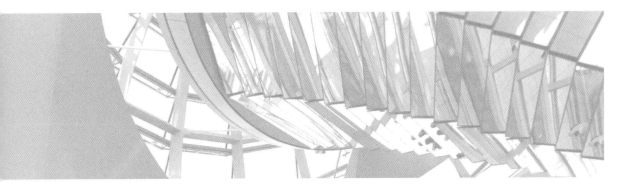

1

# CHAPTER 01

# International human resource management: its growth and significance

❖ *LEARNING OBJECTIVES*

❖ To appreciate the complexities of studying and practising international human resource management (IHRM)

❖ To define the subject matter of IHRM

❖ To identify the potential benefits and pitfalls associated with comparative study

❖ To appreciate international, regional and national 'levels of analysis' pertaining to

the operations of multinational corporations (MNCs)

❖ To consider how 'globalization ' impacts on IHRM

❖ To gain insight into contemporary developments in offshoring with reference to the financial services sector

## Introduction: what is IHRM?

International Human Resource Management (IHRM) is a relatively new field of study, the emergence and popularity of which has occurred since the early to mid-1990s. While IHRM represents something of a new departure in the study of business and social sciences, its academic orientation is fundamentally conditioned by its 'root' discipline of human resource management (HRM), which has possessed mainstream appeal since the early 1980s. The literature on HRM has rotated around the 'enlightened' organizational notion that employees represent 'valued assets' and that their deployment in a 'smart' and strategic fashion will pay not only corporate, but also national, dividends (Beer et al.,1984).

HRM has emphasized the pivotal themes of 'strategic integration', that is, enmeshing policies for the recruitment, training, payment and severance of staff with overarching corporate strategies, 'flexibility', which refers to the need to finely-tune the staff resource base with an eye to business needs, and 'quality', which recognizes the strength of the connection between employee competence and commitment and organizational outputs in terms of products and services (Guest, 1988). New management thinking concerning HRM has frequently emanated from the USA (Hollinshead and Leat, 1995) and is associated with the business drive to become 'closer to the customer' in an ever-intensifying competitive environment (ibid.). As Table 1.1 illustrates, the functional areas associated with IHRM may be correlated with 'standard' HRM activities, although, in the case of the former, there are clearly greater degrees of ambiguity and risk as internationalization may be regarded as something of a step 'into the unknown'.

While the primary concerns of IHRM remain apparent in the internationalized business environment, including the flexible utilization of human resources, a further layer of managerial skills is necessitated as companies straddle national boundaries in the era of globalization. Briscoe and Schuler (2004) assert that IHRM is potentially ambivalent and complicated as it demands:

1 responsibility for a greater number and complexity, of activities, including managing expatriation;
2 a broadening of expertise to include knowledge of foreign countries, employment laws, and so on;
3 involvement with a greater mix of employees;
4 coping with external influences and multiple cultures;
5 greater involvement in employees' lives, particularly in the case of expatriation;
6 ability to manage difficulties and risk, particularly if a subsidiary is being established in a developing country.

The added complexities of IHRM are delineated in Table 1.1, which reviews typical areas of 'standard' HRM (column 1) and then transposes these into potential international functional requirements (column 2).

Table 1.1 demonstrates that IHRM may indeed constitute an intriguing and challenging area for study and practice. If a company is planning to internationalize it may need, for example, to obtain information concerning skill availability, demographics and rates of pay in the host country environment. If recruiting, training or paying staff in the subsidiary location, expectations confronting the international company may be powerfully conditioned by structures, norms and values 'embedded' in local labour market and other circumstances. If a US-owned MNC is operating in Germany, it cannot assume that taken-for-granted approaches to non-unionism can be transposed to an institutional context in which 'social partnership' arrangements between management and trade unions have been the norm, and in which the worker consultation is a legal requirement. Moreover, once a company internationalizes, it will need to address vital questions and strategic dilemmas concerning international staffing. Should the subsidiary of an international company be managed by home or host country nationals? If the former, what are the recruitment and training corporate obligations to ensure international assignees are fully effective and comfortable in different cultural settings? If the latter, then how can this grouping be effectively coordinated and controlled?

**Table 1.1  Functional differences between HRM and IHRM**

| HRM function | International HRM complexity |
| --- | --- |
| *Human resource planning* – matching staff resources to the anticipated direction of the business, whether diversifying, expanding or contracting. Mapping future staffing needs, in terms of quantity and quality of human resources, by examining trends in retirement, turnover, and so on. This function represents a conceptual lynchpin of HRM as it (ideally) forms the basis for decisions concerning recruitment, training and staff severance | *International HR planning* – understanding labour market trends in the host (i.e. subsidiary as opposed to home 'parent') country environment. Obtaining and acting on data concerning skill availability, demographics (age, gender, racial mix) surrounding the subsidiary and market rates of pay. Awareness of indigenous laws impacting on recruitment or severance processes that may constrain desired policy in these areas. Planning for management (and worker) mobility between parent and subsidiary, and across subsidiary operations in order to meet international business needs. Dealing with higher degrees of risk and less predictability in the political, economic and social environment, particularly in developing countries |
| *Recruitment* – sourcing staff from local or national labour markets to fill vacancies or enhance the staffing complement. Recruitment will incorporate the processes of **selection** and **induction** or **socialization**, the former referring to the techniques used to screen and identify suitable candidates (e.g. interviews, psychometric tests) and the latter to the preliminary developmental action taken to ensure the new recruit is incorporated into the corporate ethos and is familiarized with job requirements | *International recruitment* – gaining familiarity with educational and training qualifications in the host country, and with varying international approaches to recruitment and selection. If recruiting staff for overseas vacancies, that is, recruiting potential expatriates, testing for appropriate qualities and competences; for example, language skills, cross-cultural sensitivity and personal adaptability |
| *Training and development* – enhancing the skills, knowledge and competence base of the organization either through in-house training initiatives, or through supporting staff in attending educational/professional development institutions. In recent years training and development emphasis has tended to shift from 'harder' technical skills towards 'softer' competences such as customer responsiveness, leadership, effective communication, and so on | *International training and development* – if a company is straddling international boundaries, gaining awareness of diverse institutional approaches to training and development in the national systems in question. This may, for example, relate to the extent of active collaboration between educational and work establishments, and more generally to the level of national or corporate investment in training and education. If preparing international managers for assignments overseas, a distinctive set of training needs is likely to emerge relating to competence in intercultural working and communication |

| | |
|---|---|
| *Pay* – structuring pay relativities within the enterprise taking account of labour market rates. As appropriate, negotiating collective rates of pay with trade unions and other employee representatives. A growing trend in pay has been to link it with individual, group or corporate performance | *International pay and reward* – understanding various national pay structures and philosophies in host national environments. Thus, for example, in some countries the state has a major role in pay determination, thus lessening corporate discretion in the formulation of pay. Moreover, notions of 'fairness' in reward vary from region to region, with certain global regions (e.g. Scandinavia) leaning towards egalitarianism, while others (e.g. the USA) tolerate significant differentiation. In the area of international staffing and expatriation, a major policy issue confronting the international company is whether to pay the expatriate 'home' rates while undertaking an assignment overseas, or whether to adjust the pay package to take account of local conditions |
| *Performance management* – seeking to enhance employee motivation and formulating policies and practices to ensure that managers (and workers) are 'adding value' to corporate operations. A frequently used mechanism for performance management is the performance appraisal interview, which is a periodic structured discussion between manager and subordinate focusing specifically on areas of strength and weakness in the interviewee's performance and formulating corrective measures through proposed developmental activity | *International performance management* – in the case of expatriation, complications arise as a result of physical distance of the international assignee from the parent. Face-to-face communications between manager and subordinate are potentially rendered problematic. If responsibility for managing expatriate performance is delegated to a line manager in the host country difficulties may occur in defining accurate and objective criteria for success (or failure) across cultural boundaries |
| *Employee consultation and involvement* – involving disclosure of information and potentially sharing of corporate decisions with trade union, or other employee, representatives. Employee consultation may be obliged by law on certain corporate issues, and many organizations regard the establishment of effective systems for collective employee involvement as a prerequisite to high employee commitment and corporate success | *International consultative obligations* – legal and corporate obligations concerning employee involvement and participation vary quite considerably from country to country. In the USA, for example, as a dominant structural feature is non-unionism, companies have considerable discretion concerning the principle and form of employee involvement. By way of contrast, in Germany, works councils are obliged by law at shop floor level. Accordingly, managers are bound to gain the consent of worker representatives on policies affecting their working lives (e.g. recruitment, job changes, layoffs) prior to their implementation. A concern of IHRM is therefore the possible need for MNCs to adapt consultative procedures to the prevailing institutional circumstances affecting the subsidiary |

Close reading of the second column in Table 1.1 reveals that two major trajectories of thought and action are apparent in IHRM. The first concerns the need to manage the careers of expatriates and others in the context of the international organization. This brings into play issues such as international team working and cross-cultural management, and applies the repertoire of HRM techniques (e.g. recruitment, pay, training, communications) to managing the international enterprise. The second demands knowledge of specific host country contexts (regarding political, economic and social environments, as well as embedded HR and employment systems) as a prerequisite of managing the relationship with host operations in a productive and sensitive fashion. Following from the title of this book, the first trajectory can be described as *international*, while the second can be defined as *comparative*.

> The *international* trajectory may be referred to as the study of human resource policies and practices in multinational enterprises. This involves strategic considerations in formulating policies (e.g. recruitment, training and reward) affecting the staffing of headquarters and subsidiaries in international enterprises. A central focus of this approach has been on expatriation.
>
> The *comparative* trajectory refers to the investigation of embedded contexts, policies and practices in specific national and regional domains. This might be referred to as the '*National Geographic*' perspective as it concerns 'terrains' of organizational and employment structures and practices as conditioned by indigenous socio-political and economic factors.

Holden (1997) points out that IHRM can be studied in an organizational and comparative context. This has been acknowledged in definitions of IHRM, notably, as provided by Boxall (1995: 6), who states that IHRM is 'concerned with the human resource problems of multinational firms in foreign subsidiaries (such as expatriate management) or, more broadly, with the HR issues that are associated with the various stages of the internationalisation process.'

Holden (ibid.) identifies various 'schools of thought' in the approach to the study of IHRM.

The first is derived from the burgeoning literature on international business (e.g. Bartlett and Ghoshal; 1989, Gauri and Prasad, 1995; Hodgetts and Luthans, 2003) and places a focus on the strategic orientation of MNCs, but also includes consideration of IHRM and employment issues, for example expatriation. The second is concerned with IHRM mainly at a country, or region, specific level; for example investigations into 'HRM in Europe' and other regions (Brewster and Harris, 1999; Budhwar and Yaw, 2001; Kamoche et al., 2004). The third, which may be regarded as somewhat tangential to the 'mainstream', relates to comparative and employment and industrial relations issues (e.g. Bean, 1994; Eaton, 2000; Hyman and Ferner, 1994). A fourth approach, which is widely in evidence, deals with primarily organizational issues , locating IHRM in MNCs, and exploring strategies of the organization relating to factors such as succession, expatriation, recruitment, selection, appraisal, reward, training and development (Briscoe and Schuler; Dowling and Welch, 2004). A final stream, although frequently not labelled as IHRM, impinges onto the subject by dealing with culture and acculturation, often with reference to MNCs and their staffing (Hofstede, 1994; Jackson, 2002; Tayeb, 2005).

Recently, the links between IHRM and business strategy have been emphasized, in the context of the growth of international alliances being fostered by MNCs. Thus, Schuler (2000) brings to the fore of analysis the challenge confronting MNCs in seeking to control and coordinate foreign subsidiaries while engendering adaptation to the host environment. As Scullion and Linehan (2005) assert, recent definitions have been extended to cover localization of management, international coordination, global leadership development and the emerging cultural challenges of global knowledge management.

We should also note a growing body of literature on the subjects of 'knowledge transfer' and 'cross-cultural management', which potentially posseses explanatory value in investigating the challenge of managing people across borders. According to Burton-Jones

(1999), managerial knowledge may be regarded as a form of capital which transcends firms, industries and national boundaries. Thus an international joint venture may be represented in terms of its potential for engendering transfer of knowledge primarily from parent to subsidiary, and also across subsidiaries and from subsidiaries to parent. Such knowledge may relate to state-of-the-art systems in strategy, finance, marketing, production, technology and other managerial functions, which imply the need for learning across the MNC. It is also possible that institutionally or culturally based factors serve to constrain or modify the flow of knowledge from country to country in circumstances where 'western'-based managerial knowledge is transposed into transitional or developing economic settings. Similarly, in the growing number of cross-cultural encounters between groups of managers in various international settings, the possession of differing fields of knowledge by these groupings, depending on their internationally grounded positions, will provide scope for mutual learning as well as the possibility of misunderstanding, and will contribute to relative positions of power.

A well-defined occupational grouping of international human resource managers has yet to be established. Nevertheless, following Briscoe and Schuler (2004), it is clear that IHRM may be subject to two major functional structures.

First, IHRM activity may be located in the headquarters of the parent corporation, engaging in matters such as selecting and training expatriates, determining expatriate pay and benefits packages and establishing HR policies and practices for foreign operations.

Second, managers with responsibility for IHRM may operate in the subsidiary operation; for example, the local facility of Hewlett Packard in Belgium. Here, the concern of practitioners would be the integration of the philosophies and practices of the parent into indigenous operations. Accordingly, for example, US expectations concerning corporate communications may need to be renegotiated to comply with Belgian employment regulations and prevailing norms and values.

As a third, 'catch-all' category, it may be asserted that all managers, and indeed other professional groupings, are being required to manage internationalism as globalization impacts on all walks of everyday life. So, for example, restaurants, building contractors, insurance companies and educational establishments may be involved in recruiting migrant workers, sourcing supplies from overseas, or being subject to a foreign takeover. In such circumstances, cross-cultural awareness and sensitivity is becoming a vital organizational skill.

## Levels of analysis

Following Edwards and Rees (2006), it is possible to identify 'levels of analysis' in understanding patterns of influence on IHRM strategies and practices. While it is recognized that the rapid pace of internationalization of business provides the global backdrop for IHRM, it should be borne in mind that specific HR policies are invariably formulated by independent actors at enterprise or organizational level. Such actors may be portrayed, however, as operating across and within the patterns of influence exerted from three concentric geographical spheres (see Figure 1.1). Thus, as Edwards and Rees ibid. suggest, the reality of practice in IHRM may be understood by considering the interplay of factors situated at *global, regional, national* and *organizational* levels.

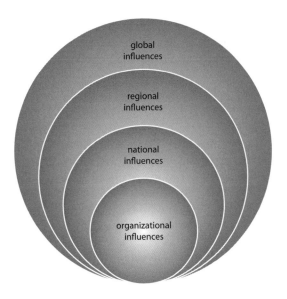

**FIGURE 1.1**  Levels of analysis of IHRM

Source: Edwards and Rees (2006).
Harlow: Prentice Hall. Reproduced with permission from Pearson Education Limited.

### Global/international

The 'globalization effect' (Edwards and Rees, 2006) manifests a set of universal influences on organizations regardless of their geographical location. Of note is the new global electronic economy in which 'fund managers, banks, corporations, as well as millions of individual investors can transfer vast amounts of money from one side of the world to another with the click of a mouse' (Giddens, 2002: 9). A further factor that has revolutionized and universalized the international context for business has been the growth of new forms of information technology (IT) and satellite-based communications; these have facilitated an instantaneous flow of information from one side of the world to another. As mentioned above, MNCs are dominant actors in the global environment and frequently serve as conduits for the dispersion of new technologies and ideas across national boundaries. A related concept is that of 'Americanization', which refers to the transposition of US norms and standards as the 'benchmark' for development in other global regions; this process has frequently been driven by US-owned MNCs. Associated with globalization has also been the emergence of a transnational cadre of managers and knowledge workers who have been highly mobile in controlling subsidiary operations and disseminating corporate know-how in overseas localities.

### Regional

While globalization offers a generic reference point for observed changes in international business activity, closer scrutiny of the dynamics of global investment and trade tend to concentrate on three global regions, namely, North America, western Europe and East Asia. These blocs represent a 'triad' of global economic powerhouses, the bulk of international trade occurring either between them, or within them (Edwards and Rees, 2006). Moves towards regionalization have been consolidated by the regulatory frameworks and the freeing of trade inherent in the European Union (EU) and North American Free Trade Agreement (NAFTA). Moreover, identification of indigenous organizations with regional, as opposed to global, reference points may be cemented by cultural bonds fostered by geographical proximity and historical legacy.

## National

The third tier of analysis is the nation state, which in many cases continues to provide the primary source of 'identity' to indigenous organizations. In a real sense, the regulatory, institutional and cultural frameworks inherent in national systems powerfully mould strategies and structures of business and other organizations. According to Whitley (2002), variations in 'business systems' can be found from country to country or from region to region, a business system comprising of a collection of institutions in a society or economy that shape transactions, cooperation and control within and between business organizations. Critically, forms of ownership and corporate governance vary across national systems, thus affecting the propensity of companies to take a longer-term view of investment prospects, including investment in human resources, or to emphasize profitability in the short term. This theme is developed in Chapter 2. Theories of culture (e.g Hofstede, 1994; Trompenaars and Hampden-Turner, 1997) also place a primary focus on the nation state, suggesting that country-specific norms and values guide the behaviour of individual and organizational subjects.

## Organizational

Fourth, the organizational effect recognizes that companies and other commercial and non-commercial concerns, in the context of the parameters exerted by the above three effects, are able to formulate strategies in an autonomous fashion. MNCs, in particular, however, will invariably be subject to cultural and institutional influences at national, regional and global levels. As Dicken (2003: 20) states:

> 66 An especially important bounded territorial form in which production networks are embedded is that of the *state*. All the elements in the production network are regulated within some kind of political structure whose basic unit is the national state but which also includes such supranational institutions as the International Monetary Fund and the World Trade Organization, regional economic groupings such as the European Union or the North American Free Trade Agreement, and 'local' states at the subnational scale. 99

Nevertheless, in embarking on study of IHRM, acknowledging the concept of strategic choice at organizational level is vital as it reaffirms that private or public concerns in the same country, or indeed in the same sector, may be contrasted in terms of managerial styles and strategies adopted in conducting their affairs.

The relationship between the four levels of analysis, global, regional, national and local, is clearly complex and certainly may not be envisaged as a 'top-down' dynamic in which each level conditions the stratum below. Instead, a complex interplay is apparent between the various affects, including patterns of reciprocity between organization and state. The representation of levels of analysis provides a useful conceptual point of departure for this text. In general, global influences are considered in Chapter 3, while Part 2 (International Themes) places a focus on the organization and Part 3 (Comparative Themes and Regional Studies) is pitched at the level of the nation state and the region.

## The theoretical benefits of cross-national study

According to Hollinshead and Leat (1995), taking a cross-national perspective helps to throw domestic institutions, practices and processes into sharper relief, which leads us to evaluate critically taken-for-granted aspects of organizational life. As the British newspaper, *The Guardian*, has pointed out:

> 66 An event seen from one point of view gives one impression. Seen from another point of view it gives a quite different impression. But it's only when you get the whole picture you fully understand what's going on.
>
> © *The Guardian*, cited in Collins (1997: 32). 99

Taking a comparative perspective not only provides the opportunity to enrich and extend knowledge of organizational practices, but also demands the comparison of international 'stories' as to how to manage people at work, which inevitably leads to the airing of contradictory and competing prescription concerning 'best practice'. Consider, for example, the following questions:

- Is industrial competitiveness best gained through offering employees relatively high levels of employment security, pay and training (e.g. Scandinavia or Germany) or through encouraging a highly flexible and cost-effective attachment of employees to their enterprises (e.g. the USA and the UK)?
- Is pay linked to individual or group performance an important motivator (e.g. as manifest in the USA and the UK) or should pay be more egalitarian in nature, supporting social bonds at the workplace and group coherence (e.g. Japan, China, Scandinavia and developing countries)?
- Is high trade union membership, and trade union involvement in corporate decisions (e.g. Scandinavia) reconcilable with innovation and competitiveness, or should trade unions occupy a relatively marginalized position to allow the 'right to manage' to prevail (e.g. the USA)?
- More generally, is a single 'model' of management transferable across national and regional systems, or do management styles and structures need to be adapted to local cultural and institutional configurations?

We should also note, however, that engaging in international comparisons carries with it some potential methodological pitfalls. As Nicholls (1994) states, the following 'health warnings' should apply to learning by comparison:

- By the time explanations of particular overseas phenomena have been studied, popularized and given currency in the domestic system, the original situation could well have changed significantly.
- The tendency to over-stereotype international practices, identifying various national 'models' available for exportation, despite evidence of practices that fall outside of the norm. For example, the USA is widely regarded as the archetypal 'free market' economy

despite protectionist policies recently enacted in financial and manufacturing sectors. National stereotyping also disregards variations in observed practice from enterprise to enterprise, or sector to sector.

- The tendency to idealize international practices. For example, during the 1980s, Japan was widely regarded as a 'miracle economy' despite evidence of high levels of workplace stress and excessive manifestations of alcoholism and suicide. Similarly, the USA has frequently been regarded as an exemplar for managerial practice despite periods of poor economic performance at corporate and national levels.

- Data concerning employment and other practices may be incomplete or unreliable in various national settings. This is likely to be a particular problem in developing countries. Once collected, there may be difficulties in comparing 'like with like' in international data sets.

## IHRM in a global context

This text focuses on the world of work, and specifically the management of people, in the era of globalization – thus referring to phenomena and developments in the uppermost stratum of the 'levels of analysis' hierarchy defined above. Debate continues to surround the significance and extent of globalization. On one 'side of the fence', 'hyperglobalizers' argue that a new global order has transpired, in which national borders have been rendered superfluous by powerful flows of cross-border trade and production (Giddens, 2006). This position is typified by Ohmae (1990, 1995), who refers to a 'borderless world' in which international market forces place national governments in a position of relative powerlessness. Similarly, it is argued that much corporate life is being subordinated to transnational enterprises that are accountable only to global capital markets (Edwards and Rees, 2006). A related proposition is that national economic policies, organizational forms and management practices are converging to emulate the most efficient international prototypes as a result of global competition (Edwards and Rees, ibid.). Globalization is catalysed by factors such as the revolutionary developments in information and communications technology, information flows and the electronic economy (Giddens, 2006).

By way of contradiction, the 'sceptics' would contend that economic interdependence between nations is by no means a recent phenomenon (ibid.), with high levels of international trade and migration occurring in the era prior to the two world wars (Edwards and Rees, 2006). It is argued that globalization, in its contemporary manifestation, is limited in its embrace as trade, investment and financial flows concentrate on the 'triad' of Europe, Japan and North America (ibid.). Also confounding the view of the hyperglobalizers is the realization that most large MNCs maintain strong roots in their country of origin, retaining strong linkages with domestic financial systems and filling most senior management positions with home country nationals (ibid.).

Nevertheless, it is clear that virtually every company, as well as public or even voluntary organization, is now touched by the forces of internationalization in some way. This may, for example, take the form of tapping into international markets to match the activities of competitors, by taking over, or being taken over by, a foreign concern, or by gaining economies of production by setting up site or 'outsourcing' abroad.

The following factors may be regarded as vital in establishing the global context for IHRM.

## Internationalization of production

As Held et al. (1999) point out, MNCs, which may also be termed 'transnational corporations', represent 'the linchpins of the contemporary world economy'. MNCs are companies, which may be gigantic (e.g. Exxon-Mobil, Coca-Cola, Mitsubishi, Nike, Microsoft) or small, and that have operations and produce goods and market services in more than one country (Giddens, 2006). Such corporations account for two-thirds of all world trade, are instrumental in the international diffusion of new technology and are major actors in financial markets (ibid.). The world's largest MNCs are larger economically than most countries. While globalization possesses many forms and manifestations, it is the internationalization of productive or service operations that tends to epitomize new international forms of work and organization. Many household name products and services are now assembled or delivered on the basis of a type of 'global production line', or global commodity chain. The following is a quotation derived from a documentary on UK Carlton Television:

> When one typical U.S. car was examined to see how 'American' it was, it turned out that nine countries were involved in some aspect of its production or sale. Roughly 30% of the car's value went to South Korea for assembly, 17.5% to Japan for components and advanced technology, 7.5% to Germany for design, 4% to Taiwan and Singapore for minor parts, 2.5% to the U.K. for marketing and advertising services, and 1.5% to Ireland and Barbados for data processing. Only 17% of the car's marketing value was generated in the USA.
>
> (Pilger, 2001)

This example from the motor industry is by no means exceptional. In clothing, footwear, computing and electronics the economic and strategic benefits of geographical relocation of elements of the production process have been realized over the past four decades. More recently, service sector organizations have sought to replicate the experience of manufacturing, decentralizing components of their business to overseas destinations; for example in banking and finance, where call centres and related activities have been relocated from the USA and the UK to India.

Dicken (2003) suggests that the international sourcing of products is not new, certain items having been international in character for centuries, notably spices and other exotic goods. In the 'pre-global' system, a type of international value-added chain was apparent (Hoogvelt, 2001), with lower value, bulk or volume production invariably occurring in developing countries, where labour was relatively unskilled and labour costs low, while higher value activities (e.g. design, assembly and retailing) involved the deployment of more highly skilled, and highly paid, staff in the affluent consumer societies. Accordingly, a 'core/peripheral' global dichotomy was apparent (Dicken, 2003) in which the peripheral (Third World) economies provided raw materials and foodstuffs and provided a market for manufactured goods, while the core (developed) economies undertook more specialist productive activity.

Over the past few decades, associated with the new era of globalization, the apparently simple core/peripheral system of international trade flow has been subject to fragmentation, which makes the relationship between developed and developing countries more complex and ambiguous. Krugman (1995) suggests that it is now possible to 'slice-up' the chain of production, so as to locate labour intensive elements of relatively high-technology processes in low-wage international locations. Similarly, Dicken (2003) states that a new *kaleidoscopic* picture of international production is apparent, with geographical relocation of production on a global scale in a way that intersects national boundaries, and with newly industrialized economies (such as India and China) offering centres of production. The 're-sorting of the global jigsaw puzzle' (ibid.) concerning the organization of international production has occurred in the context of related shifts in the global economy.

First, systems of mass production associated with heavy industry, with their fixed, immobile, quality, have given way to computer-based flexible forms of technology that may be reproduced at various global locations.

Second, the shift towards knowledge or information-based society has been based on electronic and digital technologies which, by their nature, establish a form of instantaneous production and organization across national borders.

Third, profound changes have occurred in global financial systems, enabling the instantaneous flow of capital across financial centres and into financial cyberspace. The ability to switch investment instantaneously from region to region not only serves to accentuate the interconnectedness of international economies, but also makes all economies, and managers and workers within them, susceptible to the volatilities of global financial markets.

## Freedom of movement of capital

The internationalization of business activity has occurred against a global political and economic backcloth in which it appears that 'free market' ideology is becoming ever more pervasive. Of considerable significance was the Uruguay round of the General Agreement on Tariffs and Trade (GATT) in 1994, which comprised representatives from mainly western countries, and which removed many of the barriers to international trade, including import tariffs and quotas. As a result, the volume of world trade rose by over 50 per cent in the subsequent six years. Since the early 1990s, major economies that existed outside the sphere of international capitalism have been incorporated into it, including the former planned and socialistic economies of Russia and central and eastern Europe, China, India and Brazil. The influential Washington-based agencies the International Monetary Fund (IMF) and World Bank, which have responsibility for extending loans to developing countries, have frequently, as a condition, stipulated that such countries should open up their economies to foreign investment and privatize state-owned utilities, thus exposing them to international market forces (Stiglitz, 2002).

At regional level, apparently irreversible moves have been made from economic protectionism towards the breaking down of economic barriers within and between nations. Notable examples would include the removal of trade barriers in the North American Free Trade Agreement (NAFTA) involving the USA, Canada and Mexico and the inception of the Single European Market in 1992 that has promoted the transferability of capital, services and people across an enlarging Europe. While trade liberalization within economic blocs has been designed by policy makers to act as a catalyst for growth and competitiveness, switches of capital both within and between international regions can have a devastating effect on jobs. A well-publicized and controversial example of international shifts in investment spurred by the imperative of cost reduction was the shedding of approximately 15,000 software programming jobs from the USA and western Europe by the German electronics giant, Siemens, in 2004, this function being devolved to lower cost labour in eastern Europe, China and India.

## Freedom of movement of labour

According to Castles and Miller (1993), the current era may be described as the 'age of migration', with around 3 per cent of the world population living in a country other than where they were born (International Migration Report, 2002). Although migration from country to country to enhance economic status has been a fact of life for centuries, the international flow of labour has been accentuated in recent years through the removal of protectionist barriers between member states of major trade blocs, for example the EU and NAFTA. In the case of the EU, the accession of the former socialist states in 2001 has facilitated the mobility of workers from eastern European countries (e.g. Poland, Hungary and the Czech Republic) into western Europe, although countries in the latter region differ in their openness to economic migrants. While such labour has served to fill skills gaps in the developed economies, it has also been argued that migrants and their families place undue pressure on welfare states, negatively impact the security and status of indigenous workers, and that the flow of skills from poorer countries adversely affects their economic growth potential (Dicken, 2003). In general there has been increased integration of ethnic minorities into the workforces of developed economies over the past few decades, which has promoted a climate of international diversity across many sectors of industry, commerce and public activity and affairs.

## International regulations

Morrison (2006) suggests that international companies may be depicted as operating in interacting spheres of regulation, consisting of national legal systems, regional authorities and international structures. While most of the legislation impacting on business transactions emanates from national legal authorities, particularly in the case of the EU, affected parties are subject to European-wide directives and regulations. Companies across Europe, or indeed those operating outside Europe with responsibilities for European-based subsidiaries, are affected by a raft of measures affecting minimum pay, working time, health and safety, equal opportunities, employee consultation and other matters. As a result of the European Works Council Directive passed in 1994, multinational corporations locating across Europe are obliged to consult employee representatives about matters affecting their workforces at a pan-European level at regular intervals.

   MNCs are also subject to international regulations that aim to provide employment standards across global regions, enacted by bodies such as the International Labour Organization (ILO) and the Organization for Economic Co-operation and Development (OECD). While such regulations are voluntary in nature, they may nevertheless be taken seriously by MNCs that are increasingly concerned about their ethical profile and corporate social responsibility (CSR) issues.

### Case Scenario: The offshoring of financial services

The financial services industry offers a contradictory picture of the international division of labour at the start of the new millennium. On one hand, the sector exemplifies 'path-dependent' tendencies towards concentration of people and processes in major metropolitan centres. On the other, the 'light' and electronically transmittable nature of the financial product has permitted the reorganization of productive activity into international 'financial factories' with scant regard for national borders.

Following the deregulation of financial services during the 1980s and 1990s, firms have gravitated to major financial centres, which has promoted geographical concentration of headquarters (Dicken, 2003). As Martin (1999: 19–20) states:

> " Foreign banks and related institutions have moved into these centres precisely because of geography, that is to expand their presence or gain access to specific markets, to capitalize on the economies of specialization, agglomeration and localisation (skilled labour, expertise, contact, business networks etc.) available in these centres, or to specialize their own operations and activities geographically. "

Dicken (2003) suggests that tendencies towards concentration may be attributed to the distinctive features of the finance industry, which relies upon cooperation between firms as well as competition. Relationship management is an essential activity in a profession where personal contacts are vital for generating business and business-related information (Thrift, 1994). Similarly, Dicken (2003) argues that 'micro networks' perform a vital function in price setting and related activity, resting upon the twin needs of sociability and proximity (Thrift, 1994). In the leading financial metropolises strong cultures are established that are conducive to the interpretation of complex information in a reflexive fashion and economies of scale are created in factors such as linked services, including accounting, legal and computer based (Dicken, 2003). The relational nature of the factors that have contributed to the agglomeration of financial institutions in leading metropolitan centres have clearly accumulated over a period of time and possess a highly localized quality, scarcely being amenable to replication beyond distinct geographic boundaries.

Offsetting the trend towards concentration of 'higher-order' functions, there has been a strategic realization in recent years that economies can be gained in a highly competitive market environment by separating out 'back office' activity and relocating its performance to lower cost locations. The introduction of microcomputers and networked computer terminals has added impetus to the decentralization of more routine functions, which leads to a 'spatial bifurcation' (Warf, 1989: 267) in many large finance firms. Gordon et al. (2005) point out that, although there have been earlier examples of near-and offshoring of business services, particularly in the USA, large-scale interest in the relocation of a range of service activities has become most pronounced over the past five years or so in the City of London and more widely across Europe. Gordon et al. (2005) cite three key factors that serve to explain such developments:

- technical developments in Internet use and telecommunications connectedness on a more global basis;
- heightened and persistent pressures to bring costs down across a range of advanced service activities, after a period of easy growth;
- the discovery – and, to some extent, creation – of new pools of appropriately skilled labour (and credible sub-contractors) at sites within cheap labour economies.

Accordingly, three main sets of servicing functions are subject to relocation (ibid.):

- call centres of various kinds for marketing, routine business enquiries and more sophisticated technical support;
- IT functions, including data-processing, code checking, software development and modification, operations support, publishing and statistical analyses;
- wider business support functions of various kinds, including accounting/payroll operations, para-legal work and record maintenance.

According to a recent report by the leading financial services consultancy Capco:

> Recent research conducted jointly by a team drawn from Capco and the London Business School highlights how the world's top financial services firms are deploying new sourcing strategies and models to move up the process innovation curve. This closely resembles events that have already occurred in the manufacturing sector, wherein best-in-class companies like General Electric have developed sophisticated sourcing models to optimize the value chain of their operations. By componentising their business processes, the financial services firms have begun to look at each component independently of the other components while selecting the best sourcing option ... Should the trend continue tomorrow's banks would look and behave no differently to a factory.
>
> (Gupta, 2006: 43)

However, in considering the anatomy of offshoring, it is necessary to guard against a simplistic assumption that high added value, or core, functions will be retained in house, while low added value, peripheral, functions will be subject to relocation. Gupta (ibid.: 43) contends that there is a growing incidence of vertical business functions being subject to near- and offshoring. Gupta (ibid.) provides an example of an investment bank that planned to offshore as much of a derivative-related process to India as possible in order to reduce costs. As a first move, the bank decided to offshore confirmation processes. The offshore centre in India took over responsibility for initiating phone calls, emails, and so on, while the more experienced staff based in London processed exceptions. Using this model, the investment bank was able to minimize investment in knowledge transfer and training of staff in India, while saving around 40 per cent of operating costs (ibid.: 46).

However, in early 2005 two major North American-based consultancies predicted that 50 per cent of offshoring contracts signed by US companies between 2001 and 2004 would fail to meet expectations. In such circumstances, Aron and Singh (2005) note that 'in-shoring and in-sourcing' have enjoyed a growth in popularity in business circles. Critical explanations for the failure of offshoring relate essentially to mismanagement of the process by less than exemplary organizations. Thus, despite the 'best practice' recommendations of consultancies and agencies such as Capco, companies in practice fail to systematically differentiate and measure the added value of discrete operational elements to establish a value hierarchy, and therefore relocate functions in a relatively arbitrary fashion (ibid.). In the field of employment, serious concerns have been expressed about the effects of offshoring on work in both home and host environments. From a home country perspective, workers engaged in routine activities are threatened by shifts in their functions to lower cost global regions. The potential for 'backlash' in the West has been flagged by Taylor and Bain (2003), who note two prominent trade union campaigns in the UK; first to prevent the transfer of call centre jobs from Reading to Mumbai and, second, to oppose British Telecom's decision to establish call centres in Bangalore and Delhi. The expression of alarm and despondency by those most adversely affected by the restructuring of international employment systems has occurred across many western countries, including the USA.

From the perspective of the recipient or host environment, a cause for concern is that higher value, knowledge-based, financial functions are invariably retained in house, while routine activity is subject to relocation overseas. While closer scrutiny of the anatomy of offshoring reveals that, in exceptional cases, 'vertical' functions' may be subject to international devolution, such moves are invariably accompanied by close control from the centre as well as the possibility of technological 'shadowing' and backup of critical computational functions. Where 'voice', or call centre, operations are offshored, as these demand vital interface with customers, the contribution of overseas employees is frequently subject to rigid codification and, following Taylor and Bain (2003), 'neo-colonial' forms of socialization and training may be asserted.

*Source*: © Hollinshead and Hardy (2009).

---

### Activity

Consider the strategic reasons in the above case study scenario, as to why financial services are engaging in offshoring and the potential drawbacks of such 'process re-engineering' from a strategic and employment/HR perspective.

---

## Summary

This chapter has identified the particular complexities associated with IHRM, as opposed to purely domestic HRM. It has been asserted that influences on the conduct of international business emanate from global, regional and national levels, and that strategic actions of organizations are constrained by regulatory and other influences at each of these levels. The benefits and potential pitfalls of engaging in comparative study have been identified. The dynamic international context for IHRM has been considered, illustrated by a critical examination of a modern manifestation of a 'global commodity chain' in the financial services sector.

## Further reading

**Edwards, T. and Rees, C.** (2006) *International Human Resource Management: Globalization, National Systems and Multinational Companies*, Harlow: Prentice Hall.

This edited book is subdivided into two major themes. First, the context of IHRM is explored through examining the process of globalization and national business systems. Second, HR policies and practices in multinational companies are examined and the transfer of practices across operations.

**Scullion, H. and Linehan, M.** (2005) *International Human Resource Management: A Critical Text*, Basingstoke: Palgrave Macmillan.

This edited book offers an analytical approach to contemporary debates and issues in IHRM. Drawing on original research, the text offers an original and critical insight into the nature of this disciplinary area, new policy developments and the strategies and operations of global companies.

## References

**Aron, R. and Singh, J.V.** (2005) Getting offshoring right, *Harvard Business Review*, 63(3): 79–91.

**Bartlett, C.A. and Ghoshal, S.** (1989) *Managing Across Borders: The Transnational Solution*, London: Hutchinson.

**Bean, R.** (1994) *Comparative Industrial Relations: An Introduction to Cross-national Perspectives*, London: International Thomson Business Press.

**Beer, M., Spector, B., Lawrence, P.R., Quinn-Mills, D. and Walton, R.G.** (1984) *Managing Human Assets*, New York: Free Press.

**Boxall, P.** (1995) Building the theory of comparative HRM, *Human Resource Management Journal*, 5(5): 5–17.

**Brewster, C. and Harris, H.** (eds) (1999) *International HRM: Contemporary Issues in Europe*, London: Routledge.

**Briscoe, D.R. and Schuler, R.S.** (2004) *International Human Resource Management* (2nd edn.), London: Routledge.

**Budhwar, P. and Yaw, D.** (2001) *Managing Human Resources in Asia Pacific*, London: Routledge.

**Burton-Jones, A.** (1999) *Knowledge Capitalism: Business, Work and Learning in the New Economy*, Oxford: Oxford University Press.

**Castles, S. and Miller, M.J.** (1993) *The Age of Migration: International Population Movements in the Modern World*, London: Macmillan.

**Collins, A.** (1997) Human resource management in context, in I. Beardwell and L. Holden (eds) *Human Resource Management: A Contemporary Perspective*, London: Pitman.

**Dicken, P.** (2003) *Global Shift: Reshaping the Global Economic Map in the 21st Century* (4th edn.), London: Sage Publications.

**Dowling, P.J. and Welch, D.E.** (2004) *International Human Resource Management* (4th edn.), London: Thomson.

**Eaton, J.** (2000) *Comparative Employment Relations: An Introduction*, Cambridge: Polity Press.

**Edwards, T. and Rees, C.** (2006) *International Human Resource Management: Globalization, National Systems and Multinational Companies*, Harlow: Prentice Hall.

**Gauri, P.N. and Prasad, S.B.** (1995) *International Management: A Reader*, London: Dryden.

**Giddens, A.** (2002) *Runaway World: How Globalization is Reshaping Our Lives*, London: Profile Books.

**Giddens, A.** (2006) *Sociology* (5th edn.), Cambridge: Polity Press.

**Gordon, I., Haslam, C., McCann, P. and Scott-Quinn, B.** (2005) Off-shoring and the City of London, ISMA Centre, University of Reading.

**Guest, D.E.** (1988) First annual Seear lecture at the London School of Economics and Political Science, 'Human Resource Management – is it worth taking seriously?', June.

**Gupta, S.** (2006) Financial services factory, *Journal of Financial Transformation*, Capco Institute, 18: 43–50.

**Held, D., McGrew, A., Goldblatt, D. and Perraton, J.** (1999) *Global Transformations: Politics, Economics, and Culture*, Cambridge: Polity Press.

**Hodgetts, R.M. and Luthans, F.** (2003) *International Management, Culture, Strategy and Behaviour* (5th edn.), New York: McGraw-Hill.

**Hofstede, G.** (1994) *Cultures and Organizations: Software of the Mind*, London: HarperCollins.

**Holden, L.** (1997) International Human Resource Management, in I. Beardwell and L. Holden (eds) *Human Resource Management: A Contemporary Perspective*, London: Pitman.

**Hollinshead, G. and Hardy, J.** (2009) The offshoring of financial services: a re-appraisal, working paper, University of Hertfordshire Business School.

**Hollinshead, G. and Leat, M.** (1995) *Human Resource Management: An International and Comparative Perspective*, London: Pitman.

**Hoogvelt, A.** (2001) *Globalization and the Postcolonial World: The New Political Economy of Development*, Basingstoke: Palgrave Macmillan.

**Hyman, R. and Ferner, A.** (1994) *New Frontiers in European Industrial Relations*, Oxford: Blackwell.

**International Migration Report** (2002) United Nations Department of Economic and Social Affairs, New York.

**Jackson, T.** (2002) *International Human Resource Management: A Cross-cultural approach,* London: Sage.

**Kamoche, K., Yaw, D., Horwitz, F. and Muuka, G.** (2004) *Managing Human Resources in Africa,* London: Routledge.

**Krugman, P.** (1995) *Development, Geography and Economic Theory,* Cambridge, MA: MIT Press.

**Martin, R.** (1999) The new economic geography of money, in R. Martin (ed.) *Money and the Space Economy,* Chichester: Wiley.

**Morrison, J.** (2006) *The International Business Environment* (2nd edn.), Basingstoke: Palgrave Macmillan.

**Nicholls, P.** (1994) Learning by comparison: the search for new ideas, *Work and Employment,* Spring Issue, Bristol Business School.

**Ohmae, K.** (1990) *The Borderless World: Power and Strategy in the Industrial Economy,* London: Collins.

**Ohmae, K.** (1995) *The End of the Nation State: The Rise of Regional Economies,* London: Free Press.

**Pilger J.** (2001) The New Rulers of the World, a Carlton programme for ITV transmitted in July. Booklet prepared in conjunction with the World Development Movement.

**Schuler, R.S.** (2000) The internationalization of human resource management, *Journal of International Management,* 6: 239–260.

**Scullion, H. and Linehan, M.** (eds) (2005) *International Human Resource Management: A Critical Text,* Basingstoke: Palgrave Macmillan.

**Stiglitz, J.E.** (2002) *Globalization and its Discontents,* New York: W.W. Norton & Company.

**Tayeb, M.H.** (2005) *International Human Resource Management: A Multinational Company Perspective,* Oxford: Oxford University Press.

**Taylor, P. and Bain N.P.** (2003) *Call Centres in Scotland and Outsourced Competition from India,* University of Stirling, Scotland: Scotecon.

**Thrift, N.J.** (1994) On the social and cultural determinants of international financial centres: the case of the City of London, in S. Corbridge, R. Martin, and J. Thrift (eds) *Money, Power and Space,* Oxford: Blackwell.

**Trompenaars, F. and Hampden-Turner, C.** (1997) *Riding the Waves of Culture, Understanding Cultural: Diversity in Business* (2nd edn.), London: Nicholas Brealey, Publishing.

**United Nations Conference on Trade and Development** (2008) *World Investment Report,* New York and Geneva: UN.

**Warf, B.** (1989) Telecommunications and the globalization of financial services, *Professional Geographer,* 41: 257–271.

**Whitley, R.** (2002) Business systems, in A. Sorge (ed.) *Organization*, London: Thomson Learning.

# 02

# Institutional and cultural influences on international human resource management

## Introduction

Despite the all-pervasive talk of globalization, the seasoned international business traveller will be acutely aware of differences in the 'way of doing things' from country to country and from region to region. Such differences are seldom more apparent than in the field of organization and management. Not only will the traveller be aware that conventions for doing business are culture-bound, but also that systems and structures for 'the management of people' are uniquely determined by forces of tradition. If the business traveller were to discuss the issue of fairness of pay with a Japanese worker, the latter could well reiterate the proverb 'The nail that sticks out should be hammered down', thus stressing the need for egalitarianism and group compliance. The counterpart of this worker in the USA however, particularly if a high performer, may well be aggrieved if his or her superior contribution to enterprise success is not individually recognized in financial terms. Similarly, as the recent case of the highly contested closure of the Paris branch of the UK-owned retailer Marks & Spencer (M&S) demonstrated, French employees' expectations of job security (and consultation in the case of job loss) are considerably higher than those of their British counterparts.

It is the purpose of this chapter to assist understanding as to *why* observed manifestations of HR and employment practices demonstrate distinctiveness and 'embeddedness' within specific geographic territories. It is therefore pitched at the intermediary level of analysis defined in Chapter 1, capturing regional and national influences on IHRM. We pursue two complementary lines of theoretical explanation, the first relating to *institutional arrangements*, which may be regarded as the 'hardware' of underlying systems for HRM, and the second concerning *cultural stereotypes*, which, continuing the metaphor, relate to the more intangible and psychological determinants of international diversity, or the systems 'software'.

## Institutional perspectives

According to the *Concise Oxford English Dictionary* (2002), an institution may be defined as 'an official organization with an important role in a country' or 'an organization founded for a religious, educational, or social purpose'. In the era of globalization there has been serious debate concerning the status and viability of existing institutional arrangements, including nation states. Giddens, for example, argues that many institutions have become 'shell' like, and 'have become inadequate to the tasks they are called upon to perform' (2002: 19). Nevertheless, a common set of institutions can be found in most societies, including public and private enterprises, public utilities, financial establishments, educational institutions, trade unions and government/quasi-governmental agencies. The relative strength of these institutions can vary, as can the manner in which they interact.

Dore (2000: 45–47) refers to 'institutional interlock' as typifying national economies and the relationship between the economy and the broader society. Thus, it may be argued that in some societies, as a result of socio-political traditions, institutions operate in an interlocking, mutually supportive fashion, while in others, there exists a greater 'space' between key institutions, and an emphasis on institutional autonomy and self-support. For the purpose of this analysis, various complementary institutional perspectives are offered. First, broad policy prescriptions concerning the role of the state and related institutional arrangements are explored. Second, variations in 'business systems' from region to region depending primarily on patterns of ownership will be examined.

## Neo-liberalist, neo-corporatist and socialist/Marxist perspectives

Current debates and controversies relating to globalization and, more generally, to the way in which economic systems should be ordered, are invariably based on ideologies that present a general plan of action for structuring economic and social orders. Such plans, which may emanate from politicians, policy makers, academics, management consultants and the like, are seeking to prescribe ideal forms of institutional states of existence to guide macro-level reforms. For our purposes, three influential ideologies are expounded.

### Neo-liberalism

This doctrine has been substantially attributed to the late Nobel prize-winning economist Milton Friedman at the University of the Chicago's School of Economics, although its origins can be traced back to the work of Adam Smith and his treatise *The Wealth of Nations* published in 1776. In essence, this perspective emphasizes the potency and desirability of market forces in allocating resources and engendering economic efficiency and wealth.

Freedom of movement of capital and labour is assumed, as is the ability of the individual economic actor to take responsibility for his or her own actions (Hollinshead and Leat, 1995). Thus, the essential concern of policy makers is to ensure that economic structures remain *deregulated*, that is, the state does not interfere in the behaviour of primary economic actors, and that 'freedom to manage' can occur without constraint.

According to Steger (2003), concrete neo-liberal measures include:

- privatization of public enterprises;
- deregulation of the economy;
- liberalization of trade and industry;
- tax cuts;
- 'monetarist' measures to keep inflation in check;
- control of organized labour;
- the reduction of public expenditure, particularly social spending;
- the downsizing of government;
- the expansion of international markets;
- the removal of controls on global financial flows.

Flowing from this, a negative view is taken of state-owned industry and trade unionism, both of which are regarded as possessing a monopolistic and collectivistic orientation that serves to impede the free flow of market forces. The doctrine is also consistent with the removal or reduction of state-funded provision for social welfare. Neo-liberalism became a highly influential political force in the USA and the UK in the 1980s and was associated with the wholesale privatization of state-owned and nationalized industries in the latter. These economies have also been referred to as *liberal market economies*, or LMEs (Edwards et al., 2005).

Moreover, in recent years neo-liberalism has been the guiding economic philosophy for powerful international agencies such as the World Bank and the International Monetary Fund (IMF) (Stiglitz, 2002), both operating from Washington, and instigating 'shock therapy' economic treatment in transitional and developing economies (e.g. in Latin America, East Asia, central and eastern Europe and Africa), which invariably involves the rapid privatization of formerly state-owned enterprises and the 'opening up' of these economies to western capital.

While neo-liberalism has been in the ideological ascendancy over the past decade or so, its tendency to create 'winners' and 'losers' at national and global levels has been the subject of protestation and controversy, a theme that is taken up in Chapter 3. Recently, the principles of neo-liberalism have been openly and robustly questioned across national and political spectrums as a result of the global financial crisis leading to the injection of billions of dollars of state-provided funds into the US finance and automobile sectors, and into the economy at large. Currently, the G20 group of advanced industrial nations are to discuss the establishment of a 'new global financial structure'.

## Neo-corporatism

Neo-corporatist ideology, in contrast to neo-liberalism, envisages an active role for the state in seeking to mediate and integrate the interests of various powerful societal groupings, particularly those representing labour and capital. An underlying presumption of neo-corporatist philosophy is that the unbridled flow of market forces potentially leads to unpredictable outcomes (Hollinshead and Leat, 1995), and is associated with considerable material inequity within societies, which is detrimental to the public good and longer-term economic competitiveness. Consequently, neo-corporatism upholds that market orientation should be tempered by social awareness of market outcomes, which is instigated through consensus decision making involving major societal actors.

A dominant institutional paradigm advocated by the neo-corporatist school is therefore 'social partnership' that engages representatives of labour and capital in decision making at various economic levels. This 'stakeholder' model of economic management is consistent with high levels of worker skill acquisition and commitment to corporate objectives, and is founded on highly developed national infrastructures and systems for social welfare. Neo-corporatist ideology has been influential in continental Europe, notably in Germany, the Netherlands and Scandinavia, which have also been referred to as *coordinated market economies*, or CMEs (Edwards et al., 2005).

Concrete neo-corporatist measures include:

- the involvement of 'stakeholder', including worker, interests at national, industrial and enterprise level;
- Consensus decision making;
- government intervention into economies in order to moderate market forces and protect social priorities;
- relatively high taxation rates;
- highly developed national infrastructures and considerable public expenditure;
- high levels of social expenditure;
- constructive engagement of trade unions.

Neo-corporatism has guided the formulation of EU institutional and procedural arrangements as well as the rationale for numerous social and employment policy measures. In recent years, however, neo-corporatist tendencies in the EU and its core economies have tended to give way to a powerful agenda of deregulation in the context of global competition and the associated needs for cost reduction and employment flexibility.

### Marxism

Marxist ideology, which has inspired socialist movements across countries, is fundamentally critical of modes of capital accumulation associated with market economies, and particularly neo-liberalism. In essence, the Marxist view holds that political equality is a 'myth' (Miliband and Panitch, 1993), and that the state always works in the interests of the ruling economic class and supports 'capital' (Macionis and Plummer, 2002). Central to Marxist analysis is the conviction that unequal power relations in industry do not exist in isolation, but are buttressed by patterns of inclusion and exclusion associated with various institutional arrangements, including education, health and housing. Marxist ideology holds that unemployment and insecurity is an integral feature of capitalist systems, enabling employers to promote intensification of work among those who fear redundancy. Alienated employees are systematically denied 'the fruits of their labour' in terms of profit or production as these are unfairly appropriated by employers and other vested interests. Marxism, then, emphasizes the divisions in society and concentrates on issues of power, struggle and inequality (Giddens, 2006).

According to Giddens (2006: 114), broad Marxist ideas are as follows:

■ The main dynamic of modern development is the expansion of capitalistic economic mechanisms.

■ Modern societies are riven with class inequalities, which are basic to their very nature.

■ Major divisions of power, like those affecting the differential position of men and women, derive ultimately from economic equalities.

■ Modern societies as we know them today (capitalist societies) are of transitional type – we may expect them to become radically re-organized in the future. Socialism, of one type or another, will eventually replace capitalism.

■ The spread of western influence across the world is mainly a result of the spread of capitalist enterprise.

Marxists would assert that modern patterns of foreign direct investment and the activities of western-owned MNEs in emerging and developing economies may only be understood against the backcloth of post-colonialism and international dependency (ibid.)

As a legacy of colonial rule, under which richer countries exploited the natural resources of 'Third World' nations, as well as creating markets for finished products in the latter countries, post-colonial countries have developed economic dependency on 'the West'. It should also be noted that, despite the global influence of neo-liberalism over the past few decades, Marxist and socialist political persuasions remain a potent political force in various countries, particularly a number in Latin America, southern and eastern Europe, Russia and China.

## Business systems and varieties of capitalism

Neo-liberal and neo-corporatist perspectives outlined above would support the assertion that 'varieties of capitalism' serve to order political and economic structures across global regions. This theme has been taken up by various commentators. Albert (1993) draws a distinction between 'Anglo-American' and 'Rhineland' capitalism. The characteristics of each are presented in Table 2.1.

**Table 2.1   The characteristics of Anglo-American and Rhineland capitalism**

|  | Anglo-American (liberal market economic orientation) | Rhineland (coordinated market economic orientation) |
|---|---|---|
| Source of finance | Stock market | Institutional investors |
| Primary responsibility of management | Shareholders | A wide variety of stakeholders, including employee representatives |
| Restraints on takeovers | Low | High |
| Perspective | Long term/investment | Short term/cost-effectiveness/ minimization |

*Source:* Adapted from Hyman (2004).

Hyman (2004: 140) states that, in CMEs reflecting neo-corporatist ideology, a dense network of institutions exists, sustained by law, custom and moral values that subject the decisions of managers and trade union representatives to extraneous and regulative influences. In LMEs, in keeping with neo-liberalist principles, 'freedom to manage' is well established, with primary economic actors enjoying considerable autonomy and little statutory or regulative interference into their affairs (Hall and Soskice, 2001; Hollingsworth and Boyer, 1997; Kischelt et al., 1999; Streeck, 2001).

Institutional analysis is integral to Whitley's (2002) representation of regional typologies of *business systems*. According to Whitley, a business system constitutes a collection of institutions serving to shape economic transactions, cooperation and control inside and between business organizations (Sorge, 2004). For Whitley, means of ownership represents a key determinant of the form of business system, as well as degrees of competition or collaboration between industrial and commercial concerns and the quality of relationships between management and employees/trade unions.

The following typologies manifest various configurations of business system characteristics in various global regions, and are derived from Sorge (ibid.).

### Fragmented

- Small owner-controlled firms engaged in high levels of competition.
- Short-term results orientation.
- Flexibility to convert the firm from one product or service to another.

Example: Hong Kong

### Coordinated industrial district

- Links exhibited between competing firms and across sectors.
- Economic coordination geared to long-term perspectives.
- Cooperation, commitment and flexibility emphasized in the sphere of work relations and management.
- Economic cooperation not necessarily achieved via trade unions.

Example: Italian industrial districts and other European regional districts

### Compartmentalized (*associated with LMEs*)

- Large enterprises that integrate activities between sectors, in the industrial chain and through shareholdings.
- Little cooperation between firms.
- In product and labour markets, adversarial competition and confrontation occurs.
- Owner control exercised at arm's length through financial markets and shareholding.

Example: the UK and former UK colonies

### State-organized

- More or less socialist, but dependent on state coordination, support and governance.
- Integration across and within production chains.

- In capitalist systems may involve family ownership of firms.

Examples: Korea and France

### Collaborative (*associated with CMEs*)

- Substantial associative coordination (through industrial, employer and employee associations and quasi-governmental agencies).
- Credit financing of enterprises and alliances of share ownership as opposed to dispersed ownership as in 'compartmentalized' systems above.
- Emphasis on long-term interests and development of high trust between major institutional actors.

Examples: Western Continental Europe, German-speaking and Scandinavian

### Highly coordinated

- Alliance form of owner control.
- Extensive alliances between large companies that are usually conglomerates.
- Differentiated chain of suppliers.
- High levels of employer–employee interdependence.
- A major part of workforce 'incorporated' into the enterprise.

Example: Japan

It is argued that different elements of business systems interrelate in a complex whole, giving characteristic patterns of business behaviour in different countries that persist over time in such areas as corporate governance, managerial structures and labour market issues.

## Implications of institutional perspectives for HRM

How, then, do institutional factors impact on the policy and practice of HRM? While the over-generalization of corporate orientations within nation states and regions should be avoided, Marginson (2004) suggests that enterprises embedded in LMEs (such as the USA and the UK) tend to place more emphasis on short run financial performance, and adopt investment strategies that are driven by purely financial criteria. In such systems, employees are likely to be regarded as disposable resources, or even liabilities, which conditions employment and HR policies. So, for example, the employer operating in the LME is likely to be orientated towards closely managing individual performance, possibly through the use of financial incentives (and penalties) and may tend to see training and development as an 'overhead' assuming low priority when competition is high. There is likely to be considerable movement of labour between enterprises, and, within enterprises, an emphasis placed on the 'flexible' deployment of staff. Management teams and line managers will be empowered to take control of many aspects of HRM and employee motivation. LMEs place an emphasis on international competitiveness, cost-effectiveness and flexibility, yet potential drawbacks, in a climate of competitive 'leanness' are lack of employee commitment, morale and inferior quality of product and service.

Organizational and HR principles associated with liberal market economies are as follows:

- 'freedom to manage';
- emphasis on short-term competition;

- flexible deployment of staff;
- pay linked to individual performance;
- training regarded as an 'overhead'.

On the other hand, enterprises embedded in CMEs (such as Germany and Scandinavia) are likely to prioritize longer-run performance and to pursue investment strategies involving product and process innovation and associated skill development (Marginson, 2004). Employees tend to be regarded as enduring assets constituting a valuable resource for competitive advantage, an emphasis being placed on their training and development, and on the nurturing of 'internal labour markets', that is, the existing body of employees. Related features of employment would include relatively high levels of job security, including protection for staff in the event of takeovers and mergers, and robust arrangements for employee consultation and involvement in order to engender employee commitment. In such systems managerial decision making is frequently constrained by extraneous influences, including employment laws and regulations imposed by government, and other stakeholder (particularly trade union) agendas. In CMEs, employee motivation and commitment is likely to be high, this being associated with high-quality products and services, yet such economies may run the risk of lack of global competitiveness due to high cost and 'rigid' employment practices.

Organizational and HR principles associated with CMEs are as follows:

- constraints on managerial freedom through state regulations and other influences;
- longer-term orientation;
- investment in training;
- relative job security;
- employee involvement and participation.

While institutional analysis assists with understanding the 'embedded' determinants of HRM policy and practice across nations, the use of 'business systems' and related approaches for calibrating national diversity needs to be accompanied by certain academic provisos.

First, following Pollert (1999), the concept of the business system provides an imperfect device to explain national variations in employment/HR structures. Even as an 'ideal type', it is argued that the notion of national business systems obscures non-national institutional differences, such as those between different corporate cultures within nation states, or the 'merging' of institutions through regional convergence; for example, via pan-European integration policies.

Second, there is, in reality, not a simple 'cause and effect' and highly delineated relationship between business systems and observed manifestations of HRM and employment practice. As Hardy (2002) asserts, 'local isomorphism', that is, the conditioning effects of the local environment, is more likely in certain areas of HRM because of the constraints of host country regulations and practices. For example, issues such as wage determination, hours of work, job contracts and redundancy procedures are highly subject to local institutional influence. On the other hand, in respect of systems for employee involvement and consultation, or equal opportunities and health and safety at work, enterprises may be subject to regulative effects at regional or international level, which occur 'outside the reach' of the national business system.

---

*Activity*

Imagine you are the HR team for a medium-sized, domestically owned, engineering company in a country of your choice. Formulate a PEST (political, economic, social and technical) analysis of the contextual factors impacting on your business. To what extent are they indicative of an 'LME' or 'CME' national institutional context?

---

## The psychological 'software': cultural perspectives

To what extent are differences in national practices in HRM attributable to cultural differences? This is a difficult question to answer, not least because of the intangible nature of culture itself. Geert Hofstede (2001), a seminal writer on culture, has referred to culture as the 'software of the mind', while Hodgetts and Luthans (2003) suggest that it possesses the following attributes:

- It is *learned.* Culture is not inherited or biologically based. It is acquired by learning and experience.
- It is *shared.* People as members of a group, organization or society share culture. It is not specific to single individuals.
- It is *transgenerational.* Culture is cumulative, passed down from one generation to the next.
- It is *symbolic.* Culture is based on the human capacity to symbolize or use one thing to represent another.
- It is *patterned.* Culture has structure and is integrated. A change in one part will bring changes in another.
- It is *adaptive.* Culture is based on the human capacity to change or adapt, as opposed to the more genetically driven adaptive process of animals.

Dahl (2004), drawing on the work of Hofstede (2001), Trompenaars and Hampden-Turner (1997) and Spencer-Oatey (2000), asserts that there are various levels to culture (resembling the layers of an onion), ranging from the easily observable and changed outer layers (such as behavioural conventions, artefacts and conventions, observable practices) to the more 'difficult to grasp' inner layers (such as assumptions and values). This is a valuable insight in the context, for example, of international joint ventures as internationally diverse teams may appear, at face value, to possess cultural consonance, yet more rigorous interaction may become dysfunctional as a result of deeply held preconceptions of key actors. In this section we explore seminal theories of culture.

## Hall and Hall's high and low context cultures

Hall and Hall (1990) contend that context refers to 'the information that surrounds an event; it is inextricably bound up with the meaning of that event'. In low context countries (including the former West Germany, Switzerland, Scandinavia and North America), interaction between individuals tends to be explicit, unambiguous and formal in tenor. An emphasis is placed on time management, deadlines and punctuality, and work and home life is quite rigidly separated.

In high context cultures (e.g. Japan, Asia, Africa, Latin America, the Middle East and southern Europe), it is assumed that most information resides in the person and therefore greater emphasis is placed on 'interpersonal chemistry' and 'body language' as manifested in informal, word-of-mouth, face-to-face communication. In such cultures activities may be carried out simultaneously; there is less emphasis on time management, and a blurred division between work and domestic activities. This theoretical contribution would seem to have particular value as joint ventures between low and high context regions are becoming more commonplace, potentially creating clashes in values, norms and mutual expectations.

## Hofstede's study

The study of Geert Hofstede, originally based on survey data obtained from two company attitude surveys conducted in 1968 and 1972 and involving 116,000 IBM employees across over 60 countries, has provided influential insights into varying cultural predispositions across national barriers. Initially, four dimensions were identified that possessed universal applicability across cultures, with a fifth subsequently being added. For each dimension, Hofstede presented possible origins as well as consequences for management behaviour.

*Power distance* reflected the extent to which members of society are prepared to accept a hierarchical or unequal power structure. Tracing the anthropological roots of this cultural predisposition to the Islamic and Roman empires, it is apparent that in some societies the relationship between superior and subordinate is adhered to with greater rigidity and reverence than in others. This dimension clearly has explanatory value concerning varying degrees of organizational hierarchy and propensity towards managerial consultation across cultures. Northern Europe and the USA tend to have relatively low power distance, while those in southern Europe, Asia, Latin America and Africa are relatively comfortable with hierarchy and paternalism.

*Uncertainty avoidance* relates to the extent to which members of a society are prepared to tolerate ambiguity and risk. In risk-averse countries or organizations, regulations or institutional arrangements tend to be put into place to mediate the threat of uncertainty and ambiguity. Rule-making and bureaucracy would be a common feature of working life in such countries. In Europe, Germany, Italy and France tend to be risk-averse, while Britain and Sweden are relatively orientated towards risk. Japan and Latin American and Mediterranean countries also score highly on uncertainty avoidance. As Hofstede astutely observes, it is not necessarily the risk-taking countries (the USA and Great Britain) that have achieved the highest levels of economic performance in recent years.

*Individualism versus collectivism.* Individualism is prevalent in those societies in which the primary concern of people is to endure the well-being of themselves, or their immediate kin. In collectivistic societies, wider groupings and networks share extended responsibilities and loyalties. Hofstede asserts that modern management policies and practices tend to emanate from more individualistic societies (e.g. performance-related pay) and that they therefore possess limited applicability in collectivistic and developing countries. It is postulated that countries become more individualistic as they become more economically advanced.

English-speaking countries tend to be highly individualistic (notably the USA), while higher degrees of collectivism are to be found in continental Europe, Asia, Latin America, the post-socialist bloc and developing countries.

*Masculinity versus femininity.* This dimension represents the extent to which stereotypical male values such as high earnings, personal recognition and a challenging career take precedence over 'feminine' preferences for good personal relations, employee well-being and satisfaction, consensus orientation, nurturing and sharing. Highly masculine societies include Japan, Austria and Latin countries, while Scandinavian countries and the Netherlands are relatively feminine in orientation.

*Long-term versus short-term orientation.* This dimension was added in 1987, with the assistance of researcher Michael Bond, to counter the potential western bias of the IBM questionnaire and to embrace Asian values. Long-term thinking, prevalent in eastern 'Confucian'-oriented thinking, stresses virtues such as persistence and perseverance and is consistent with organizations building strategic plans over an extended time frame, while western, short-term, thinking is associated with results 'here and now' and puts pressure on businesses and employees to demonstrate immediate achievements.

Hofstede's study has been highly influential in academic and commercial circles as it has highlighted the significance of culture in international business engagements and in shaping managerial behaviours across national boundaries. The study, through its strong empirical orientation, sought to make tangible and quantifiable the nebulous notion of culture.

However, Hofstede's contribution may be criticized on a number of counts:

- It is out of date. The empirical studies carried out in the late 1960s and early 1970s occurred before the intensification of globalization and related developments (such as the invention of the Internet), which has impacted on values and attitudes on a global scale. Similarly, key concepts may be regarded as somewhat passé, such as stereotypical masculine and feminine values, which predated much feminist thinking.
- The concentration on the nation state as the primary cultural reference point might now be regarded as misguided as social and commercial interactions now frequently transcend national borders, which has created new and eclectic cultural 'hybrids'.
- Social sub-groupings within the nation state, fragmenting its cultural unity, have become increasingly apparent; for example, ethnic and religious minorities and economic migrants.
- The theory tends to present culture as a static phenomenon, thus rendering it measurable, while in reality it is clear that homogeneity in culture may not be taken for granted over time.
- It is methodologically flawed. Not only may one take issue with the notion that components of culture can be dissected and scored, but also the exclusive sample of IBM employees may be regarded as offering only a partial picture of national norms and values.

## Trompenaars and Hampden-Turner

The work of Trompenaars and Hampden-Turner (1997) serve to supplement Hofstede's study by offering an alternative set of cultural dimensions, and by placing a focus on meanings, or humans' interpretations of the world around them. Trompenaars' empirical investigation occurred in the early 1990s and involved the distribution of questionnaires to over 15,000 managers in 298 countries. He identified five 'relationship orientations', as follows:

*Universalism versus particularism* relates to the extent to which individuals are inclined to apply universal principles or rules to social situations or events or whether they are prepared to modify those principles according to each specific occurrence. While formal notions of fairness and truth are regarded as significant in universalistic cultures, particularism places a greater emphasis on the building and protection of relationships. Thus, according to Trompenaars, in particularistic cultures witnesses to a road accident in which the driver was breaking the speed limit would feel obliged to testify in favour of that driver if he or she is a friend or relative. Western countries such as the USA, Australia and the UK ranked high on universalism, while China, Latin and developing countries were more particularistic in orientation.

*Individualism versus communitarianism* is reflective of Hofstede's equivalent dimension and essentially refers to whether the individual's primary orientation is towards the self or to common goals and objectives. In embracing a wider range of nation states in a later era, Trompenaars interestingly unearths national cultural predispositions that would seem to contradict the thrust of Hofstede's analysis. Thus, following the relatively recent inception of market liberalism in their domains, Mexico and the Czech Republic tend towards individualism. Japan, on the other hand, remains strongly collectivist in orientation.

*Achievement versus ascription* refers to the extent to which social status is achieved either by what people have *done*, that is, what they have achieved through their own exertions (educational qualifications, performance measurements, etc.), or through who they *are*, as a product of birth, family, gender, age or religion. It is argued that the USA, the UK and western societies tend to be achievement oriented, while Asian cultures and those in developing societies place greater value on ascribed characteristics.

*Neutral versus affective* relates to the extent to which feelings and emotion, or impersonality and rationality, are expressed in interpersonal encounters. According to Trompenaars, and Hampden-Turner (1997), Japan has a highly neutral culture, while Mexico is strongly affective or emotional.

*Specificity versus diffuseness* relates to the distinction drawn between the individual's private and public spaces. In specific cultures, compartmentalization occurs between work and private life, while in more diffuse societies various spheres of life are closely integrated, and the 'whole person' is involved in business relationships. As with other dimensions, a broad separation is apparent between western societies and others, with western countries tending towards specificity.

*Sequential versus synchronic* distinguishes cultures on the basis of their perceptions of time. Some nationalities and regions are most oriented towards *monochrony*, which assumes that time is linear and sequential, while others are *polychronic*, where time is multiple and diffuse. In the former, activities tend to be separated into sequences, while in the latter, individuals are inclined to undertake several activities at the same time. This dimension also relates to the extent societies are oriented towards the past, present or future.

*Inner versus outer directedness* reflects fundamental notions as to whether individuals and groups can control their own destiny, or whether external factors and luck play a decisive part. In inner-directed societies, it is believed that strategic choices and planning are important in shaping organizations and their environment, while outer directedness emphasizes the force of political conditions and 'acts of God'. Personal networking has a high premium in outer-directed societies.

While both Hofstede and Trompenaars have provided highly influential insights on cultural diversity, it may be argued that other, perhaps less vaunted, works provide equally valid insights for understanding the cultural complexities of international business (Kupta et al., 2008).

In particular, Lewis (1999) draws distinctions between 'clusters of countries' (Ronen and Shenkar, 1985) on the basis of *Linear-Active-Multi-Active* (LAMAS) and *Dialogue-Oriented -Data-Oriented* (DODOS) scales. According to these classifications, cultures that follow multi-active (DODOS) time systems, such as Mediterranean and Latin American cultures, tend to engage in various activities simultaneously, are more flexible and have less rigid management conversational rules. In contrast, Swedes, Swiss, Dutch or Germans, in relatively 'linear' (LAMAS) societies, exhibit sequential action patterns, focus on single acts, time consciousness and punctuality. Lewis (1999) suggests that DODOS countries tend to have more closely knit social networks, which enable them to gather information about business partners through informal networks of friends and families. In contrast, Germans, Swiss, North Americans and New Zealanders 'love to gather solid information and move steadily forward from that database' (Kupta et al., 2008)' (ibid. 46).

## The World Values Survey

The World Values Survey has provided a wide-ranging and contemporary survey of international value systems in the era of globalization. A wide spectrum of countries is covered, ranging from impoverished to affluent global extremities. Results are derived from interviews, using a standardized questionnaire, with representative national samples measuring changing values concerning religion, gender roles, work motivations, democracy, good governance, social capital, political participation, and tolerance of other groups, environmental protection and subjective well-being (World Values Survey, 2008).

Even though the survey encompasses a number of cultural zones and embraces both liberal and authoritarian regimes, two major dimensions of cross-cultural variation are identified: *traditional/secular-rational* and *survival/self-expression*. Figure 2.1 depicts how societies manifest these two dimensions.

The traditional/secular dimension refers to the extent to which religion is important in societies. 'Traditional' societies emphasize parent–child ties, deference to authority and traditional family values while rejecting divorce, abortion, euthanasia and suicide. In nearly all industrial societies values have shifted from traditionalism to secularism/rationalism, which rejects the traditionalist worldview specified.

The survival/self-expression dimension embodies value changes associated with the shift from industrial- to knowledge-based societies. While survival is a priority in pre-industrial and even in industrial society, in knowledge societies an increasing proportion of the population, comprising mainly young people (Inglehart, 2000), has grown up taking survival for granted. The World Values Survey (2008: 6) states:

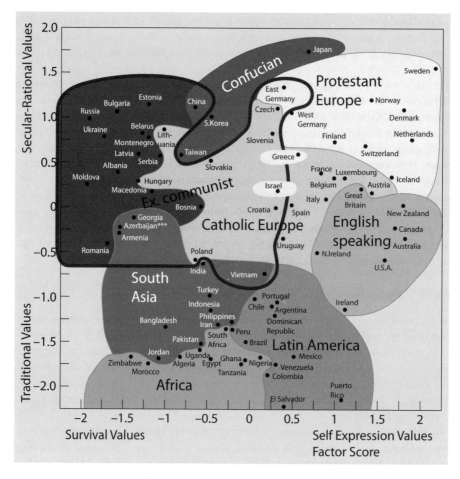

**Figure 2.1   Cultural map of the world**

*Source:* Ronald Inglehart and Christian Welsel, *Modernization, Cultural change and Democracy*, Cambridge University Press, 2005, p. 63. Reproduced from www.worldvaluessurvey.org.

> 66 Their priorities have shifted from an overwhelming emphasis on economic and physical security toward increasing emphasis on subjective well being, self-expression and quality of life. Self expression values give high priority to environmental protection, tolerance of foreigners, gays and lesbians and gender equality, and rising demands for participation in decision-making and political life. 99

This shifting worldview in developed societies has been described by Inglehart (2000) as 'post-materialist' and is associated with looser and flatter, rather than bureaucratic, organizational forms, and with a work/life balance that promotes imagination and individual freedom rather than hard work.

The World Values Survey provides a number of insights that are potentially useful for policy and practice in IHRM. First, referring to the traditional/secular dimension, there are clear implications for joint ventures and similar concerns emanating from 'rationalist' cultural contexts and operating in 'traditional' contexts. Essentially, such concerns run the risk of being insufficiently sensitized to deeply-held religious and other convictions in the host environment, tending to impose westernized, yet perhaps inappropriate, organizational cultural and structural frameworks.

The worldview shift towards 'self-expression' identified by the Survey implies that younger generations across national frontiers possess a remarkably different outlook on work and life than their predecessors. If tolerance and a less materialistic orientation indeed represent primary facets of emerging international value systems, this will have implications for the motivation of future generations of international managers, who may be disposed towards quality of life benefits rather than financial reward, and who should be well disposed towards international team working and the assimilation of diversity. The dimension also has a bearing on preferred organizational structures in respect of which informal and democratic systems are likely to be valued above hierarchy and bureaucracy.

## Implications of cultural perspectives for IHRM

Clearly, there are some powerfully intuitive connections between the cultural stereotypes and orientations theorized by Hall and Hall (1990), Hofstede (2001) and Trompenaars (1993), and observed manifestations of HRM across regions. Although such connections are far from empirically proven, the following example of organizational practice might be regarded as being influenced by culture:

- preferred organizational structures – flat/tall, consultative/authoritarian, and so on (power distance);
- recruitment, whether based on merit or nepotism (achievement v. ascription, high context);
- whether pay is individually determined (individualism v. collectivism);
- the level of statutory regulation in employment (uncertainty avoidance);
- maternity, paternity, childcare provisions, and so on (masculinity v. femininity).

While, however, cultural theory can provide a useful conceptual tool for understanding and judging comparative manifestations of HRM across borders, arguably its most telling contribution relates to the awareness it provides of the potential for cross-cultural ambiguity and misunderstanding in international team working.

Together, institutional and cultural theories provide a powerful conceptual frame for analysing and explaining international variations in HR and employment practices. While care needs to be taken to avoid overly deterministic links between such theoretical perspectives and actual manifestations of HR within national or regional settings, which denies the significance of enterprise autonomy and independent corporate strategies, complementarities exist in the 'predictions' of institutional and cultural theory. For example, a high incidence of performance-related pay may be found in countries that score highly on 'individualism' and which are strongly oriented towards neo-liberalism; each of these theoretical contributions captures the value of individual competition and material gain. Similarly, some correlation may be perceived between neo-corporatist and uncertainty avoidance tendencies, each of which are associated with commercial climes that manifest relatively high degrees of regulation and a preference for longer-term planning.

Case Study: Marks and Spencer

# 'FROM CONTINENTAL CHOCOLATES TO CONTINENTAL CLOSURE'
## By Moira Calveley, University of Hertfordshire Business School

### The company background

Marks and Spencer (M&S) is a well-known high street retailer in the UK with stores nationwide. It was formed in 1894 by a partnership between Michael Marks and Tom Spencer and became a public company in 1926. During the 1970s the company began to expand on a global basis, opening its first overseas store in Canada in 1973 and in France and Belgium in 1975. In the late 1980s it acquired stores in the USA (which remained trading under the Brooks Brothers name) and opened stores in Hong Kong. By the mid-1990s, M&S had stores in around 30 countries worldwide, incorporating Europe, North America and Asia.

Known for its high quality, good service and value for money, the company developed into a highly profitable organization, even branching out into financial services in 1985. M&S was to become one of the most profitable retailers in Europe. However, when the recession hit the retail industry in the UK in the late 1990s, M&S began to make the news as its profits dropped sharply.

In 1999 M&S responded to the fall in profits by reviewing its management structure, stopping recruitment to its graduate training programme and reviewing its business operations. The first major overseas investment to go was in Canada, where in 1999 it closed its 38 stores, reportedly cutting approximately 900 jobs and paying around $35 million in severance payments and closure costs (Warson, 1999). It also sold its Brooks Brothers stores in the USA in November 2001. It was, however, the closure of shops in France and Belgium in March 2001 that put M&S in the headlines, as we shall see below.

### M&S's approach to people management

The company takes a paternal approach to managing people and, although not without its critics, it is often viewed as a 'good' employer. M&S prided itself on introducing staff 'welfare' services in the early 1930s that included the provision of pensions, subsidized staff canteens, health and dental care, hairdressing, rest rooms and camping holidays. Such practices have continued over the years and the company works at being seen to be fair with people. For example, when it was decided to freeze graduate recruitment in 1999, as a gesture of goodwill it gave the equivalent of one month's salary (around £1,500) to each of the graduates to whom it had withdrawn its offer of employment (Welch, 1999).

The company has promoted good human relations because, as Lord Sieff a former Chairman explained, 'we are human beings at work not industrial beings' (1984, quoted in Blyton and Turnbull, 1998) and 'good human relations at work pay off; they are of great importance if a business is to be efficiently run' (1990: 245, quoted in Blyton and Turnbull, 1998). The company's approach to trade unions is that employees have a right to join one, but that unions are not recognized for negotiation purposes – except where legislation requires them to do so, as in mainland Europe. With good HR practices, M&S believe that trade unions are not necessary. However, although M&S have traditionally put a strong emphasis on personnel management, giving it strategic importance (Blyton and Turnbull, 1998), Clara Freeman lost her position as Executive Director for UK stores and personnel in September 2000 as part of the management restructuring programme (Cooper, 2000). An M&S spokesperson denied that the HR function was being downgraded as HR was being represented at executive level by the chief legal adviser and company secretary; nevertheless, a company analyst commenting on the situation suggested that 'personnel directors do not make money' (Cooper, 2000).

## Continental closures

In order to retrench and cut costs, in 2001 M&S decided to close stores across Europe, and an announcement was made on 29 March that the shops in France and Belgium were to close. It is estimated that this restructuring involved around 38 stores in total and upward of 4,000 employees; in France, the numbers were reported as 18 shops and 1,700 workers.

The announcement caused great controversy and uproar, particularly in France. It was alleged that managers were informed by email and that the closure announcement took place only five minutes after the initial, informal, meeting with worker representatives, which reportedly did not constitute a consultation that conformed to the French work code. The timing of the announcement corresponded with the opening of the London Stock Exchange, 8.00 a.m.

Although trade unions are not recognized by M&S in the UK (as discussed above), some French workers were. On their behalf, several trade unions filed a complaint against M&S, claiming that it had broken French labour law by only informing the staff at the same time as it informed the UK Stock Exchange of the decision to close the stores. A French court later ruled that M&S had acted illegally by not consulting with employees before announcing closure; the company was told that it had to suspend its plans until a full consultation had taken place.

M&S denied having acted in any way to contravene legislation in France, claiming that it was abiding by UK law and the rules governing listed companies. It argued that under these rules a quoted company has to inform the market of any major developments in its activities without delay. Further, it was only announcing that it intended to close stores by the end of the year. The implication is clearly that worker consultation would have leaked the news and this may have affected stock market activity and share prices; as it was, M&S shares jumped 7 per cent on the day.

M&S appealed against the ruling that was later overruled. However, the jobs were saved as the stores were bought by the department-store group Galeries Lafayette which, as part of the deal, secured the jobs of the workers. Both trade unions and works committees in France were consulted prior to the deal.

## Reaction to the closures

Following the announcement of the store closures, emotions were running very high. It was perceived that M&S was intent on restructuring due to a business crisis, but with little thought for the French workers. The French government encouraged trade union action against M&S's decision: the Labour Minister called for a Europe-wide trade union protest; the Prime Minister, Lionel Jospin, described the company's actions in closing the stores as 'unacceptable' and called for the Labour Ministry to launch its own enquiry.

In protest over the closures, M&S workers took to the streets. It was reported that more than 1,000 workers from across Europe protested outside the company's main UK store in London on 17 May 2001. There were also protests in Paris and at the European Parliament in Strasbourg.

In the UK, the French workers were supported by the Trades Union Congress (TUC), who supported the London demonstration. The TUC General Secretary was reported as saying, 'M&S thought they could export the UK's easy hire-and-fire rules to the rest of Europe' (Benham and Freeman, 2001). Contrary to this, an M&S spokesperson is quoted as saying, 'We're convinced that we complied with all legal requirements ... we're surprised by the reaction of the authorities' (*The Guardian*, 2001b).

## French labour law, custom and culture

The French government takes an interventionist approach to employment relations. Their reaction discussed above was partly as a result of their drive to reduce unemployment in the country. Works councils were created by law in France in 1945 and are one of the channels of worker representation, the other two being workforce delegates and trade unions. In most companies these organizations coexist; however, works councils are playing an ever-increasing role. They are made up of elected employee representatives and they have the right to information and consultation that includes issues such as redundancy (EIRO, 1998; Hollinshead and Leat, 1995). It was the perceived failure of M&S to follow these consultation laws that caused unrest following the announcement of store closures.

Although not a direct result of M&S's action but spurred on by it, the French government rushed through proposals to increase employment rights in order to protect workers' jobs. The resulting 'social modernization' bill included: the doubling of minimum redundancy pay; increased powers for works councils with regard to redundancy and a longer time period for consideration of redundancy plans; and nine-month redeployment leave for redundant workers (EIRO, 2001a).

One of the factors that M&S may not have taken account of in its decision to announce the shop closures the way it did is the culture of the French people. The French are renowned for 'taking to the streets' to demonstrate for social and political reasons. In 1968, 10 million people went on strike to demand a fairer form of capitalism that would create an economy to benefit all; in June 2003, people took to the streets to demonstrate over pension reforms. The French people believe that organizations have a social responsibility. Books of condolence were set up in M&S shops and were filled by people who had empathy with their fellow workers. The feeling of the people was perhaps summed up by French Prime Minister Jospin when he stated, 'the employees who enriched shareholders deserve better treatment. Such behaviour should be punished' (*The Guardian,* 2001b).

*Sources*: BBC (2001a, 2001b) CNN (2001a, 2001b) EIRO (2001a, 2001b) Marks (2003) *People* (2001) *The Guardian* (2001a, 2001b, 2001c).

## Discussion questions

**1**  From the M&S experience described above:

    **a**  Discuss to what extent an institutional perspective would have assisted management in analysing and understanding cross-national employment relations.

    **b**  Discuss to what extent a culturalist perspective would have assisted management in analysing and understanding cross-national employment relations.

**2**  What appear to be the overarching ideological frames of reference employed by institutions in France? Give examples for your answer.

**3**  In your opinion, what is the ideological perspective in which M&S were operating? Give examples for your answer.

**4**  As the HR manager of a multinational organization, which analytical approach would you adopt when considering employment matters in a country different from your own? Explain your reasons.

*Source*: Adapted from Calveley (2005).

---

### Activity

Imagine you are the management team of a US-owned pharmaceutical company entering into a joint venture with a partner in a Latin American country of your choice. Using Geert Hofstede's cultural dimensions, and other relevant materials, explore the potential cross-cultural problems in international team working between parent and subsidiary managers. Make recommendations as to how these problems might be overcome.

## Summary

This section has offered two complementary strands of analysis to comprehend diversity in international HR systems – institutional and cultural. Institutional forms and structures, which may be regarded as the 'hardware' of national and regional business systems, impact fundamentally on the comparative status of the human resource. Institutional perspectives also cast light on the nature of pervasive 'neo-liberal' ideology emanating from the USA, associated with liberal market economies and the 'alternative' doctrine of 'neo-corporatism' that is associated with coordinated market economies of Europe.

Cultural perspectives may be represented as the 'software' conditioning international variations in values and mindsets. While major tenets of cultural theory may be regarded as being in need of updating to account for new global developments, intuitive connections may be established between cultural stereotypes and observed manifestations of country-specific HR practices. The World Values Survey offers a contemporary and comprehensive picture of changing and contrasting value systems at a global level, accounting particularly for distinctive worldviews in developing and developed countries, as well as among the 'post-materialist' generation.

## Further reading

**Harzing A.W. and Van Ruysseveldt, J.** (2006) *International Human Resource Management* (2nd edn.), London: Sage Publications.

This edited volume offers theoretically grounded material on the role of IHRM in internationalization, multinational structures and strategies, and the role of HRM in mergers and acquisitions. A major part of the book is also devoted to the analysis of comparative HRM and industrial relations. Part 2, in particular, provides in-depth analysis of cultural and institutional perspectives on IHRM.

**Crouch, C. and Streeck, W.** (1997) *Political Economy of Modern Capitalism*, London: Sage Publications.

This book provides an in-depth explanation and analysis of business systems in European countries and the USA, delving into international variations in corporate governance and industrial relations.

**Hofstede, G.** (2001) *Culture's Consequences: Comparing Values, Behaviors, Institutions and Organizations Across Nations* 2nd edn., Thousand Oaks, CA: Sage Publications.

This book represents a seminal work on culture, management and organization. An in-depth explanation is offered for the formulation of the renowned cultural dimensions, drawing on anthropological perspectives. Analysis is informed by intriguing illustrative material.

## Useful websites

www.geerthofstede.com
An accessible digest of Hofstede's cultural theory, with brief explanations of key cultural dimensions.
www.worldvaluessurvey.org
As 'the world's most comprehensive investigation of political and socio-cultural change', this site provides links to detailed survey findings, surveys and publications.

## References

**Albert, M.** (1993) *Capitalism Against Capitalism*, London: Whurr.

**Benham, M. and Freeman, C.** (2001) Rally piles pressure on M&S, *London Evening Standard*.

**Blyton, P. and Turnbull, P.** (1998) *The Dynamics of Employee Relations*, Basingstoke: Palgrave Macmillan.

**Calveley, M.** (2008) Competencies of international human resource managers, in M. Özbilgin, M. (ed.) *International Human Resource Management: An Eight-point Framework for Global HR Management*, London: Palgrave Macmillan.

***Concise Oxford English Dictionary*** (2002) Oxford: Oxford University Press.

**Cooper, C.** (2000) Freeman's departure marks end of an era for HR at troubled Marks and Spencer, *People Management*, 28 September.

**Dahl, S.** (2004) Intercultural research: the current state of knowledge, discussion paper no. 26, Middlesex University.

**Dore, R.** (2000) *Stock-market Capitalism, Welfare Capitalism: Japan and Germany versus the Anglo-Saxons*, Oxford: Oxford University Press.

**Edwards, T., Almond, P., Clark, I., Colling, T. and Ferner, A.** (2005) Reverse diffusion in US multinationals: barriers from the American business system, *Journal of Management Studies*, 42: 6.

**EIRO** (1998) Works Council reveals major differences in practice, European Industrial Relations Observatory, Dublin.

**Giddens, A.** (2002) *Runaway World: How Globalization is Reshaping Our Lives*, London: Profile Books.

**Giddens, A.** (2006) *Sociology* (5th edn.), Cambridge and Malden MA: Polity Press.

***Guardian, The*** (2001a) France calls for protests at M&S closures, 6 April.

***Guardian, The*** (2001b) French say M&S closure may have been illegal, 2 April.

***Guardian, The*** (2001c) Sacked European workers march on M&S in the rain, 18 May.

**Hall, E.T. and Hall, M.R.** (1990) *Understanding Cultural Differences*, Yarmouth, MA: Intercultural Press.

**Hall, P.A. and Soskice, D.** (2001) An introduction to varieties of capitalism, in P.A. Hall and D. Soskice (eds) *Varieties of Capitalism: The Institutional Foundations of Comparative Advantage*, Oxford: Oxford University Press

**Hardy, J.** (2002) An institutionalist analysis of foreign direct investment in Poland: Wroclaw's second great transformation, unpublished PhD thesis, University of Durham.

**Hodgetts, R.M. and Luthans, F.** (2003) *International Management, Culture, Strategy and Behaviour* (5th edn.), New York: McGraw-Hill.

**Hofstede, G.** (2001) *Cultures' Consequences: Comparing Values, Behaviors, Institutions, and Organzations Across Nations* (2nd edn.), Thousand Oaks, CA: Sage Publications.

**Hollingsworth, J.R. and Boyer, R.** (1997) Co-ordination of economic actors and social systems of production, in J.R. Hollingsworth and R.Boyer (eds) *Contemporary Capitalism: The Embeddedness of Institutions*, Cambridge: Cambridge University Press.

**Hollinshead, G. and Leat, M.** (1995) *Human Resource Management: An International and Comparative Perspective*, London: Pitman Publishing.

**Hyman, R.** (2004) Varieties of capitalism, national industrial relations systems and transitional challenges, in A.W. Harzing and J. Van Ruysseveldt (eds) *International Human Resource Management* (2nd edn.), London: Sage Publications.

**Inglehart, R.** (2000) Globalization and postmodern values, *The Washington Quarterly*, 23(1): 215–228.

**Inglehart, R. and Welsel, C.** (2005) *Modernization, Cultural Change and Democracy*, Cambridge: Cambridge University Press.

**Kitschelt, H., Lange, P., Matks, G. and Stephens, J.D.** (1999) Convergence and divergence in advanced capitalist economies, in H. Kitschelt, P. Lange, G. Marks and J.D. Stephens (eds) *Continuity and Change in Contemporary Capitalism*, Cambridge: Cambridge University Press.

**Kupta, B., Everett, A.M. and Cathro, V.** (2008) Home alone and often unprepared – intercultural communication training for expatriated partners in German MNCs, *International Journal of Human Resource Management*, 18(10): 1765–1791.

**Lewis, R.D.** (1999) *When Cultures Collide: Managing Successfully Across Cultures* (2nd edn.), London: Nicholas Brealey Publishing.

**Macionis, J.J. and Plummer, K.C.** (2002) *Sociology: A Global Introduction* (2nd edn.), Harlow: Pearson.

**Marginson, P.** (2004) The Eurocompany and European Works Councils, in A.W. Harzing and J. Van Ruysseveldt (eds) *International Human Resource Management* (2nd edn.), London: Sage Publications.

**Miliband, R. and Panitch, L.** (1993) *Socialist Register 1993: Real Problems, False Solutions*, London: Merlin Press.

**Pollert, A.** (1999) *Transformation at Work in the New Market Economies of Central Eastern Europe*, London: Sage Publications.

**Ronen, S. and Shenkar, O.** (1985) Clustering countries on attitudinal dimensions: a review and synthesis, *Academy of Management Review*, 10(3): 435–454.

**Smith, A.** (1776) *An Enquiry into the Nature and Causes of the Health of Nations*, London: Strahan and Cadell.

**Sorge, A.** (2004) 'Cross-national differences in human resources and organization, in A.W. Harzing and J. Van Ruysseveldt (eds) *International Human Resource Management* (2nd edn.), London: Sage Publications.

**Spencer-Oatey, H.** (2000) *Culturally Speaking: Managing Rapport Through Talk Across Cultures*, London: Continuum.

**Steger, M.B.** (2003) *Globalization: A Very Short Introduction*, Oxford: Oxford University Press.

**Stiglitz, J.E.** (2002) *Globalization and its Discontents*, New York: W.W. Norton & Company.

**Streeck, W.** (2001) Introduction: explorations into the origins of nonliberal capitalism in Germany and Japan, in W. Streeck and K.Yamamura (eds) *The Origins of Nonliberal Capitalism: Germany and Japan in Comparison*, Ithaca, NY: Cornell University Press.

**Trompenaars, F. and Hampden-Turner, C.** (1997) *Riding the Waves of Culture: Understanding Cultural Diversity in Business* (2nd edn.), London: Nicholas Brealey Publishing.

**Warson, A.** (1999) Marks and Spencer and other U.K. firms exit Canada, *Shopping Centers Today*, September.

**Welch, J.** (1999) Marks and Spencer and its graduate programme, *People Management*, June, p. 14.

**Whitley, R.** (2002) Business systems, in A. Sorge (ed.) *Organization*, London: Thomson Learning.

**World Values Survey** (2008) World Values Survey Association.

# 03

# Multinational corporations (MNCs)

## ❖ LEARNING OBJECTIVES

❖ To consider why companies become multinational in their operations

❖ To expose seminal theories relating to multinationals and structure, with particular reference to the relationship between parent and subsidiary

❖ To examine the employment policies of multinationals, and to consider how they are responding to ethical concerns

## Introduction

This chapter focuses on the pivotal corporate actor in international human resource management (IHRM), the multinational corporation (MNC). With reference to 'levels of analysis' referred to in Chapter 1, the MNC may be viewed as occupying the 'lower tier' organization level, although it is important to note that in their operations MNCs straddle local, national, regional and international boundaries and are therefore impacted by regulatory and other influences at each of these levels. MNCs, given their size and international scope, also exert a powerful influence on the global environment and the process of globalization itself. Gaining insight into the internal strategies and structures of MNCs is vital for the student of IHRM, as these serve to condition staffing policies; for example, whether expatriates or local managers will administer subsidiary units.

The growth of MNCs as dominant economic actors has occurred in global economic and political environment subject to the intensification of market liberalization over the past two to three decades. At a regional level, protectionist barriers between nation states have given way to the establishment of 'single markets' in Europe (the EU) and North America (NAFTA). Over the same period, nations that were previously removed from global economic structures, such as Russia, China, the former communist regimes in central and eastern

Europe, India and a number of Latin American countries have undergone political revolutions or transformations, which have meant that they are now 'open for business'. At an international level, moves towards international market liberalization have been orchestrated by powerful international bodies operating from Washington, notably the World Trade Organization (WTO), the World Bank and the International Monetary Fund (IMF). Since the 1986–94 Uruguay round of GATT (the General Agreement on Trade and Tariffs), which may be regarded as the predecessor of the WTO, there has been a virtually unbridled agenda towards the freeing of international trade incepted and catalysed by these bodies. The underlying philosophy of the WTO, as captured by Hoekman and Kostecki (1995), is that 'open markets, non discrimination, and global competition in international trade are conducive to the national welfare of all countries' (p. 1).

Established in 1995, the WTO assumed responsibility for the administration of multilateral trade agreements negotiated by its members. Industrialized market economies represent the most influential participants in the WTO, with the EU, Japan and the USA constituting a 'triad' of major players, reflecting their global economic positions. Countries such as Brazil and India have also exerted substantial influence, partly as a result of their economic size, but also due to their acting as spokespeople for other developing countries (ibid.). While the WTO, the World Bank and the IMF have distinctive mandates, there is also interdependence between these agencies. As Hoekman and Kostecki (1995) state, the World Bank mobilizes support in support of poverty alleviation and sustained development in low income countries. The IMF provides short-term financing to countries that confront macro-economic imbalances, while the WTO induces countries to adopt non-discriminatory policies and to reduce their barriers to trade.

It is in the context of global economic liberalism that the MNC has become a dominant organizational form as well as, frequently, an awesome economic power. At the outset of this chapter, it is worth reflecting on the precise nature of MNCs in order to distinguish them from primarily domestic concerns involved in exporting or importing. An MNC is a company *physically* active in more than one country (i.e. it has plant, technology and employees in a country other than its country of origin). This definition therefore would not merely embrace household names such as Shell, Ford, Mitsubishi or McDonald's, but also much smaller companies in the services as well as the manufacturing sector. Examples of the latter are in finance or property investment. There are 63,000 MNCs in the world and they are now responsible for two-thirds of global trade and 80 per cent of investment. Recent international reports by the UN Conference on Trade and Development (UNCTAD, 2000) and the UN Development Programme (UNDP, 2000) have demonstrated that the largest MNCs have annual sales greater than the entire economic output of many medium-sized countries. Based on this formulation, General Motors is bigger than South Africa and Shell is twice as big as Nigeria. Of the largest 100 economic actors in the world today, 51 are corporations and 49 are countries (Pilger, 2001).

The dominant flow of foreign direct investment (FDI) has been between developed economies, or, less frequently, from developed to developing economies. As a concomitant, the 'nerve centres' of MNCs have retained concentration in Europe (see Figure 3.1), North America and Asia. Nevertheless, there is some evidence of a breach in this global 'economic order' in recent years. According to *The Economist* (2007), the world is becoming 'more bumpy' as more MNCs are owned and controlled by non-western sources. The following quotation from *The Economist* (ibid). is instructive:

"" Indian and Chinese firms are now starting to give their rich world rivals a run for their money. So far this year, Indian firms, led by Hindalco and Tata Steel, have bought some 34 foreign companies for a combined $10.7 billion. Indian IT-services companies such as Infosys, Tata Consultancy Services and Wipro are putting the fear of God into the old guard, including Accenture and even mighty IBM. Big Blue sold its personal computer business to a Chinese multinational, Lenovo, which is now starting to get its act together. PetroChina has become a force in Africa, including, controversially, Sudan. Brazilian and Russian multinationals are also starting to make their mark. The Russians have outdone the Indians this year, splashing $11.4 billion abroad and are now in the running to buy Alitalia, Italy's state airline.

(*The Economist*, 2007) ""

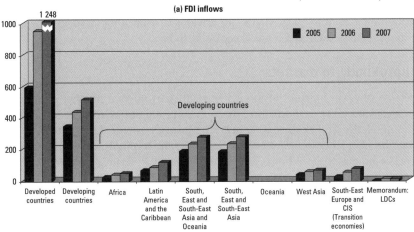

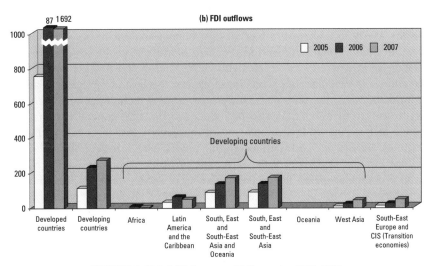

**FIGURE 3.1** Global FDI flows: top 20 Economies, 2005–2007

*Source*: UNCTAD (2008).

What are the factors that drive companies to expand their operations across national borders? Following Ghertman and Allen (1984) and Barrell and Pain (1997), some key explanatory factors are as follows.

## New markets

Undoubtedly, a critical driving force towards the internationalization of corporate forms and structures is the need to create and respond to new markets. This is not a new phenomenon. The Dutch economy, for example, is reputed for its international orientation and as being a home base for such giants as Philips and Royal Dutch Shell. Yet initial moves to internationalize were the response to obvious limitations of national demographics and land space. Now there is broader recognition across business that, as markets become more volatile and contested, there is a need to spread sales and distribution networks beyond national boundaries. Furthermore, MNCs are anxious to gain a foothold in emerging markets in transforming regions such as China, Russia and India

## Physical proximity to markets

More generally, physical location in foreign marketplaces offers a number of strategic advantages over and above exportation. These include the ability to draw on indigenous supplies of knowledge and skills (e.g. concerning tastes, customs, laws and social networking), the avoidance of import restrictions and the ability to capitalize on local inducements or grants. It should also be pointed out that in some sectors the perishable nature of products renders exportation impossible. This is the case, for example, in dairy products and in newspapers, where there is nothing much staler than yesterday's headlines.

## Internationalizing production

A clear strategic benefit possessed by MNCs, which is not available to the purely domestic concern, is the ability to undertake a type of cost–benefit analysis of physical and human resources on an international basis and to organize productive processes accordingly. Factors in the equation as to where to locate elements of the production process would include knowledge and skills of indigenous workers set against the cost of labour, availability and quality of local suppliers, the state of advancement of local technology and the availability of raw materials. Inward investors may also be influenced by more general national political and economic factors such as the complexion of the government in power, or the nature of taxation regimes. Indeed, as 'cash rich' economic actors, MNCs reserve the right to switch funds from one country to another if the financial and strategic rationale underlying operations in a particular region falters. The capacity of MNCs to juggle investments on an international basis has particular significance in the field of labour relations, where threats of industrial unrest from local workers can be met with threats of closure from parent company management. Such a scenario has been evidenced at Ford's plant in Halewood, Liverpool, during its chequered history.

## Host country incentives

While MNCs have been subject to robust criticism concerning employment and other matters in overseas subsidiaries, it is undeniably the case that governments and other primary stakeholders in the host country environment are aware of the economic benefits in offering a favourable climate for the receipt of FDI. This may relate to financial incentives, tax concessions, or more generally offering a cost-effective and flexible context for business operations. MNCs have argued that their overall effect on work and employment has been positive. Not only do they create jobs (approximately 50 per cent of employment in the UK and Ireland is dependent on FDI) but also there is an indirect boost for suppliers, services and infrastructures when an MNC subsidiary locates in a host locality. We should note also that these job creation effects are magnified in developing regions of the world, particularly in Asia. It has been argued that MNCs assist with the process of industrialization or modernization in host countries. As conduits for the diffusion of the 'state-of-the-art' ideas and practice, MNCs have taken credit for the exportation of new technologies and managerial 'know-how' such as branding, performance management and total quality systems. Finally, MNCs have contended that they are disposed to offer in excess of local labour market rates of pay.

## Multinational structures and strategies

A key issue for many multinationals is to combine being highly differentiated, so that there is sufficient flexibility to be able to respond to local conditions, and particularly market requirements, with a level of integration that will promote corporate cohesiveness, image and economies of scale. It has become clear that there is no single model multinational organization, but rather a set of typologies exist that are contingent on the market and other circumstances in which the MNC finds itself, as well as the strategic intent of the MNC. In a seminal work, Bartlett and Ghoshal (1989) define four such typologies, which are represented as dominant forms in sequential historical eras, but nevertheless still possess explanatory value regarding various industrial sectors.

*Multidomestic* was a dominant form between the two world wars, at which time changing customer preferences were apparent and logistical barriers impeded international trade. In these circumstances, products or services were differentiated to meet local demands, and products themselves were often produced locally. Within MNCs, organizational structures were decentralized, with a low level of control from the centre. This typology has been common in the food and drinks sector and in French and British MNCs.

*International* represented a dominant organizational form in the post-war years, in which product demand was booming, with the USA enjoying unrivalled productive capacity. This typology is associated with a retrenchment of organizational power to the (US) parent, with subsidiaries being dependent on the centre for new products and ideas. Technological innovation was diffused from home to host in a sequential fashion and the corporate culture was based on professional management with limited delegation. It has been a dominant model in the telecommunications industry.

*Global* typology was prevalent in the 1960s and 1970s in a period when tariff barriers were being reduced, combined with lower transport costs and homogenous consumer demand. At this time, as price competition was vital, MNCs integrated and rationalized production to deliver standard products in a cost-efficient manner. Personal and bureaucratic forms of control were apparent and dependent subsidiaries performed a 'pipeline' role for the parent. This has been a common configuration in consumer electronics, computers and automobiles and in Japanese and German MNCs.

*Transnational* became a dominant model in the late 1970s, in which MNCs were seeking to tap into niche markets across national borders while seeking to maintain economies of scale in an increasingly competitive market environment. Thus, there was a need to respond simultaneously to the conflicting strategic needs of global efficiency and local responsiveness. In these circumstances, while subsidiaries were 'empowered' with corporate responsibilities (such as research and development), a high degree of parental control remained through socializing subsidiary managers (and workers) into the corporate ethos, and through establishing interactive networks encompassing parent and subsidiaries. This form of MNC began to embody the notion of flexibility, using computer-aided design and manufacturing, and formulating strategy in an incremental and adaptive fashion (Mintzberg, 1988). Pharmaceutical and food MNCs approximate to the transnational model, which is also typical of US, Dutch and Swiss corporations.

In a complementary and influential study, the US management theorist Howard Perlmutter (1969) provided stereotypes to understand the 'tortuous' nature of the relationship between multinational parent and subsidiary. The typologies below (see also Table 3.1) depict the phases of development of multinational corporations, as international subsidiaries move from infantile dependency towards mature autonomy:

- The *ethnocentric* concern bases its operations on the assumption that tried and tested approaches to management can be extended from the country of origin to operating sites in other countries. Underlying this is the preference to keep the reins of power in the country of origin. This is reflected in the centralization of managerial authority. Ethnocentric concerns are also likely to retain research and development and other 'knowledge' activity in the country of origin.

In HRM terms, while host country labour will be recruited to carry out routine activity, expatriates from the country of origin will be primarily responsible for the management of subsidiaries. The possible dysfunctions associated with expatriation include failure of assignees to adjust to the host country due to language and cultural difficulties, problems for dual career couples, schooling for children, as well as organizational re-entry on completion of the assignment. From the point of view of the host country population, *ethnocentricity* is problematic as local talent is confronted with a 'glass ceiling' impeding promotion to senior positions that remain the preserve of parent company nationals. Similarly, training and development activity is focused on such managerial and professional staff, viewed as the 'brains' of the organization, while indigenous employees are treated as unskilled operatives. While Perlmutter (1969) viewed this typology as a primary stage of multinational development, it nevertheless retains explanatory value. For example, a number of western-owned international companies have now become established in the Moscow region. While local observers welcome the modernizing potential of such firms, there has been some consternation expressed regarding the sight of the 'suitcase' westerner in Red Square. As a result of such strategic dysfunctions, the MNC is disposed to devolve areas of decision-making authority to local managers, taking it to the next stage of development.

- A *polycentric* company bases its operations on the assumption that local managers and employees are best placed to formulate policies that most realistically reflect local needs. This approach therefore rests on a preference for decentralization and provision of autonomy for operating sites. In essence, moves towards empowerment of locals are based on the strategic realization of the value of indigenous knowledge as a vital organizational asset. It should be pointed out, however, that the divestment of decision-making authority to local level management teams is invariably partial. While the parent company may be prepared to delegate aspects of the HRM or marketing portfolio, typically critical areas of financial management and research and development are retained at a central level.

From an HRM perspective, the move towards polycentricity is beneficial as it removes many of the problems associated with expatriation and vests continuity of managerial approach with host country managers. More detailed elements of HRM policy flow from the overall paradigm shift; most notably, payment systems will be closely related to local structures and systems, the organization may well take account of local arrangements for the expression of employee 'voice'; for example, works councils in many European countries, and training and development activity will be dispersed more widely throughout the organization. Nevertheless, following Perlmutter's assertion that the move towards polycentricity is complex, parent companies are scrupulously careful in screening the competence of host country management teams, as well as their commitment to organizational values, before delegating any authority to them. In this respect HQ staffs need to be convinced that they can *trust* the managerial acumen of subsidiaries, as well as retain *control* over operations, even if in a more indirect fashion. However, reflecting Bartlett and Ghoshal's (1989) 'transnational' classification, MNCs are invariably striving to strike an optimum balance between local responsiveness (differentiation) and international organizational coherence (integration). This takes us to the final stage of Perlmutter's evolutionary model.

- *Geocentricity* captures the status of the truly global concern, and combines local and international strengths. At senior corporate levels in particular, managers will be able to take a global view of the organization, being able not only to respond flexibly to local needs but also to transcend them in the pursuit of corporate goals and values. A modern interpretation of geocentricity would highlight organizational characteristics such as flexible, as opposed to hierarchical, organizational structures, the devolution of responsibility to teams of staff, and the sharing of knowledge throughout the organization.

HR priorities for geocentric concerns would include, first, an integrated approach towards recruitment ignoring national demarcation, especially at managerial level; second, the balancing of internal relativities in pay on an international basis; and third, an emphasis on language and cross-cultural training. The global organization therefore seeks to facilitate the emergence of staff networks and teams, quite often appearing spontaneously and connected through virtual technologies. Shell, for example, recently spawned clusters of global centres of excellence. These emerge as individuals with a strong interest in a certain area gather like-minded people around them, many using virtual networks. Although it is not easy to find examples of truly global concerns, one possible case is Asea Brown Boveri, the electrical engineering conglomerate. Its characteristics reportedly include horizontal networking through *ad hoc* task groups, which then transfer knowledge among decentralized, and semi-autonomous, operating units.

**Table 3.1 MNC strategic typologies**

| Typology | Strategic characteristics | Strategic concerns | HR policies |
|---|---|---|---|
| Ethnocentric | Values, cultures and strategic decisions determined by parent company that gives very little power to overseas subsidiaries | MNC not reaping the benefits of local knowledge or adapting to local environment<br>Local managers and workers feel imposed upon by parent, limited influence/promotion prospects, and so on for locals | Subsidiaries largely managed and controlled by expatriates or former HQ staff<br>One-way lines of communication |
| Polycentric | Each overseas subsidiary regarded as autonomous business unit, controlled and managed by local managers<br>Key decisions (e.g. financial investment and strategy) controlled by parent, which retains key positions<br>'Tortuous' devolution based on differential trust | Not fully adaptive to local environment as areas of strategic control retained by parent<br>Not fully gaining advantages of strategic integration/economies of scale across MNC as a whole | HRM decisions may be devolved to subsidiary<br>As parent/local managers are interacting there is a need for cross-cultural training, and so on<br>Possible tensions between parent/local managers<br>Less reliance on expatriation<br>Need to socialize local managers (and workers) into corporate values |
| Geocentric | World orientation<br>Acting locally but thinking globally, combining responsiveness to local markets and environments with international coordination and integration<br>Aiming for collaborative approach between parent and subsidiaries and between subsidiaries | Difficult to arrive at desired 'balancing act' of integration and differentiation | Multidirectional communication and mobility of managers/staff<br>Virtual team working across subsidiaries, and so on<br>Establishment of global centres of excellence<br>Corporate values shared throughout the organization |

In a later study, Heenan and Perlmutter (1979) identified a fourth international organizational form, defined as *regiocentricity*. This strategic orientation may be regarded as a midway position between ethnocentricity and a truly global profile (Harzing, 2004). Regiocentricity implies the devolution of corporate responsibilities to headquarters at regional level, for example in Europe, East Asia or North America. An associated staffing policy is the staffing and movement of key managerial positions at a regional level (ibid.). Regiocentricity arguably possesses particular validity in the current era of globalization as patterns of FDI and the physical location of subsidiaries continue to rotate around the 'triad' of Europe, North America and Asia (Edwards and Rees, 2006).

In a more recent study, Mayrhofer and Brewster (1996) suggest that ethnocentricity offers various advantages as well as disadvantages, and that many MNCs are still fundamentally ethnocentric in orientation (Table 3.2).

**Table 3.2 Advantages and disadvantages of ethnocentricity**

| Advantages | Disadvantages |
|---|---|
| ■ Efficient coordination<br>■ Effective communication<br>■ Direct control of foreign operations<br>■ Diffusing central values, norms and beliefs throughout the organization<br>■ Broadening the view of expatriates and the chance of growth for expatriates<br>■ Rapid substitution of expatriates possible<br>■ No need for a well-developed international internal labour market<br>■ Appropriate for entry into international business | ■ Adaptation of expatriates uncertain<br>■ Selection procedures prone to errors<br>■ High costs<br>■ Complicated personnel planning procedures<br>■ Private life of expatriates severely affected<br>■ Difficulties in mentoring during stay abroad<br>■ Reduced career opportunities for locals<br>■ Potential failure rate likely to be higher<br>■ Government restrictions |

*Source*: Mayrhofer and Brewster (1996).

The evolutionary tendencies of MNCs are also recognized by Adler and Ghadar (1990), who suggest that MNC strategies and structures accord to phases in the product life cycle. Adler and Ghader draw on Vernon's (1966) life cycle theory that distinguishes three phases in the international product life cycle (Scullion and Paauwe, 2005). The first phase prioritizes the product, and research and development, as a vital functional area. The second is associated with the development and exploitation of markets at home and abroad, while the third is most concerned with the lowering of prices and cost control in the face of intensive competitive pressures. Adler and Ghadar, while recognizing that cycles of product development and marketing have dramatically shortened since Vernon's theorization in the mid-1960s, nevertheless draw a connection between international marketing strategy, the significance of foreign culture in operational terms and resultant HR policy formulations. According to Adler and Ghadar (1990), MNCs may pass through the following ideal typical stages (note the usage of the same terms as Bartlett and Ghoshal (1989), which are however varied in their application to corresponding developmental phases):

■ *Domestic*: in the first phase, an emphasis is placed on home markets and exports, and management operating from an ethnocentric perspective, with little attention given to foreign cultures. Adler and Ghadar (1990: 242) exemplify this stage with the statement, 'We allow you to buy our products'. In HR terms, this phase may only involve brief visits of parent country managers to the host environment on a project basis, with technical skill being the most vital resource (Scullion and Paauwe, 2005).

■ *International*: here, the focus shifts to local responsiveness and the transfer of learning. This phase is associated with Perlmutter's *polycentric* classification, and indigenous cultures become highly important in entering into external relations (ibid.). It may well be the case that production is transferred to the host environment, and considerable strategic attention is given to obtaining a good match between the product and local market preferences. In this phase IHRM considerations become more manifest as parent country managers are expatriated to provide general management, technical expertise and financial control (ibid.). Expatriates operating in the fields of sales, marketing and HR are likely to require language skills and cross-cultural sensitivity.

■ *Multinational*: in the third phase, a focus is placed on low cost and price competition. Foreign-based operations are significant as a means to achieve cost-effectiveness on the basis of production factors differentials and economies of scale. Accordingly, although cross-cultural sensitivity is less vital than is the case for the 'International' typology above, awareness of cultural diversity in the global concern is still required (ibid.). The primary concern of IHRM is to recruit the most effective managers for international positions, regardless of their country of origin. The sharing of a common organizational ethos across diverse managerial groupings will contribute to unity of purpose, which necessitates appropriate management development activity, career counselling and international transfers within the enterprise (ibid.).

■ *Global*: Adler and Ghadar's (1990) fourth typology is closely associated with Perlmutter's (1969) *global* configuration, emphasizing particular challenges in international competition and organization in the global era. This typology places a focus on both local responsiveness and global integration in seeking to combine cost advantages and low prices with high-quality products or services, and adaptability to local tastes. For this typology, cultural sensitivity is vital both inside and outside the enterprise, as the international organization needs to be highly responsive to its environment. In HR terms, a premium is placed on capitalizing on cultural diversity within the organization to generate creative and innovative responses to environmental challenges. A climate for continuous learning will be a valued organizational asset (Scullion and Paauwe, 2005).

The theories of Bartlett and Ghoshal (1989), Perlmutter (1969) and Adler and Ghadar (1990), despite being highly 'ideal typical' in nature, provide useful insights into organizational dynamics and tensions within MNCs, and offer a useful conceptual background for understanding staffing issues in MNCs. A key lesson to be drawn from these, and related, contributions is that structures and strategies of MNCs are powerfully conditioned by factors in their economic and political environment, and that the relationship between parent and subsidiary may evolve over time.

## The transfer of HR practices in MNCs

In straddling geographical boundaries, the MNC represents an important conduit for the international flow of practices and ideas. Edwards and Rees (2006) assert that notions of 'best practice' in MNCs are likely to flow from their country of origin. As these authors state, 'MNCs from countries that have been economically successful have an incentive to diffuse those practices that are seen as having contributed to this success to their foreign subsidiaries' (p. 100). Thus, a 'dominance' effect is apparent as MNCs originating from the most successful global regions (the USA, Europe and Asia) are disposed towards dispersing home-centred practices across their global productive facilities. As the leading global economy, there is a history of US-inspired practices being disseminated far beyond North American borders through overseas corporate operations. Notable examples include the spread of 'Fordist' mass production systems from the 1940s to 1960s, and 'Taylorist' work organization and formalized systems of payment in the post-war period. More recently, the international dispersion of 'HRM' philosophies and practices has been attributed to the USA

(Hollinshead and Leat, 1995). Abating North American global influence in the 1980s, Japanese-owned MNCs frequently transposed systems of lean production, just-in-time manufacturing and quality standards to their North American and European subsidiaries (Edwards and Rees, 2006).

Edwards and Rees (ibid.) point out that the 'country of origin' effect may be offset by various other factors impacting on the relationship between parent and subsidiary. Following on from the analysis above, diffusion from headquarters to subsidiary units may well be rendered problematic if an MNC possesses a multi-domestic or ethnocentric structure. In these circumstances, limited contact between home and host staff and intra-organizational barriers constrain the free flow of knowledge and techniques in the MNC. On the other hand, in the global/geocentric or highly integrated concern, transference of know-how and mobility of staff is facilitated by multi-dimensional and deep linkages between international sub-units, which promotes liberal diffusion. Edwards and Rees also suggest that the status and function of the subsidiary will also have a bearing on diffusion possibilities. Thus, a 'greenfield' or new site in the host location is likely to be amenable to transposition of knowledge and practice from the MNC 'centre' as it is not 'embedded' in local institutional and cultural arrangements that may promote resistance.

Indeed, Edwards and Rees (2006) and Almond et al. (2005) identify the mitigating effect of the host country 'business system' on unidirectional transference of managerial policies from the parent. So, for example, robust 'coordinated market economy' (CMC – see Chapter 2) institutional arrangements evident in continental Europe (e.g. works councils, restrictions on staff severance) may represent a significant barrier to the unbridled assertion of liberal market- inspired practices (e.g. relative freedom to 'hire and fire') by a US-owned MNC (Ferner et. al.), 2005. While not a common phenomenon, Edwards (2005) highlights some relatively minor examples of 'reverse diffusion' from subsidiaries of US-owned MNCs to the parent, relating to matters such as team working and performance management.

It should also be borne in mind that MNCs are not politically neutral organizations, and that practices and ideas asserted from the home country may be resisted by interests in the host environment, or vice versa (Dörrenbächer and Geppert, 2006). Indeed, in the 'micro-political' climate that characterizes the 'real' culture of international and domestic organizations, exerting proprietary control over particular fields of knowledge and expertise may enhance the power position of vested interest groups, epitomizing the notion that 'knowledge is power'.

## Multinationals – a force for good?

### Employment and ethical concerns

There has been much public controversy and debate generated in recent years by the apparently unbridled power of MNCs, which found its most vehement form of expression in street protests in cities such as Seattle and Genoa. The allegations levelled against MNCs are wide ranging, from environmental neglect to flagrant breaches of human rights in developing countries. Sachder (2006) provides the following statistics to demonstrate the economic prowess of MNCs:

- The profits of the world's ten largest firms are equal to the GDP of 29 African countries (Elliott and Denny, 2003).

- The 12 most important global industries, such as textiles and the media, are each more than 40 per cent controlled by five or fewer corporations (McIntosh et al., 1998).
- The coffee trade is said to be dominated by four transnationals that account for 40 per cent of worldwide retail sales (Fairtrade Foundation, 2002).

As Sachdev (2006) asserts, the 'vacuum' left by the withdrawal of the state from various domains of economic and social activity – for example, healthcare, education and, more recently, reconstruction activity following war and other crises (Klein, 2007) – has frequently been filled by MNCs and associated subcontractors, which reflects the unprecedented elevation of the power of international capital (Korten, 1995).

It has been observed that the onset of the 'global village' is clearly associated with a growing dichotomy between rich and poor, both within national systems and between 'northern' and 'southern' hemispheres. A General Electric Shareholder Resolution (1998), for example, found that, in 1997, the chief executive officer (CEO) of General Electric was paid more than 1,400 times the average wage earned by his blue-collar workers in the USA. However his earnings were 9,571 times the average wage of Mexican industrial workers, who made up an increasing percentage of the workforce as production moved over the border.

A persistent allegation levelled against MNCs has been an apparent propensity towards creative accounting, taking the form of 'transfer pricing'. This means that higher profits are declared in regions where it is most financially expedient to declare such profits (given varying national taxation systems, etc.) and, conversely, losses are also declared where this is financially convenient. This alleged practice is significant in the field of labour relations as well-organized trade union movements will typically justify substantial wage claims by referring to high levels of profitability. In other words, transfer pricing offers the technical possibility not only of sidestepping unfavourable national financial regimes, but also assertive trade unionism.

In a climate of unrelenting global competition, there have been a number of well-publicized examples of MNCs demonstrating an instrumental attachment to employees and other stakeholders in their host country. Such companies have decided to 'take flight' if a seductive set of economic and employment inducements appear in another region. A recent case that alarmed British observers was that of James Dyson, the colourful home-grown entrepreneur who invented the 'bagless' vacuum cleaner. Despite crediting Britain as a 'powerful manufacturing nation', in 2002 he announced the plan to shift production from Malmesbury to Malaysia, entailing the loss of 800 jobs in the Wiltshire town. Undoubtedly, a critical factor in the decision was the significantly lower cost of employment in Asia. The matter is of particular concern in the UK, where a series of 'business flights' in sectors ranging from motor components to textiles to low-cost economies have been witnessed, which reflect the relative ease of business closure in the country's deregulated business environment. By way of contrast, in Germany, employers have needed to satisfy a series of legal and consultative provisions prior to securing closure.

Some prominent commentators are now drawing attention to a new order of globalization in keeping with a 'brand' new world that proselytizes the 'meaning' of commodities rather than the 'stuff' they are made of. In her best-selling and provocative book *No Logo*, journalist Naomi Klein (2000) draws attention to modern manifestations of corporate and consumerist cultures in which the true value of a product relates to the 'lifestyle' or 'attitude' it evokes. Consequently, according to Klein, western corporations such as Nike and Gap have channelled hugely disproportionate resources into product branding and distribution while reducing costs of production to the lowest possible levels. This process has entailed subcontracting production to 'export processing zones' in developing countries such as Indonesia, the Philippines, Sri Lanka and China. In a survey of 'sweatshops' in China, Klein finds that the predominantly young female workers are subject to conditions such as 12-hour shifts over seven days a week, being fined for not working overtime and corporal punishment and fines for becoming pregnant. There were also examples of child labour being recruited. Average rates of pay in the utilities surveyed were less than $2.5 per hour.

## The response of MNCs

Multinational corporations are increasingly recognizing the need to adhere to ethical standards and to observe notions of corporate social responsibility (CSR). A rethinking by MNCs of their ethical stance has been prompted by high-profile scandals, such as Enron in the USA, active campaigning by public opinion leaders, students and members of the public in developed and developing regions, and as a result of the enlightened self-awareness that adverse publicity affects sales. The CEO of Heineken, cited in Klein (2000: 424), defending the company's withdrawal from Burma in 1996, stated: 'Public opinion and issues surrounding this market have changed to a degree that could have an adverse effect on our brand and corporate reputation.' Threatened boycotts have directly impacted the operations of companies such as PepsiCo, Philips, C&A, Ralph Lauren, Motorola, Carlsberg and Kodak (Sachdev, 2006), while the Internet has been employed to radically enhance the potency of global campaigning against MNCs (Carmichael, 2001). In response to public concerns, a number of household-name MNCs, particularly those operating in the clothes and apparel sector, have been highly visible in promoting their codes of ethical standards, gaining endorsements from world-renowned celebrities. Sachdev (2006) reports that Gap now employs more than 80 people whose sole responsibility is to ensure that factories comply with ethical sourcing criteria, and Nike has quadrupled the number of employees dealing with labour practices (Murray, 2002).

Those with an interest in exposing and regulating the ethical breaches of MNCs have recognized that it is clearly inadequate to allow MNCs to monitor their own affairs, and have sought to bring a set of international standards to bear on the operations of MNCs. As Sachdev (2006) points out, the FTSE4Good Index, for example, will require companies exposed to supply chain risks to demonstrate policies of labour standards, including non-discrimination, forced labour, child labour and worker representation, while over a period of decades the International Labour Organization (ILO) has been active in establishing minimum standards to apply across national borders (World Link,1995). These include:

- employment: creating and promoting jobs, job security, eliminating discrimination in the workplace;
- vocational training;
- conditions of work and life, wages, benefits, and job safety and health;
- industrial relations, freedom of association, right to collective industrial dispute resolution.

Despite the benign intention underlying these and similar provisions passed by other interested agencies, their effectiveness has been hampered by their primarily voluntary status. An ILO review of 215 codes, examining coverage of labour practices, found 'significant discrepancies' in content and operation between them (Sachdev, 2006). As Sachdev asserts, there is widespread concern that the adoption of these codes may constitute little more than 'greenwashing' or 'corporate gloss' (ibid.). This is borne out by various commentators (Hutton, 2000; Joseph, 2002), who reveal that actual investment into CSR matters has increased little over the past decade. At an operational level, where multinationals subcontract operations to developing countries, the necessary international regulative mechanisms do not exist to compel factory inspection and to ensure compliance to minimum employment standards. Indeed, it is sometimes difficult for western MNCs to control employment and ethical practice as chains of command are diffuse and subject to contractor changes at local level.

---

### Case study: An East European Joint Venture

## THE EDEN BEVERAGE GROUP RAPIDLY EXPANDS IN EUROPE AND ENTERS SERBIA

### The case of Eden Weisser Brewery, Pancevo

Press release to the public, 15 August 2003

'Eden Breweries has acquired the majority shares of the **Pancevo Brewery** ('**Pancevo'**) in **Serbia**, located on the outskirts of Belgrade.'

Therefore Eden has added Serbia to its portfolio of European markets currently comprising of Russia, Ukraine, Romania and Moldova. The total number of markets that EBI operates, thus, has increased to six, including Kazakhstan, one of the major markets in Central Asia.

The Serbian beer market, where the competition consists of local breweries, has an estimated total consumption exceeding 470 million litres and per capita consumption of around 58 litres as of 2002. Pancevo operates with three brands: 'Weisser', 'Karlbrew' and 'Starivo'. Pancevo planned a capital investment programme of approximately $10 million until 2005 to increase the capacity from the current level of 40 million litres.

Eden has acquired a 63% stake in Pancevo through a cash contribution to the capital increase of the company and has become the first international brewer to invest in Serbia. The fresh capital injected in Pancevo, amounting to around $6.5 million, was to be used to improve the product quality and the technical infrastructure of the brewery.

Mr Mahmed Kari, President and CEO of the Eden Beverage Group, has said: 'We will integrate Pancevo's 250 years of brewing heritage with Eden's proven technological as well as marketing capabilities to be a leading brewer in Serbia. We will act with speed to fully leverage our advantage of being the first international brewer to enter into Serbia.'

This case study focuses on the local and multinational parties to the joint venture, and considers the organizational and HRM challenges it has created.

### Historical background

Pancevo is the oldest brewery in the Balkans, which was established on 22 May 1722. Since that time it has never stopped working and has gradually developed its technological capacity. A critical stage in its development occurred at the end of the nineteenth and beginning of the twentieth century when the German family, Weisser, took charge and developed the first steam brewery. The brewery's international connections were useful in learning brewing techniques from abroad, particularly from Austria and Germany.

During the 'Tito' era, Pancevo was nationalized, family ownership giving way to the socialistic organizational form of 'social ownership'. Accordingly, the brewery was owned by the workers themselves and managed by their representatives. For one year Pancevo merged with Belgrade-based BYP, but this was unsuccessful and evidently short-lived. In 1970, the brewery became a subsidiary entity within the Amish holding company, which also possessed interests in agriculture and other sectors. In the early 1980s, the brewery enjoyed rapid development and increased capacity, serving markets in Serbia, Montenegro, Macedonia, Bosnia and Croatia through the establishment of distribution centres in these regions. In June 1989, Pancevo became a legal entity through the provisions of the first law on companies.

As with other Yugoslav organizations during the 1990s, Pancevo suffered as a result of war and sanctions, as well as losing valuable markets as the former Yugoslavia disintegrated. Over this period the brewery was not in a position to attract new investment from government and it was unable to import technology and equipment. Nevertheless, the Serbian demand for beer remained buoyant throughout this time of crisis and domestic producers, such as Pancevo, possessed a stranglehold over the market. In 1991, the brewery became one of the first privatizing organizations in Serbia, with shareholders acquiring 60 per cent of socially-owned capital.

## Eden

Eden is a system of companies listed on the Istanbul Stock Exchange producing and marketing beer, malt and soft drinks across a territory ranging from the Adriatic to China, consisting of 14 breweries, four malteries and nine Coca-Cola bottling facilities in ten countries. It has an annual brewing capacity in excess of 1.8 billion litres, malting capacity of 150,000 tonnes and Coca-Cola bottling capacity of around 420 million unit cases per year. The group is among the ten largest European brewers by sales volume. Eden Beverage Group brands are enjoyed in over 35 countries worldwide, and Eden Pilsen, the Group's primary brand, is one of Europe's top ten brands worldwide. At the end of 2003, total beer sales volume reached 1,175 million litres, growing by 29 per cent on 2002 levels.

In Turkey, sales volumes increased by 7 per cent, which represents the highest increase since 2000. Including exported volumes, which grew by 31 per cent in 2003, total sales volume of Turkish beer operations reached an all-time high of 642 million litres.

International beer operations, conducted by EBG, commenced production in two state-of-the-art breweries in Rostov, Russia and Almaty, Kazakhstan. In addition to Pancevo, EBG acquired breweries in Chisinau, Moldova and Ufa, Russia in 2003.

Eden Group management had set itself a long-term goal in 1999 to generate 50 per cent of its beer volume through international sales by 2004. This objective was achieved in 2003, one year ahead of target.

## The joint venture

The joint venture was officially registered on 25 August 2003, following the agreement reached the previous April. Eden Weisser (EW) became the new company name, as the protocol for merging was formulated and a joint 'transition team' of senior managers from EBG and Pancevo was appointed to steer the process of organizational integration. This team included the former general manager at Pancevo, as well as legal, sales, technical and finance managers. It was joined, on a project-by-project basis, by temporary expatriate experts offering assistance and advice on matters such as information technology and quality control. The vast majority of the new management team (including sales, legal, purchasing, logistics and HR functions) possess Serbian nationality, some of these being recently appointed, while the general manager appointed in 2003. is a Belgian who previously worked for Interbrew.

The immediate contribution of Eden, in addition to an injection of capital, was to engage in product quality enhancement measures, including pasteurization, product rebranding through the use of a new logo, reshaping bottles and crates, and introducing new plastic bottles. In December 2003, the Weisser brand was relaunched, followed by strong marketing support.

## Organizational/HRM implications

Throughout its recent history, Pancevo has been concerned to maintain a relatively small, as well as efficient and committed, workforce. Until recently, as a legacy of the socialist era, workers were used to virtually total job security as well as generous social benefits, including sports and welfare facilities. Although wages were low, an egalitarian philosophy embraced all workers and management at the enterprise. At the time of the joint venture, the total headcount was 340 employees. Understandably, at the time of the merger, there was concern about job security.

Changes in employment practice have been negotiated with the two unions represented at the brewery. The newly established HR department has devoted considerable attention to communicating and explaining new policies to trade union representatives who have generally acted in a 'partnership' capacity and as mediator in dealing with the workforce. Although the management team recognizes that the process of organizational transformation has only just started, if rapidly gathering momentum, some important HR policy developments have already occurred or are in the pipeline.

First, a 'technological surplus' agreement has been implemented whereby the labour force has been 'downsized' to 235 employees. In agreement with the trade unions, and in accordance with relevant law and collective agreement, surplus staff have been redeployed or transferred where possible. Where compulsory redundancies have occurred, severance pay has been used to create further job opportunities; for example, some ex-drivers have bought trucks and continue their relationship with the company on a self-employed basis.

Second, as part of a wider programme of 'culture change', standard rates of pay across job categories and for managers are being modified in favour of a 'performance-related' scheme, whereby company, unit and individual performance will determine individual rates of pay. As a concomitant of this scheme, 'performance appraisal' is to be introduced, which involves qualitative assessment of individual performance on a periodic basis by supervisory 'line' managers. The form of payment is itself to be modernized, to be made on a gross and annual basis. This significant HR policy initiative is being introduced slowly, accompanied by full consultation with trade unions and an 'educational drive' using appropriate examples of practice delivered by the HR department. However, a negative aspect of this development from the point of view of workers is that social benefits will be lost. It is also the case that the new management team is earning approximately ten times the average worker rates.

Third, organizational developments are occurring within the HR department, with separate functions being established for personnel administration, payroll, safety and protection, security and canteen, industrial relations and training and development. Certain of these functions are 'outsourced', including payroll and security.

Such initiatives are integral to rapid organizational changes that have occurred over the past year or so, involving the establishment of entirely new departments, not only in HR, but also in marketing, quality assurance and logistics.

*Source:* Adapted from Hollinshead and Maclean (2007).

## Discussion questions

1 Examine the strategic attractiveness of Pancevo as a partner for Eden. What does Pancevo bring to the alliance?
2 To what extent is HRM a relevant concept in the new joint venture?
3 Should Pancevo management and workers welcome the purchase by Eden? What does Eden offer them? Should they have any reservations?
4 Identify the key challenges for the new HR department at Pancevo. What are the barriers to successful implementation of the desired change and how may they be overcome?
5 Can other organizations learn from Pancevo's experience, both in terms of receiving FDI and implementing subsequent organizational change?

### Activity

Access the labour behind the label website (www.labourbehindthelabel.org). Using corporate examples, present in bullet point form the major criticisms levelled against MNCs in the clothing industry relating to their employment and ethical practices.

## Summary

This chapter has noted the power and significance of MNCs as global economic actors. The strategic relationship between parent and subsidiary has been examined, with particular reference to the notion of devolution or differentiation, which serves to condition IHRM and staffing policies. Finally, ethical concerns considering the operations of MNCs, particularly in developing countries, and the response of MNCs, have been considered.

## Further reading

**Dickens, P.** (2004) *Global Shift: Reshaping the Global Economic Map in the 21st Century* (4th edn.), London: Sage Publications.

This book has become a sociologically-based standard work on globalization, covering the nature of the globalization debate and the interplay between multinational corporations, states and changing technologies. It investigates themes such as development inequality, environment and governance. In-depth sectoral analysis is provided on textiles and garment, automobile, semi-conductor and financial services and distribution industries.

**Bartlett, C.A. and Ghoshal, S.** (1989) *Managing Across Borders: The Transnational Solution*, Boston, MA: Harvard Business School Press.

A seminal contribution to the debate on multinational strategies, highlighting the relationship between 'parent' and 'subsidiary' units and placing an emphasis on systems and processes.

**Manea, J. and Pearce, R.** (2004) *Multinationals and Transition: Business Strategies, Technology and Transformation in Central and Eastern Europe*, Basingstoke: Palgrave Macmillan.

This research-based book provides insight into the strategic rationale impinging on multinational 'parent–subsidiary' relations in central and eastern Europe. In an exposition that has more general applicability to international mergers and acquisitions and joint ventures, the authors delineate 'efficiency', 'market' and 'knowledge' seeking motivations for corporate internationalization.

**Klein, N.** (2007) *The Shock Doctrine: The Rise of Disaster Capitalism*, London: Penguin/Allen Lane.

A provocative critique of the application of US-inspired 'neo-liberal' economics in various global regions following military interventions and other 'shock' tactics, casting a negative light on current conceptions of globalization and the activities and affairs of multinational corporations.

## Useful websites

www.mallenbaker.net/csr/CSRfiles/nike.html
Provides news on corporate social responsibility

www.gapinc.com/public/About/abt_milestones.shtml
Real case material on a high-profile MNC in the clothing/apparel industry. This site also provides material specifically for students on Gap's corporate social responsibility policies and related matters.

www.labourbehindthelabel.org
A campaigning organization for international garment workers. Working conditions of household name suppliers are highlighted.

www.johnpilger.com/page.asp?partid=12
The site of journalist John Pilger offers a critical view of globalization, providing links to material on global institutions, privatization and regional studies.

Other websites:
www.naomiklein.org
www.ilo.org
www.cepaa.org
www.unctad.org
www.nikebiz.com

## References

**Adler, N.J. and Ghadar, F.** (1990) Strategic human resource management: a global perspective, in R. Pieper (ed.) *Human Resource Management: An International Comparison*, Berlin: De Gruyter.

**Almond, P., Edwards, P., Colling, T., Ferner, A., Gunnigle, P., Müller-Camer, M., Quintanilla, J. and Wächter, H.** (2005) Unraveling home and host country effects: an investigation of the HR policies of an American multinational in four European countries, *Industrial Relations*, 44(2): 276–306.

**Barrell, R. and Pain, N.** (1997) EU: an attractive investment. Being part of the EU is good for FDI and being out of EMU may be bad, *New Economy*, 4(1): 50–54.

**Bartlett, C.A. and Ghoshal, S.** (1989) *Managing Across Borders: The Transnational Solution*, Boston, MA: Harvard Business School Press.

**Carmichael, S.** (2001) Accounting for ethical business, in T. Bentley and D. Stedman Jones (eds) *The Moral Universe*, London: Demos.

**Dorrenbächer, C. and Geppert, M.** (eds) (2006) Micro-politics and conflicts in multinational corporations, *Journal of International Management*, Special Issue, 12(3): 247–388.

**Economist The** (2007) Globalization's offspring: how the new multinationals are remaking the old, 7–13 April.

**Edwards, T. and Rees, C.** (2006) *International Human Resource Management: Globalization, National Systems and Multinational Companies, Harlow:* FT/Prentice Hall.

**Edwards, T., Almond, P., Clark, I., Colling, T. and Ferner, A.** (2005) Reverse diffusion in US multinationals: barriers from the American business system, *Journal of Management Studies,* 42(6): 1261–1286.

**Elliott, L. and Denny, C.** (2003) New issues, *The Guardian,* 8 September.

**Fairtrade Foundation** (2002) *Spilling the Beans on the Coffee Trade,* London: Fairtrade Foundation (www.fairtrade.org.uk).

**Ferner, A., Almond, P., Colling, T. and Edwards, T.** (2005) Policies on union representation in US multinationals in the UK: between micro-politics and macro-institutions, *British Journal of Industrial Relations,* 43(4): 703–728.

**General Electric Shareholder Resolution** (1998) reprinted in *A Decade of Excess: The 1990s,* Sixth Annual Compensation Survey: United for a Fair Economy/Institute for Policy Studies.

**Ghertman , M. and Allen, M.** (1984) *An Introduction to the Multinationals,* Basingstoke: Macmillan.

**Harzing, A.W.R.** (2004) Composing an international staff, in A.W.R. Harzing and J. Van Ruysseveldt (eds) *International Human Resource Management,* (2nd edn.), London: Sage Publications.

**Heenan, D.A. and Perlmutter, H.V.** (1979) *Multinational Organizational Development,* Reading, MA: Addison-Wesley.

**Hoekman, B. and Kostecki, M.** (1995) *The Political Economy of the World Trading System: From GATT to WTO,* Oxford: Oxford University Press.

**Hollinshead, G. and Leat, M.** (1995) *Human Resource Management: An International and Comparative Perspective,* London: Pitman Publishing.

**Hollinshead, G. and Maclean, M.** (2007) Transition and organizational dissonance in Serbia, *Human Relations,* 60(10): 1551–1574.

**Hutton, W.** (2000) *Society Bites Back: The Good Enterprise, the Purposeful Consumer and the Just Workplace,* London: The Industrial Society.

**Joseph, E.** (2002) Corporate social responsibility – delivering the new agenda, *New Economy,* 8(2): 121–123.

**Klein, N.** (2000) *No Logo,* London: Flamingo.

**Klein, N.** (2007) *The Shock Doctrine: The Rise of Disaster Capitalism,* London: Penguin/Allen Lane.

**Korten, D.C.** (1995) *When Corporations Rule the World,* London: Earthscan.

**Mayrhofer, W. and Brewster, C.** (1996) In praise of ethnocentricity: expatriate policies in European multinationals, *International Executive*, 38(6): 749–775.

**McIntosh, M., Leipziger, D., Jones, J. and Coleman, G.** (1998) *Living Corporate Citizenship*, Harlow: FT/Prentice Hall.

**Mintzberg, H.** (1988) Opening up the definition of strategy, in J.B. Quinn, H. Mintzberg and R.M. James, *The Strategy Process*, Englewood Cliffs, NJ: Prentice Hall.

**Murray, S.** (2002) The rapid rise of new responsibility, *Financial Times*, 11 June.

**Okleshen C.** (2000) Case provided for R.M. Hodgetts and F. Luthans, *International Management- Culture, Strategy and Behaviour,* (4th edn.), Boston, MA: Irwin/McGraw-Hill.

**Perlmutter, H.** (1969) The tortuous evolution of the multi-national corporation, *Columbia Journal of World Business*, 4(1): 9–18.

**Pilger J.** (2001) The new rulers of the world, a Carlton programme for ITV transmitted July. Booklet prepared in conjunction with the World Development Movement.

**Sachdev, S.** (2006) International corporate social responsibility and employment relations, in T. Edwards and C. Rees (eds) *International Human Resource Management: Globalization, National Systems and Multinational Companies*, Harlow: FT/Pearson.

**Scullion, H. and Paauwe, J.** (2005) Strategic HRM in multinational companies, in H. Scullion and M. Linehan (eds) *International Human Resource Management: A Critical Text*, Basingstoke: Palgrave Macmillan.

**United Nations Conference on Trade and Development** (**UNCTAD**) (2000) *World Investment Report*, pp. 72–74.

**UNCTAD** (2008) World Investment Report, Transnational Corporations and the Infrastructural Challenge, p. 8.

**United Nations Development Programme** (**UNDP**) (2000) *Human Development Report*, pp. 206–209.

**Vernon, R.G.** (1966) International investment and international trade in the product cycle, *Quarterly Journal of Economics*, May: 190–207.

**World Link** (1995) Ethical guidelines for multinationals to take to the forefront, *World Link*, September–October: 1, 4.

# PART 2
# International Themes

# 04

# Staffing the multinational enterprise: expatriation and managing across borders

## ❖ *LEARNING OBJECTIVES*

❖ To consider the strategic rationale for expatriation with reference to multinational corporation (MNC) strategies

❖ To investigate the concept of expatriate failure

❖ To examine alternatives to expatriation, notably 'localizing' management authority to the host environment

❖ To identify problems and issues associated with working across cultures

❖ To explore the concept of 'expatriate adjustment'

## Introduction: overview and the rationale for expatriation

In this section we turn our attention more fully to *international* human resource management (IHRM), which is concerned with the strategic considerations in formulating policies affecting the staffing of parent and subsidiaries in international enterprises. In Chapter 3 we described the complexity of the parent–subsidiary relationship, suggesting that the MNC configures and reconfigures its organizational form over time in a manner that enhances its international competitiveness across national boundaries. Returning to the seminal contribution of Perlmuttter (1969) in the first, *ethnocentric*, phase of development, multinational operations would typically be run by the parent in a centralized fashion, with little need for meaningful interaction between parent and host country managers (HCMs) and other interested stakeholders. However, in subsequent *polycentric* and *geocentric* phases, or in Adler and Ghadar's (1990) *international*, *multinational* or *global* configuration, when the subsidiary becomes a critical player in the realization of international corporate goals, real cross-cultural engagement between home and host country staff develops in strategic importance and IHRM issues are closer to the forefront of corporate deliberations. As a starting point, therefore, for considering international staffing we should note that it is not founded on a unidirectional notion of direct parental control over subsidiaries via expatriation, but rather on a complex and variable set of interrelationships between human agents in home and host environments that are conditioned by the overall strategic orientation of the MNC.

Expatriation has occupied a pivotal position in the (IHRM) literature in representing the most direct form of human resource intervention by the parent into the operations of subsidiaries. According to Harzing (2004), an expatriate may typically be defined as a parent country national (PCN) working in foreign subsidiaries of the MNC for a predefined period, usually 2–5 years. A recent survey by GMAC ( 2007), covering 180 small, medium and large-scale organizations from a variety of sectors, including information technology, pharmaceuticals, construction, chemicals and finance, and managing a worldwide employee population of more than 8.4 million, sheds light on the current state of expatriation. This may be exemplified by the following facts:

- 34 per cent of responding companies deployed 50 or fewer expatriates; a high percentage of respondents (56 per cent) deployed over 100 expatriates.
- 69 per cent of respondents reported the number of expatriates to have increased in 2006.
- 20 per cent of expatriates were female.
- 48 per cent of expatriates were 20–39 years old.
- 60 per cent of expatriates were married and 54 per cent had children accompanying them.
- Spouses/partners accompanied 82 per cent of expatriates; 59 per cent of spouses were employed before an assignment and 8 per cent during an assignment.
- 10 per cent had previous international experience, 14 per cent were new hires and 86 per cent were employed by the company at the time of the international assignment.
- 58 per cent were relocated to or from the headquarters country.
- The USA, the UK, China and Germany were the most frequently cited destinations.

In an in-depth investigation into the corporate rationale for expatriation, Edström and Galbraith (1977) identify three main company motives for international transfer. First, international companies may despatch expatriates in order to *fill positions* where indigenous knowledge and skills are not available. Deploying expatriates as agents for the transfer of knowledge may be particularly significant for subsidiaries in developing countries. Second, expatriation may occur for *management development* purposes. In this instance, experience accumulated through international transfer will equip the expatriate for career progression within the organization. Third, expatriation can assist with *organizational development* through establishing personal channels of communication between parent and subsidiary and through facilitating the diffusion of corporate norms and values throughout the international organization, thus promoting a common corporate culture (Caligiuri and Di Santo, 2001; McCall and Hollenbeck, 2002). The observations of Edström and Galbraith (1977) are borne out in the GMAC (2007) survey, which finds that the most common assignment objective was to fill a skills gap (27 per cent of respondents), followed by building management expertise (23 per cent) and technology transfer (18 per cent).

At a more strategic level of analysis, Colakoglu and Caligiura (2008) assert that expatriates are deployed in order to influence the performance of subsidiaries as a result of the strategic leadership positions they occupy, the knowledge from headquarters that they transfer and their potential for 'boundary spanning' between headquarters and host subsidiaries (Bonache and Brewster, 2001; Edström and Galbraith 1977). Expatriates may therefore perform a vital function in facilitating the 'outward flow' of knowledge, skills and practices from the home to the host unit, and also the 'inward transfer' from subsidiary to parent (Riusala and Suutari, 2002). Expatriates are engaged in the 'cultural control' of subsidiaries, which involves the dissemination of corporate values and norms that powerfully determine the organizational context for work processes and behaviours (Balgia and Jaeger, 1984). In asserting cultural control expatriates may directly control subsidiary operations by constituting a 'mini-headquarters' in the host environment, or may exert more indirect influence through encouraging subsidiary employees to adopt corporate norms and values, which is based on processes of 'education' and 'socialization' (Harzing, 2001). According to Colakoglu and Caligiura (2008), the greater the degree of cultural distance between parent and subsidiary environment (note cultural theories in Chapter 2), the greater the need for expatriate cultural control (Balgia and Jaeger, 1984; Boyacigillar, 1990; Kogut and Zander, 1993).

While the 'strategic mission' is performed by an elite group of expatriates, it should be borne in mind that not all international assignments require the pursuit of such elevated corporate objectives. Caligiuri and Colakolu (2007) assert that the purpose of staff deployment may be primarily functional (i.e. carrying out an assigned task in the field of finance, marketing, human resources, etc.) or technical (e.g. providing technical advice relating to systems, software, etc.). The latter two forms of assignment are clearly less demanding in terms of the requirement for cross-cultural proficiencies and skills.

While MNCs continue to place considerable reliance on expatriation as a critical mechanism for international coordination and control, Black and Gregerson (1999), in a wide-ranging and critical review, reveal that few MNCs reap the expected returns of overseas deployments due to poor expatriate practices (Verbeke, 2009). In a survey of nearly 750 US, European and Japanese firms over a decade, including the views of expatriates themselves, Black and Gregerson find that 80 per cent of all mid- to large-size MNCs send managers abroad at a significant cost to the company, with full packages costing two to three times the average equivalent domestic position. These authors found that:

- 10–20 per cent of US expatriates returned home early due to dissatisfaction with their overseas assignment and difficulties in cultural adjustment.
- The performance of more than 30 per cent of expatriates that remained in their overseas posting did not reach senior management expectations.
- For those who completed their assignments, over one-quarter left the company within a year of their return.
- More than 30 per cent of expatriates were still in temporary positions within three months of returning home.
- Over three-quarters experienced demotion and reduction and job discretion on return home.
- Over 60 per cent found that there was little or no opportunity to apply or leverage the knowledge they had acquired overseas on return to headquarters.

It is perhaps awareness of the high emotional and financial stakes associated with expatriation that leads many potential international assignees to resist a career move overseas (Dupuis et al., 2008).

## The risks of expatriation and international staffing alternatives

### Expatriate failure

Despite its continuing popularity as a method of international staffing, it is undoubtedly the case that expatriation carries with it significant risks, both to the company and to the transferee him or herself. A subject of considerable debate by researchers has been the risk of failure. Expatriate failure is normally defined as the premature return of the expatriate to the home base prior to completion of the agreed term. The GMAC/GRS (2007) survey reveals, however, that early return does not always signify failure, as 14 per cent of prematurely returning respondents successfully completed their assignment early, and 23 per cent returned to take up a new position in the parent company. Harzing (1995) contends that there are widely varying estimates as to the proportion of failed expatriate assignments in developing countries (ranging from 16–50 per cent), the estimates at the middle to higher end of this spectrum being questionable. The GMAC/GRS (2007) survey finds that 10 per cent of expatriates returned prematurely; the major explanations for this being partner dissatisfaction, inability to adapt to the host environment, family concerns and poor candidate selection. The survey found that China, the UK, the USA and Japan were the locations with the highest rate of assignment failure. Despite disagreement over the precise extent of expatriate failure, it is undoubtedly the case that it is a problem worth taking seriously. From the company's point of view, the significant costs associated with expatriate recruitment and training are forfeited, while a more 'invisible' cost is continuing underperformance as each new expatriate embarks on the lower end of a 'learning curve' (Lee, 2007). The company will also accrue costs in continually replacing failed international assignees.

From the expatriate's point of view, failure may be associated with reduced career prospects in the company, financial loss and lowering of morale; there may also be detrimental effects on partner and children if they are accompanying the expatriate. Lee (ibid.) suggests that a significant explanation for expatriate failure was a deficiency in the *relational capabilities* of international assignees (including cultural sensitivity, personal and emotional maturity, adaptive capacities in a new environment), which is being exacerbated by a tendency by both companies and expatriates to concentrate on the technical aspects of working overseas.

### Strategic alternatives to expatriation

In order to avert the risk of failure, the need to prepare the expatriate for cross-cultural engagement through training and development programmes is increasingly being recognized. However, following on from our previous analysis of various multinational strategic and structural formulations, it is not always the case that a 'traditional' expatriate is needed, and therefore it makes sense for the international company to consider alternative methods of international staffing. Briscoe and Schuler (2004: 223) note that, 'the tradition of referring to all international employees as expatriates – or even international assignees – falls short of the need for international HR practitioners to understand the options available...'.

Following these authors, Zimmerman and Sparrow (2007) identify the following types of international assignee: parent country nationals, host country nationals (HCNs), third country nationals (TCNs), international commuters, employees on short-term or intermediate foreign postings, permanent transferees or permanent cadre, international transferees (moving from one subsidiary to another), immigrants, returnees, contract expatriates, or virtual international employees in cross-border project teams.

The GMAC/GRS (2007) survey report finds that 55 per cent of companies were seeking alternatives to long-term assignments, the major reason for this being cost. For those companies endeavouring to move away from traditional expatriation, 36 per cent used short-term assignments, 14 per cent localized expatriates and 13 per cent relied on business travel. As we shall investigate in Chapter 5, as well as being a risky business, traditional expatriation is frequently also expensive as companies need to provide incentives for staff to undertake overseas assignments, and to retain a coherent package that reflects home payment criteria in the host environment. Regarding cost, therefore, both the options of shorter-term assignments (in which home country rates are paid with few extras) and permanence or localization (in which host country rates may be paid) offer attractive alternatives to traditional expatriation. Shorter international assignments also carry the quite considerable benefit that relocation will not be necessary for the partner, spouse or children of the expatriate.

## Devolving to the subsidiary

The model of traditional expatriation is perhaps most under threat from a realization of the strategic benefits associated with international devolution, or staffing senior positions in the subsidiary with HCNs, which complies with Perlmutter's (1969) notion of *polycentricity*. Harzing (2004) asserts that HCMs can contribute invaluable resources of locally-based knowledge to international companies, appertaining to socio-economic, political and legal circumstances, as well as business practices in the host environment. Furthermore, as Harzing points out, devolution of managerial authority to host country managers (HCMs) can respond effectively to the host government's demand for localization of subsidiary operations, and provides a motivational stimulus to local managers who perceive opportunities for promotion and advancement.

While the deployment of PCNs in subsidiaries manifests a country of origin 'dominance effect' in international staffing, the employment of HCNs, according to Gaur et al. (2007), helps a subsidiary conform to local laws and gain knowledge of the local environment. The employment of HCNs is likely to be an important factor in promoting the local legitimacy of MNCs, and can signal that the MNC is providing benefits to the local economy (ibid.). The deployment of local managers may also provide for greater continuity and reliability in the staffing of subsidiaries.

Brown (2008) reports that a number of MNCs are recognizing the benefits, in terms of cost and skills, of employing TCNs. This group may be defined as internationally mobile staff whose origins are neither the home country of their employer nor the country of assignment. TCNs are enlarging the candidate pool for international assignments, constituting 35 per cent of expatriates in a study of 181 companies operating in 130 countries (SHRM, 2001). The increased sourcing of international 'talent', particularly from developing countries including India, China and Russia, signifies an internationalization of recruitment approaches in MNCs. This grouping, which constitutes neither home nor HCNs, can fill corporate deficits in skills or knowledge that are not available within the existing reservoir of human resources, and may be in an optimal position to combine technical proficiency with cross-cultural sensitivity.

As a concomitant of international devolution, MNCs have become aware of the advantages of *inpatriation* as a strategic alternative to expatriation. Inpatriation involves the organization of secondments for subsidiary managers in the parent's headquarters for a particular period of time. Subsidiary managers may gain from this experience by actual exposure to norms, values and 'state-of-the-art' knowledge in the parent, as well as be able to establish informal communication networks between subsidiaries and parent (Harzing, 2004). Similarly, according to Briscoe and Schuler (2004), HCNs who have been exposed to international state-of-the-art knowledge represent a scarce resource for MNCs, as they are able to combine such knowledge with local awareness. Thus, Japanese high-technology MNCs have seen the benefits of employing 'boomerangs' (Pacific Bridge International Asian HR, 2003); this category of international staff typically comprising Japanese knowledge workers who have migrated to western countries, but are tempted to return home as they possess the necessary language and cultural skills to navigate the complex local business environment (Briscoe and Schuler, 2004).

## Working across cultures

As the strategic configuration of the MNC develops to embrace the subsidiary as a vital contributor to its international operations, so the need for interaction between home and host country nationals at an interpersonal level is likely to increase. Referring to institutional and cultural perspectives explored in Chapter 2, it can be appreciated that organizational mindsets, and general attitudes towards 'doing business' may be grounded in highly diverse national or regional traditions. So, for example, taking an institutional perspective, a US manager has lived and worked in an environment in which 'freedom to manage' has been paramount, while such a manager's French counterpart is used to significant aspects of managerial activity being subject to statutory regulation. From a cultural perspective, the US manager, according to Hofstede (1994), has been profoundly conditioned by an individualistic organizational mindset, while his or her French equivalent, while valuing individualism, is strongly oriented towards the avoidance of uncertainty. It is therefore apparent that management across cultures carries with it greater potential for complexity and ambiguity than managerial interaction within cultures. Accordingly, a critical challenge confronting not only expatriates, but all those involved in international managerial engagement (Brewster et al., 2007), is the need to operate effectively in diverse international teams. Hodgetts and Luthans (2003) suggest the following potential problems with diversity:

- *Mistrust*: difficulties in understanding 'alien' modes of interaction and business customs (e.g. US managers' bewilderment at Japanese managers 'huddling together' and discussing a problem in their own language in an international business meeting). Different perceptions of hierarchy, for example, between high-power distance-oriented French managers and low-power distance French managers may also confuse deliberations between managerial groupings from these nations (Hollinshead and Leat, 1995).
- *Stereotyping*: culturally-rooted preconceptions and prejudices concerning international colleagues. An example might be the western perception that post-socialist managers are collectivist in orientation; however, contrary evidence exists of highly individualistic tendencies (Hollinshead and Michailova, (2001).
- *Inaccurate communication*: this refers not only to potential problems of translation, but also etymological problems in establishing the meaning of words and terminology. For example, the term 'human resource management' has no literal equivalent in many east

European countries. Difficulties may also arise from the misinterpretation of 'body language' and idiosyncratic mannerisms across cultures.

■ *Different perceptions and uses of time*: this may refer to punctuality in attending meetings, preparedness to commit to an agreed course of action during a meeting, and to the scheduling of agreed tasks resulting from an international business encounter.

On the other hand, it has been acknowledged that internationally diverse teams potentially offer considerable HR-related benefits to the MNC. Indeed, Shapiro et al. (2002) suggest that multicultural teams tend to operate at extreme ends of the spectrum of high and low performance, while Adler (1997) argues that the productivity of diverse teams depends on how they manage such diversity. Following Hodgetts and Luthans (2003), multicultural or diverse teams offer advantages over homogenous managerial groupings in the following scenarios:

■ where innovative or creative ideas or solutions are required. As group members come from a host of different cultures, they are often able to create a greater number of unique suggestions.
■ where there is a need to avoid 'groupthink'. This phenomenon relates to the tendency of a homogenous 'in group' to conform to established patterns of consensus and group norms, and to discredit ideas that run against compliant thinking and behaviour.

## Case scenario: Western expatriates in Moscow

Since the early 1990s, Russia has become more integrated into the wider international economic community; western interests being fully aware of the huge market potential it offers, as well as local reserves of knowledge and skills that may be accessed through the formation of 'East/West' strategic alliances or joint ventures. The emergence of a new generation of young 'market oriented' (Puffer, 1996) managers in Russia, who are familiar with the 'repertoire' of international business, and who possess formidable language and technological skills has apparently contributed to the construction of an interpersonal 'bridge' from western countries into the former Soviet territory, promoting the real possibility of collegiality in business dealings and meaningful intercultural exchange.

However, beneath the 'veneer' of camaraderie between western and eastern managerial participants in new alliances lurks deeply rooted mutual suspicion that hinders effective cross-cultural working and which requires psychological adjustment on *both* sides to the new climate for doing business in the 'new' Russia. The 'crossed wires' that continue to blight communication and interaction between western and Russian groupings may be attributed to contrasting forms of socialization to those they were subject to in capitalist and communist structures. Contradictory and dysfunctional sentiments may be witnessed on matters such as adjustment, orientation to work, ethics and knowledge and skills issues, as the following quotations bear out.

### On psychological adjustment to the new international work setting

*Western manager:*

'It's obviously better to start the way you mean to continue, the problem is that when you come to Russia for the first time, you really cannot imagine the situation, and as a result, you either sink or swim.'

*Russian manager:*

'We need to understand what the priorities are. This is very clear to Westerners because they are working in their own system; it's not clear to us because capitalism is very new to us … we are playing a new game and the rules need to be explained clearly.'

## On orientation to work

*Russian manager:*

'In Russia we use the word "collectiv" which refers to the group or team. It's similar to communist ideas of community. We can't get away from the idea of the 'collectiv' which is like a big family – and that's why, when we go to work, we share all our problems and probably even dress as if we are going to see friends.'

*Western manager:*

'A Russian will change jobs for a difference of 50 dollars a month … Russian employees are purely money driven, there is such a contrast to how other nationalities make their choice about the place of work.'

## On ethics

*Russian manager:*

'… you can compare the arrival of Americans to the gold rush in America in the last century … the word exploitation comes to mind.'

Western manager:

'There is more willingness and greater tendency [by Russians] to be dishonest.'

*Russian manager:*

'Westerners use their connections to further their careers and business purposes, their connections are the people that they know. We look for someone who knows someone whom we could pay to help us.'

'There is a feeling that Russians are being treated as second-class citizens. They are paid much less than the expatriates, who, in addition, have large living allowances, live in better accommodation than Russians and frequently have a chauffeur.'

## On knowledge and skills issues

*Western manager:*

'… Russian managers are young and very open to learning and being trained … we are very lucky because we work with an elite section of the Russian population.'

*Russian manager:*

'… We [Russians] are chauvinistic. We were taught that we are the best and I think that deep down we still want to believe this story … I think it's insulting for Russians when westerners think they know more about Russia, especially when they know so little.'

It is clear from the above quotations that unleashing higher levels of commitment to international enterprise in Russia is conditional on entering a more positive cycle of mutual engagement, calling for learning and unlearning capacities on all sides. For westerners, not only is there a need to become more immersed in Russian culture both at home and at work, but also there is a need to be sensitive to the negative symbolic effect of overt expressions of inequality. If there is to be an optimal sharing of local and international knowledge in joint ventures, then priority needs to be attached to the intricacies of relationship building.

It is becoming incumbent on Russian managers to adapt their behaviour to meet the requirements of the rapidly changing circumstances around them. They are being required to empathize with and absorb 'western' visions of organizational purpose, thinking in a less domesticated and more international fashion, and developing 'soft' skills such as the ability to delegate and motivate others.

*Source*: Camiah and Hollinshead (2003).

## Expatriate adjustment

The case scenario above identifies the difficulties expatriates may face when undertaking an overseas assignment. The western expatriates experienced a degree of 'culture shock' and were challenged by the need to adjust or achieve comfort in a new environment. Adjustment therefore denotes the psychological change induced in individuals by a move to an unfamiliar cultural environment (Bhaskar-Shrivinas et al., 2005; Black et al., 1991; Ogri, 2009). More broadly, Hippler (2000) conceptualizes adjustment as the general satisfaction with one's life in the new environment, while Aycan (1997) refers to the degree of fit between the expatriate manager and the environment, both work and socio-cultural. Varner and Palmer (2005) affirm that inadequate adjustment is likely to be at the expense of effective job performance.

According to Zimmerman and Sparrow (2007), the adjustment process can be broken down into three facets, as follows: (1) psychological adjustment (changes of psychological and emotional states characterized by feelings of well-being and satisfaction; (2) interaction adjustment (the individual's behavioural and attitudinal changes with regard to intercultural interactions characterized by the ability to 'fit in' and 'negotiate' interactive aspects of the new culture); and (3) work adjustment (changes in reaction to the new job). In a new departure, but reflecting adjustment processes observed in the foregoing case scenario, Zimmerman and Sparrow (ibid.) characterize adjustment as involving *mutual* psychological and social movement by members of international teams as opposed to unidirectional mindset shifts on the part of expatriates.

In an influential model (see Figure 4.1), which has significant implications for the selection and training of expatriates, Black et al. (1991) distinguish between *anticipatory adjustment*, that is, those factors that will facilitate effective expatriation prior to departure, and *in country adjustment*, that is, factors relating to work, interaction with HCNs and coping with living conditions in general that will determine success following arrival in the host environment.

Anticipatory adjustment is concerned with the determination of accurate expectations on the part of expatriates, thus minimizing the risk of culture shock (Harzing, 2004). Significant

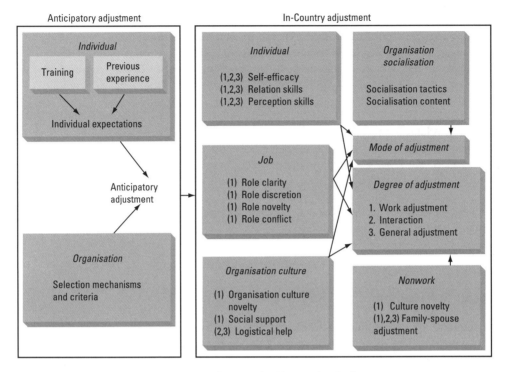

**Figure 4.1 The framework of international adjustment**

*Source*: Black et. al. (1991).

anticipatory variables relate to the accumulation of previous experience by the expatriate in foreign assignments, the selection criteria and mechanisms adopted by the organization in identifying a suitable expatriate, and the level and appropriateness of technical and cross-cultural training provision in advance of the assignment.

Turning to in-country variables, the model is premised on the notion that effective adjustment will depend not just on job-related factors, but also is influenced by behavioural characteristics of the expatriates themselves, including the ability to develop relationships, and is critically determined by non-work factors. In terms of personal orientation, a key attribute is 'self-efficacy', which is associated with the ability to learn from mistakes, and to regard inevitable set-backs as learning experiences. Such an attribute will be helpful when an individual is experiencing 'culture shock' in the first stages of an assignment, and is conducive to the acquisition of meaningful, self-generated, learning in an unfamiliar environment.

Inevitably, work itself will contribute to successful expatriation, important variables relating to the clarity of the job role, the level of discretion enjoyed, the newness of portfolio of tasks and the degree to which conflict is experienced in the job role. Of course, the job is located within a broader organizational setting, in which the conduciveness of the organizational culture and the ability of the expatriate to draw on social support represent significant contributors to success.

Finally, non-work factors relate to the ability of the expatriates, and their spouses/partners and families, to relate to the practicalities of life in the new environment. This may relate to housing, transport, food, cultural amenities, schooling, medical care, and the availability of employment for the 'trailing' partner. It is suggested by the authors of the model that the organization can assist in providing logistical and other support to assist with non-work factors.

The model also incorporates the notion that ease of adjustment is determined by the degree of cultural proximity or distance between home and host environments, thus corroborating a view that certain destinations are more challenging than others for expatriates. Shaffer et al. (1999), in an empirical testing of the model, reaffirm the importance of job design and organizational support systems. These authors, however, also stressed the significance of inclusion of the spouse in training and support programmes and language fluency as a selection criterion.

Black et al.'s (1991) model has contributed to the theory and practice of expatriation by stressing the significance of pre-departure and post-arrival experiences in determining successful adjustment, as well as work and general 'life' factors. Nevertheless, the model has not remained beyond criticism. Halsberger and Brewster (2007), in postulating a 'six adjustment domain' alternative, assert that factors such as social relations that focus on the establishment of networks, neighbourhood, contacts and friendships should be given greater priority. In general, critiques have argued for a more behavioural approach to be taken to explain success in adjustment, emphasizing individual and emotional 'fit' with circumstances in the host environment.

De Cieri et al. (1991) have provided an insight into the subjective experience of expatriation, mapping the phases of adjustment over time in graphical form (see Figure 4.2). According to these authors, psychological reactions to an assignment occur in three main phases, as follows:

- Phase 1 – *tourist* – is associated with mixed emotions, including excitement, fear of the unknown, anxiety and sense of adventure. On arrival in the host country, there may be a short-term experience of enchantment and unreality, which is referred to as the 'honeymoon' period. However, as the realities of everyday life in the new location become apparent, a downswing in mood may occur, promoting a feeling of crisis (Dowling and Welch, 2004).
- Phase 2 – *crisis* – may determine the success or failure of the assignment, depending on how the individual copes with the realities of living and working in a new environment. It is likely that 'self-efficacy' is a vital attribute during this stage, with the expatriate demonstrating an ability to learn from adverse experiences and to formulate positive coping mechanisms.
- Phase 3 – *pulling up* – assuming the individual successfully weathers Phase 2, is a time of recovery and emotional stabilization.
- Phase 4 – *adjustment* – represents a healthy recovery and integration into the new environment. As Dowling and Welch (ibid.) note, however, return home after experiencing this phase may require further adjustment on the part of the expatriate.

The 'models' of adjustment offered by Black et al. (1991) and De Cieri et al. (1991) promote vital understanding of the range of factors promoting expatriate adaptation to host countries. Each of these approaches, however, arguably runs the risk of stereotyping, over-generalizing and 'normalizing' adjustment phenomena that in practice are characterized by their

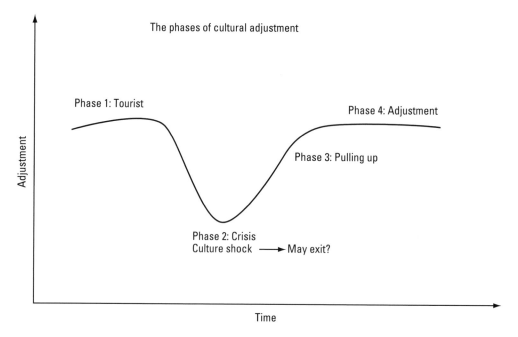

**Figure 4.2 Stages of adjustment**

*Source*: Dowling et.al. 2008, adapted from De Cieri et al. (1991).

variability and unpredictability, depending on the organization in question, the particularities of home and host environments, and the idiosyncrasies of the expatriates and their immediate relations (Halsberger and Brewster, 2007).

---

### Activity

Referring to the case scenario – Western expatriates in Moscow – above, consider the following:

- How does cultural theory (Hofstede and others) help us understand the problems in cross-cultural working between the two international management groupings forming the subject of the study?
- What should be the essential features of an expatriate training programme designed to assist the western expatriates adjusting to life and work in Russia?
- How do you interpret the motivation of the Russian managers? How might this be improved?
- Are there any useful lessons from this study for international joint ventures in general?

## Summary

This chapter has explored the staffing implications of organizing across national boundaries. It has suggested that, while expatriation remains a common HR mechanism for the exertion of parental influence on the subsidiary, various cost-effective and less risky strategic alternatives exist, including the devolution of decision-making authority to local managers. We have also investigated the organizational complexities of international team working, suggesting that multicultural management may be hampered by mistrust and miscommunication, but also offers the possibility of creativity and innovation. Finally, we have considered the factors contributing to successful expatriate adjustment in the host environment, an adjustment model forming the basis for recruitment and training approaches to international staffing.

## Further reading

**Dowling, P.J., Festing, M. and Engle, S.D., Sr**. (2008) *International Human Resource Management* 5th edn., London: Thomson Learning.

An informed and comprehensive review of the 'international' aspect of the subject is offered, presenting the various stages of the expatriation 'cycle' in an accessible form. Coverage is also offered of small- and medium-sized enterprises, managing diversity and cross-cultural management and offshoring.

**Hodgetts, R.M. and Luthans, F.** (2003) *International Management: Culture, Strategy and Behavior*, (5th edn.), New York: McGraw-Hill.

This text investigates processes and practices in staffing the international enterprise from an international business perspective. The international management of people is therefore located under the broader umbrella of international strategic management and related issues. The book contains a wealth of case studies and other stimulating learning materials. Part Four, in particular, focuses on the behavioural dimensions of IHRM.

**Black, J.S., Mendenhall, M. and Oddou, G.** (1991) Towards a comprehensive model of international adjustment: an integration of multiple theoretical perspectives, *Academy of Management Review*, 16: 291–317.

This journal article provides exposition of the rationale for the 'adjustment' model. Based on the original research of the authors, the various dimensions (work and non-work) facilitating or hindering expatriate adjustment are systematically investigated.

## Useful websites

www.gmacglobalrelocation.com/survey.html
The Global Relocation Trends Survey issued by GMAC/GRS provides up-to-date and comprehensive data on global relocation.

www.harzing.com

The personal website of Professor Anne-Wil Harzing provides information on online papers and resources on international management, including research-based insights into expatriation.

## References

**Adler, N.J.** (1997) *International Dimensions of Organizational Behavior* (3rd edn.), Cincinatti OH: South Western Publishing.

**Adler, N.J. and Ghadar, F.** (1990) Strategic human resource management: a global perspective, in R. Pieper (ed.) *Human Resource Management: An International Comparison*, Berlin: De Gruyter.

**Aycan, Z.** (1997) Expatriate adjustment as a multifaceted phenomenon: individual and organizational predictors, *International Journal of Human Resource Management*, 84(4): 491–504.

**Balgia, B.R. and Jaeger, A.M.** (1984) Multinational corporations: control systems and delegation issues, *Journal of International Business Studies*, 15: 25–40.

**Bhaskar-Shrivinas, P., Harrison, D.A., Shaffer, M.A. and Luk, D.M.** (2005) Input-based and time-based models of international adjustment: meta-analytic evidence and theoretical extensions, *Academy of Management Journal*, 48(2): 257–281.

**Black, J.S. and Gregersen, H.B.** (1999) The right way to manage expats, *Harvard Business Review*, 77: 52–63.

**Black, J.S., Mendenhall, M. and Oddou, G.** (1991) Towards a comprehensive model of international adjustment: an integration of multiple theoretical perspectives, *Academy of Management Review*, 16: 291–317.

**Bonache, J. and Brewster, C.** (2001) Knowledge transfer and the management of expatriation, *Thunderbird International Business Review*, 43: 143–168.

**Boyacigillar, N.** (1990) The role of expatriates in the management of interdependence, complexity and risk in multinational corporations', *Journal of International Business Studies*, 21(3): 357–181.

**Brewster, C., Sparrow, P. and Vernon, G.** (2007) *International Human Resource Management* (2nd edn.), London: CIPD.

**Briscoe, D.R. and Schuler, R.S.** (2004) *International Human Resource Management* (2nd edn.), London: Routledge.

**Brown, R.J.** (2008) Dominant stressors on expatriate couples during international assignments, *International Journal of Human Resource Management*, 19(6): 1018–1034.

**Caligiuri, P.M. and Colakoglu, S.** (2007) A strategic contingency approach to expatriate assignment management, *Human Resource Management Journal*, 17(4): 393–410.

**Caligiuri, P.M. and Di Santo, V.** (2001) Global competence: what is it and can it be developed through international assignments?, *Human Resource Planning*, 24(3): 27–35.

**Camiah, N. and Hollinshead, G.** (2003) Assessing the potential for effective cross-cultural working between 'new' Russian managers and western expatriates, *Journal of World Business*, 38(3): 245–261.

**Colakoglu, S. and Cagliuri, P.M.** (2008) Cultural distance: expatriate staffing and subsidiary performance: the case of US subsidiaries of multinational corporations, *International Journal of Human Resource Management*, 19(2): 223–239.

**De Cieri, H., Dowling, P.J. and Taylor, K.F.** (1991) The psychological impact of expatriate relocation on partners, *International Journal of Human Resource Management*, 2(3): 377–414.

**Dowling, P.J. and Welch, D.E.** (2004) *International Human Resource Management* (4th edn.), London: Thomson Learning.

**Dowling, P.J., Festing, M. and Engle, D. Sr.** (2005) *International Human Resource Management* (5th edn.), London: Thomson Learning.

**Dupuis, M.J., Haines, V.Y. III and Saba, T.** (2008) Gender, family ties and international mobility: cultural distance matters', *International Journal of Human Resource Management*, 19(2): 274–295.

**Edström, A. and Galbraith, J.R.** (1977) Transfer of managers as a coordination and control strategy in multinational organizations, *Administrative Science Quarterly*, 24: 248–263.

**Gaur, A.S., Deloi, A. and Singh, K.** (2007) Institutional environments, staffing strategies and subsidiary peformance, *Journal of Management*, 33(4): 611–636.

**GMAC/GRS** (2007) Global Relocation Trends, 2006 Survey Report, Woodridge, IL.

**Halsberger, A. and Brewster, C.** (2007) Domains of expatriate adjustment with special emphasis on work, paper presented at the *V1 International Workshop on Human Resource Management*, Cadiz University, Jerez, Spain.

**Harzing, A.W.K.** (1995) The persistent myth of high expatriate failure rates, *International Journal of Human Resource Management*, 6: 457–475.

**Harzing, A.W.K.** (2001) Of bears, bumble-bees, and spiders: the role of expatriates in controlling foreign subsidiaries, *Journal of World Business*, 36: 388–379.

**Harzing, A.W.K.** (2004) Composing an international staff, in A.W. Harzing and J. Van Ruysseveldt (eds) *International Human Resource Management* (2nd edn.), London: Sage Publications.

**Hippler, T.** (2000) European assignments: international or quasi-domestic? *Journal of European Industrial Training*, 24(9): 491–504.

**Hodgetts, R.M. and Luthans, F.** (2003) *International Management: Culture, Strategy and Behaviour* (5th edn.), New York: McGraw-Hill.

**Hollinshead, G. and Michailova, S.** (2001) Blockbusters or bridge-builders? The role of western trainers in developing new entrepreneurialism in eastern Europe, *Management Learning*, 32(3): 419–436.

**Hollinshead, G. and Leat, M.** (1995) *Human Resource Management: An International and Comparative Perspective*, London: Pitman Publishing.

**Hofstede, G.** (1994) *Cultures and Organizations: Software of the Mind*, London: HarperCollins.

**Kogut, B. and Zander, U.** (1993) Knowledge of the firm and the evolutionary theory of the multinational corporation, *Journal of International Business Studies*, 24(2): 625–645.

**Lee, H.W.** (2007) Factors that influence expatriate failure: an interview study, *International Journal of Management*, 24(3): 403–423.

**McCall, M.W. and Hollenbeck, G.P.** (2002) *Developing Global Executives: The Lessons of International Experience*, Boston, MA: Harvard Business School Press.

**Ogri, E.** (2009) Nigerian expatriate adjustment in the U.K., unpublished MSc International Business thesis, University of Hertfordshire.

**Pacific Bridge International Asian HR e-newsletter** (2003) Japanese boomerangs, 2(12): 2.

**Perlmutter, H.** (1969) The tortuous evolution of the multi-national corporation, *Columbia Journal of World Business*, 4(1): 9–18.

**Puffer, S.** (1996) Understanding the bear: a portrait of Russian business leaders, in S.M. Puffer (ed.) *Management Across Cultures: Insights from Fiction and Practice*, Oxford: Blackwell.

**Riusala, K. and Suutari, V.** (2000) Expatriation and careers: perspectives of expatriates and spouses, *Career Development International*, 5(2): 81–90.

**Shaffer, M.A., Harrison, D.A. and Gilley, K.M.** (1999) Dimensions, determinants and differences in the expatriate adjustment process' *Journal of International Business Studies*, 30(3): 557–581.

**Shapiro, D.L., Furst, S.A., Spreitzer, G.M. and Von Glinow, M.A.** (2002) Transnational teams in the electronic age: are team and high performance at risk?, *Journal of Organizational Behavior*, 23: 455–467.

**SHRM** (2001) Secrets of success, (article on results of 2000 Global Relocation Trends Survey by GMAC Global Relocation Services/Windham International, the National Foreign Trade Council, and the SHRM Global Forum).

**Varner, I.I. and Palmer, T.M.** (2005) Role of cultures: self-knowledge in successful expatriation, *Singapore Management Review*, 27(1): 1–25.

**Verbeke, A.** (2009) *International Business Strategy*, Cambridge: Cambridge University Press.

**Zimmerman, A. and Sparrow, P.** (2007) Mutual adjustment processes in international teams: lessons for the study of expatriation, *International Studies of Management and Organization*, 37(3): 65–88.

# CHAPTER

## 05

# Working across borders: the expatriation cycle

## ❖ *LEARNING OBJECTIVES*

❖ To consider criteria and methods for recruiting expatriates

❖ To highlight issues in the under-representation of women and ethnic minorities in the expatriate population and to consider how this might be overcome

❖ To examine the strategic issues involved in formulating a training programme for international assignees

❖ To investigate the significance of expatriate pay and the strategic tensions in formulating international reward packages

❖ To consider the value of international performance management and problems in its implementation

❖ To examine problems and issues in repatriation and to suggest why the returning assignee represents a valuable resource to the international organization

## Introduction

In the previous chapter we took issue with the notion that a single model of expatriation existed, and various forms of international assignment were identified, including international commuters, short-term postings, permanent international staff, as well as the possibility of devolving responsibility for management of the subsidiary to local managers. In this chapter, while placing an emphasis on 'traditional' expatriation, typically involving a foreign assignment for a parent country national (PCN) for around a three-year period, we continue to recognize that expatriation and the human resource (HR) policies associated with it are *contingent* in nature, being determined by the broader strategic goals of the international company and, in particular, the nature of the relationship between parent and subsidiary. In this chapter we turn our attention to the HR policies impinging on expatriation and follow through the broad *cycle* of international placement, embracing the selection of international transferees, training and development, managing pay and performance and repatriation. As Brewster et al. (2007) observe, there is a considerable gap between espoused intention and practice in international HR policy making, or, in other words, a tendency for authors and practitioners to delineate somewhat idealized 'best practice' with insufficient regard for its empirical reality.

## Expatriate selection

According to Briscoe and Schuler (2004), international companies take the following criteria into account in filling expatriate positions:

- *Job suitability*: relating to the technical expertise of the potential expatriate and his or her ability to perform job requirements.
- *Cultural adaptability*: there is a growing recognition that employees must be able to adjust to new and alien job environments while delivering their technical and managerial expertise.
- *Desire for foreign assignment* (*candidate and family*): the willingness of the potential expatriate to make the necessary effort to adjust needs to be assessed during the candidate review.
- *Profiles of successful international assignees*: companies and consultancies have established profiles of successful international assignees that are used for screening purposes. Such profiles typically include the following factors: experience, education, personal interests and activities, signs of flexibility, family situation and desire for the assignment.

While undoubtedly specifying vital skills and competences for expatriate success, this form of 'catch-all' prescriptive listing runs the risk of defining 'supermen or superwomen' (Brewster et al., 2007). Indeed, Dowling and Welch (2004) seek to explode certain 'myths' concerning international staffing, their view perhaps offering a more realistic starting point for considering expatriate selection, training and pay. In particular, these authors take issue with the notion that there is a universal approach to management, suggesting instead that evidence from cross-cultural studies points to variations in managerial ethos and style from country to country. Dowling and Welch also dispute the assumption of the body of literature on expatriate selection that there are common characteristics shared by successful international managers. Such an approach, which identifies predictors of success, holds that an individual with certain characteristics, traits and experiences is likely to perform most effectively in the international environment. These authors suggest that such predictors are difficult to measure and that factors associated with subsequent expatriate adjustment, which may not be accounted for in the selection process, can impact on the individual's performance in the foreign environment.

In an early, yet telling, contribution to the study of expatriation, Tung (1981) suggests that there has been over-reliance on technical factors in the selection and training of expatriates, with inadequate emphasis having been placed on cross-cultural competence. In order to rectify this shortcoming, she identifies four types of factor that are potentially vital to success in foreign assignments: technical competence on the job, relational abilities (social skills), ability to deal with environmental constraints (government, labour issues, etc.) and family situation. Tung (1981) advocates a *contingency* approach to the recruitment and training of expatriates, which holds that no single criterion or set of criteria is applicable to international assignments. Instead, she argues that for each assignment, the selection of the appropriate individual to fill the position should be made after careful analysis of the task (in terms of interaction with the social community) and the country of assignment (in terms of the degree to which it is similar/dissimilar to that of the home country), and the personality characteristics of the candidate (in terms of the candidate's and spouse's ability to live and work in a different cultural environment) (Kyriakidou, 2005; Tung, 1981).

A discrepancy between prescribed 'best practice' approaches and empirical reality is also apparent in the methods used to select expatriates. According to Briscoe and Schuler (2004), a variety of methods is potentially appropriate for selection of international assignees, including interviews, formal assessment, committee decision, career planning, self-selection, internal job postings, recommendations and assessment centres. In practice, however, research suggests a predominance of informal selection methods in selecting international assignees C Dowling et al., 1994; Mendenhall and Oddou, 1986). Brewster (1991) elaborates on this notion by suggesting that the outcome of selection interviews is frequently predetermined following recommendations by specialist personnel staff or line managers. Perhaps more provocatively, Harris and Brewster (1999) assert that expatriate recruitment decisions are made in a closed/informal system surrounding the office coffee machine or water cooler, such decisions subsequently ratified through formal organizational processes.

An informal approach to selection of international assignees undoubtedly has negative implications for equal opportunities and, in particular, expatriation opportunities for diverse ethnic groupings and women. The relative failure to ensure a balanced racial mix among expatriate teams would appear to increasingly run against the grain of 'best practice' in international staffing, particularly as MNCs extend their operations into developing countries. It may be argued that the ethnicity of expatriates conveys a powerful and symbolic message to subsidiary employees concerning the 'dominance effect' of the country of origin. To date, the bulk of research concerning equal opportunities in expatriate selection has referred to gender issues, which we now turn to.

## Equal opportunity issues in expatriate selection

The most recent GMAC/GLS (2007) survey reveals that only around one-fifth of expatriates are women, although this number is growing. As Harris (2004) asserts, the under-representation of females in expatriate positions represents a fundamental equal opportunities challenge for those global enterprises in which undertaking an international assignment is a prerequisite for progression to senior management. Harris also argues that the absence of female expatriates represents an opportunity cost to organizations operating in an increasingly knowledge-based economy in which it is necessary to utilize and develop all HR potential. Indeed, a number of authors have argued (Barham and Devine, 1991; Mendenhall and Oddou, 1986; Wills and Barham, 1994) that women possess particular skills that are highly conducive to effective performance in international roles, including interpersonal skills and highly communicative management styles.

The reasons for poor representation of women in international management groupings are closely related to broader patterns of discrimination at work, which are manifested in the failure of women to reach the highest management positions ('the glass ceiling') or the confinement of women to lower-status occupations ('the glass wall'). However, in the field of expatriation, there are specific factors at work that serve to hamper the progress of women.

## Organizational preconceptions

According to Adler (1984), a myth that is commonly subscribed to in international enterprises is that women do not wish to undertake international assignments. This author undertook an extensive survey of over 1,000 new MBA graduates in Canada, the USA and Europe to examine whether such a preconception could be upheld in practice, and found that new women college graduates demonstrated as much interest in pursuing international careers as their male counterparts. In a more recent study by Lowe et al. (1999), it was suggested, however, that women may be less prepared than men to accept assignments to regions that are perceived as 'culturally tough'.

A second organizational myth investigated by Adler (1987) was that host-national men would be reluctant to deal with female expatriates. Adler's study into this topic, however, revealed that US female assignees were just as successful as their male counterparts overseas, even in patriarchal societies such as Japan and Korea. Adler (1987) and Linehan (2005) argue that senior female expatriates tend to command respect in the host environment as they have had to overcome serious obstacles to achieve their positions.

Linehan (2005) argues that women will be more likely than men to be deterred from undertaking international assignments on personal grounds. Gender-related conventions concerning childcare responsibilities, both in home and host environments, may reinforce the notion that married women with children do not wish to pursue international careers, which are most amenable to young, married or single, males. Expatriation has also carried with it the emotional and economic detriment of the 'trailing' partner or spouse. As Kupta et al. (2008) contend, mode of adjustment of the expatriate's spouse/partner and other family members to the overseas environment is likely to be a major determinant of assignment success. Nevertheless, it remains the case that international companies leave decisions in this area to the family concerned and offer little assistance (Linehan, 2005).

## Organizational policies

Following from Harris and Brewster's (1999) depiction of the 'coffee machine' approach to expatriate recruitment, women may be excluded from applying for international assignments either due to informal organizational processes (not being at the right place at the right time) or as a result of formal procedures that tend to reproduce the staffing status quo. The current proliferation of males in fields of business activity that lend themselves to internationalization tends to possess a characteristic of self-perpetuation, particularly when the dominant selection approach is promotion from within (Rothwell, 1984). Furthermore, as Harris and Brewster (1999) suggest, the tendency to have unrefined and universalistic selection criteria for expatriate selection, rather than those that are finely tuned to meet precise job requirements, tends, in practice, to arbitrarily reproduce the dominant paradigm concerning suitable expatriate candidates. According to Linehan (2005), the tendency towards discrimination in expatriation may be reinforced by the prevalence of male mentors and through organizational stereotypes that are prone to exemplify the ideal international transferee in 'masculine' terms. In order to counter discriminatory tendencies in the selection of international managers, Harris (2004) suggests the following actions should be taken. Although this section has referred particularly to equal opportunities on the basis of gender, the recommendations may also have applicability concerning other forms of discrimination.

Organizations should:

- become more strategic in their planning for international assignments in order to prevent *ad hoc* and informal placements that may replicate an existing expatriate profile and prevent the adoption of alternative approaches;
- adopt a sophisticated approach to the determination of criteria for effective international managers. Competences should be developed and debated in as wide and diverse a forum as possible;
- monitor their selection processes for international management assignments to ensure access is not unfairly restricted to specific sections of employees. This includes auditing career development systems leading up to international assignments for potential unintended bias;
- run selection skills training for all employees involved in selection for international assignments. This training should include raising awareness of the advantages of using diverse groups of employees on international assignments and challenging existing stereotypes relating to women and other non-traditional groups;
- avoid assumptions as to the likely motivation of women to accept overseas assignments and the likely success rates of women expatriates;
- provide flexible benefits packages that will cater for single employee and dual career couples as well as the traditional 'married male with family' expatriate;
- define the international assignment in such as way that the chances of success are high; that is, establishing full status, permanent assignments;
- provide full support for alternative arrangements for the domestic aspect of international assignments that might influence women's perceptions of accessibility;
- work with relocation companies to ensure the female expatriate's residence will facilitate the possibility for social interaction.

In order to alleviate problems of expatriation concerning dual career couples, it may be suggested also that organizations: (1) fully consider shorter alternatives to 'traditional' expatriation; (2) consider anticipatory and in-country adjustment problems, and courses of action to support partner and spouse; and (3) implement 'family-friendly' policies; for example, helping the partner to find employment in the host country.

## Training and development

The model of expatriate adjustment (Black et al., 1991) considered in the previous chapter provides a useful basis for the identification of expatriate training needs and developmental priorities. Drawing on the model, the following observations may be made concerning the desired orientation of expatriate training programmes:

- Training should be provided both prior to departure and on arrival in the host environment.
- Training in cross-cultural proficiency (relating to general adjustment to the host environment) should accompany more job-specific, technically-oriented material.
- The training/adjustment needs of spouse/partner (and children) should be accommodated.
- Fluency in the host country language is likely to be a useful attribute.

According to the GMAC/GRS (2007) survey, although 80 per cent of expatriates reported that their companies offered formal cross-cross cultural preparation, only 34 per cent of companies provided this training on all assignments. Furthermore, only 21 per cent of respondents offering cross-cultural preparation indicated that training was mandatory, determinant factors including the grade of employee and the national destination. Training was made available to the employee and spouse in 34 per cent of cases. As the survey reveals, actual participation in cross-cultural training programmes by expatriates and their families is, in practice, likely to be low. The authors of the survey suggest that this is perplexing, given the growing sophistication of available cross-cultural tools (particularly web-based material), and the overwhelmingly positive evaluation of the quality of such programmes. As the survey report states:

> 66 With effective cross-cultural training tools available, why is participation so low? It is hard to reconcile why managers of human resource programmes continue to be challenged by family-transition problems, premature returns from assignments, and assignment failure when it appears a solution lies with increasing the mandatory participation in these training programmes.
>
> (GMAC/GRS, 2007) 99

The authors of the report indicate that the continuing corporate underestimation of the significance of cross-cultural training may be a product of the lack of influence of HR professionals at an operational level. One expatriate is cited as follows: 'human resources sees the importance quite well, but line management doesn't always view it the same, they concentrate on getting the job done only …'.

While the overall level of engagement in cross-cultural training is disappointing, research in this field has suggested that the form and method of such training should be 'fit for purpose' and finely tuned according to specific expatriate training needs. In other words, the degree and form of requisite cross-cultural preparation may vary from assignment to assignment. In an early contribution to the subject, Tung (1981) provides a two-dimensional framework for selecting cross-cultural training methods: the degree of interaction required in the host culture, and the similarity between the expatriates' home culture and the host culture. Mendenhall and Oddou (1986), elaborating on Tung's approach, identify three levels of training rigour relating to the anticipated degree of integration into the host environment, as follows:

- *Lowest level of rigour* – information giving – area briefings, cultural briefings, films/books, use of interpreters, 'survival'-level language training.
- *Medium level of rigour* – affective approach – cultural assimilator training, language training, role-playing, critical incidents, cases, stress reduction training, moderate language training.
- *Highest level of rigour* – immersion approach – assessment centre, field experiences, simulations, sensitivity training, extensive language training.

As the above spectrum of training intervention suggests, at the highest level of rigour not only is the knowledge to be assimilated most challenging, but also methods of delivery are highly interactive. At the lowest level, there is considerable emphasis on factual forms of knowledge and one-way modes of dissemination. The medium level of intervention is exemplified by the method of *cultural assimilator training*, which refers to a paper or web-based exercise in questionnaire format, frequently containing multiple-choice responses. Using this format, the designated expatriate is presented with various international scenarios or quandaries relating to day-to-day living or working issues that need to be resolved.

In a more recent contribution, Mendenhall et. al. (1995) assimilate and develop previous contributions to the field of expatriate training, drawing on social learning theory, by formulating a decision tree model that incorporates the variables of culture novelty, required degree of interaction with host nationals, job novelty and training rigour (Figures 5.1 and 5.2).

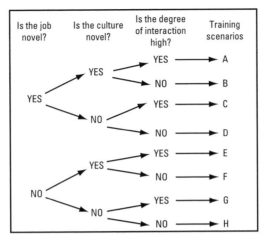

**Figure 5.1 Decision tree for selecting appropriate training methods**

*Source:* Mendenhall et. al. (1995).

| | Level of rigor | Duration | Approach | Training Content |
|---|---|---|---|---|
| **A** | High | 60–180 hours | Lecture, factual briefing, books, role plays, cases, field experiences, culture assimilator, simulations | Equal emphasis on job demands and culture (include: economic, political, historical, and religious topics) |
| **B** | Moderate | 20–60 hours | Lecture, film, books, culture assimilator, cases | Equal emphasis on job and culture |
| **C** | Moderate | 20–60 hours | Lecture, film, books, cases, role plays, simulations | Strong emphasis on job demands, less on culture |
| **D** | Low to moderate | 20–40 hours | Lecture, factual briefing, cases | Strong emphasis on job demands, little on culture |
| **E** | Moderate | 40–80 hours | Lecture, film, books, culture assimilator, cases, role plays, simulation | Little emphasis on job demands, most on culture(economic, political, historical, and religious topics) |
| **F** | Low to moderate | 20–60 hours | Lecture, film, books, cases | Little emphasis on job demands, more emphasis on culture |
| **G** | Low to moderate | 30–60 hours | Lecture, film, books, cases, role plays | Little emphasis on job demands, more emphasis on culture |
| **H** | Low | 4–8 hours | Lecture, film, books | Little emphasis on either job or culture |

**Figure 5.2 Training scenario**

*Source:* Mendenhall et. al. (1995)..

Turning more specifically to areas of knowledge required for international assignees, although these will clearly vary from assignment to assignment, Briscoe and Schuler (2004) identify the following topics as a minimum to facilitate adjustment:

- intercultural business skills (e.g. negotiating styles in different countries and cultures);
- culture shock management (e.g. what to expect and how to deal with the stress of adaptation);
- lifestyle adjustment (e.g. how to deal with different shopping and transportation systems and the different availability of familiar foods and entertainment);
- host-country daily living issues (e.g. any unfamiliar problems with water or electricity);
- local customs and etiquette (e.g. what to wear and different behaviour patterns and gestures for men and women);
- area studies (e.g. the political and religious environment and the local geography);
- repatriation planning (e.g. how to stay in touch with the home office and how to identify an appropriate assignment prior to repatriating back home);
- language learning strategies, both before leaving for the new assignment as well as after arrival.

While we have tended to present expatriate training as primarily a corporate responsibility in the above section, there has been growing recognition in the field of management learning of the need for individuals to generate and resolve their own learning needs in a proactive fashion. In keeping with the notion of *self-efficacy* referred to in the model of adjustment defined by Black et al. (1991) (see Chapter 4), a critical challenge confronting international assignees is to respond positively and creatively to learning experiences in the foreign environment in an independent fashion. Accordingly, new developments in management learning, which emphasize the significance of action learning (Revans, 1982), and which recognize that individual learning styles vary (Kolb, 1983), may be particularly applicable to those seeking to adjust and perform in unfamiliar territories. Of particular significance to expatriates is likely to be 'double-loop learning' (Argyris, 1990, 1994) that calls upon managers to question and confront the way in which problems are defined, and to query the assumptions upon which behavioural routines are based (Woodall, 2006). In contrast to 'single-loop learning' in which 'defensive routines' are adopted and uncomfortable environmental challenges are ignored (ibid.), double-loop learning demands exploration and the taking of calculated risks. For the international assignee, therefore, double-loop learning demands that mental maps in new environments should be 'reframed' in a rapid fashion, and that tried and tested manners of business and social engagement cannot be transferred in an unproblematic and complacent fashion from culture to culture.

## Pay and performance management

## International reward packages

The management of expatriate compensation constitutes a critical function in the IHRM portfolio (Bonache, 2006), and inevitably involves the reconciliation of strategic tensions (Dowling and Welch, 2004).

- On the one hand, international companies are increasingly seeking to ensure that expatriation is justified in terms of cost. In the GMAC/GRS (2007) survey, 60 per cent of respondents required a clear statement of assignment objectives before funding and 43 per cent required a cost–benefit analysis to justify the relocation assignment. On the other, there is a need to provide sufficient financial incentive to recruit capable international transferees, and to promote optimal adjustment and performance during the course of the assignment, as well as facilitating return to the home environment. The needs of partner/spouse and children are also likely to come into the reckoning in the formulation of international reward packages.

■ Various international relationships will be placed under the microscope in seeking to establish fairness and equity in payment structures. Not only will groupings of expatriates compare their packages when transferring to various destinations, but also the relative remuneration of home and host country counterparts is subject to scrutiny (Camiah and Hollinshead, 2003).

Complexities may also arise in the administration of international reward relating, for example, to high rates of inflation in developing countries, currency conversion and realization of legal tender, varying taxation systems, general difficulties of obtaining financial and related information in the host country, and the need to upgrade payroll systems and software to account for extra components and variables in international reward packages.

The formulation of international reward packages, as with other aspects of IHR policies, may vary according to the type of international engagement. Accordingly, following Briscoe and Schuler (2004), shorter-term expatriates, including categories such as international commuters, are experiencing little dislocation from their home environment, and so are likely to expect little variation in their pattern of remuneration. On the other hand, 'traditional' expatriates, undertaking a foreign assignment for approximately a three-year period, will expect to retain at least the home country standard of living in the host country, and also an inducement to undertake the assignment. This grouping is also likely to desire provision for partner/spouse and children. The 'permanent' cadre of international staff, normally consisting of high-status professionals and 'knowledge workers' moving from subsidiary to subsidiary, may expect to receive a desirable benefits package that is 'global' in its reference points, transcending organizational or national market rates and instead being established by comparison to equivalent internationally prestigious occupational groupings. Finally, permanent transferees, that is, those who convert from long-term assignee to local status, might appropriately be rewarded according to market rates in the local (host) environment.

## Approaches to rewarding international managers

The most widely used method of expatriate compensation is the *balance sheet* approach, which is designed to equalize the purchasing power of employees living overseas and in the home country, and to provide incentives to offset variations in the quality of life between assignment locations (Reynolds, 2000). Thus, Dowling et al. (2008) summarize the key features of the balance sheet approach as follows:

■ The basis objective is maintenance of home country living standard plus financial inducement.
■ Home country pay and benefits are the foundations of this approach.
■ Adjustments are made to the home package to balance additional expenditure in the host country.

■ Financial incentives (expatriate/hardship premium) are added to make the package attractive.

The fairness and equity of this approach may be argued on a number of grounds (ibid.). First, a comparable rate will be maintained for the international assignee transferring from subsidiary to subsidiary in different countries. Second, comparisons can be sustained in respect of expatriates from the same parent in various subsidiary destinations. Third, the return of the expatriate to the home environment will be facilitated, with the logic of the payment structure connecting home and host remaining intact. On the other hand, a disadvantage of the balance sheet approach is the material and symbolic separation it serves to reinforce between expatriates and host country managers and employees.

As an alternative to counter the perceived drawbacks of the balance sheet approach, the *going rate* (ibid.) or *localized* approach may offer not only a cost-effective alternative, but also a re-orientation of the international reward structure to comply with local conditions. The establishment of going rates is founded on local market rate information, and survey comparisons of both home and country managers operating in the region. Upward adjustments are likely to be in the case of transfer to low-pay countries, while the expatriate stands to benefit from transfer to a destination with relatively favourable conditions of employment. The adoption of the going rate approach may be hampered by difficulties in obtaining information pertaining to the host environment. While the going rate approach promotes identification on the basis of similar status with local managers, it tends to disrupt relativities with expatriate counterparts on the basis of variations in standards of living in their destinations, and difficulties may occur in reconstructing pay progression on re-entering the parent environment. As a possible consequence, the GMAC/GRS (2007) survey reports a number of international enterprises transitioning away from their expatriates' original benefits structure to local standards, primarily on grounds of cost. Such a move is perhaps significant in signalling the strategic desirability of localization on the part of the international company, and the loosening of parent company control over the terms and conditions of employment of international management groupings.

Balance sheet and going rate approaches may be regarded as the primary strategic alternatives in international reward, although, as the above analysis implies, the dividing line between them may be indefinite after overseas inducements and adjustments are accounted for. Other pecuniary options are also being recognized by MNCs, including:

■ *lump sum*: the firm determines a total salary for the expatriate, frequently at the commencement of the assignment, covering all incentives and adjustment. This avoids unnecessary intrusion into the expatriate's privacy and lifestyle as he or she can decide how much to spend on housing, transportation, education, and so on (Briscoe and Schuler, 2004; Littlewood, 1995);
■ *cafeteria*: primarily designed for senior executives, this approach allows expatriates to choose from a range of benefits up to a predetermined monetary value (possibly including company car, company-provided housing, healthcare) that relieves the individual and company of tax obligations (Briscoe and Schuler, 2004).

## Performance management

Given the aforementioned concern with the cost-effectiveness and 'added value' of expatriation, it might be expected that MNCs would devote considerable attention to monitoring the contribution of the international assignee to corporate objectives. The GMAC/GRS (2007) survey, however, reveals that only 42 per cent of respondents used host country performance reviews, while 34 per cent used home and host country reviews. Such evidence that assessment of expatriate performance is far from common has been corroborated by various authors, including Brewster (1991) and Fenwick et al. (1999). The under-utilization of performance management for expatriates is perhaps perplexing, as systems for managing individual contribution have become widely utilized in many sectors of commercial activity. A major performance management tool has been the performance appraisal interview, typically between first-line manager and subordinate, despite some scepticism having been expressed concerning the reliability and validity of this method (Pym, 1973). As Briscoe and Schuler (2004) assert, the transposition of performance management into the international arena can help stabilize the experience of expatriation by contributing towards feedback on performance, the identification of training needs, development planning, and pay and motivation. An overriding benefit of performance management for expatriates is that it offers an effective channel for interpersonal communication, thus avoiding the 'out-of-sight out-of-mind' syndrome, and provides a tangible system of mentoring in unfamiliar and ambiguous circumstances, potentially alleviating the risk of expatriate failure.

Despite the potential benefits associated with expatriate performance management, its adoption 'on the ground' has been hampered by a variety of factors (ibid.):

■ Choice of evaluator – should the appraiser be the home or host country line manager?
■ Communication difficulties between host country appraiser and expatriate.
■ Difficulties in long-distance communication with headquarters.
■ Parent company ethnocentrism/indifference to international business issues and lack of understanding of the foreign environment.
■ Inadequate establishment of performance objectives of the foreign operations and means of recording individual and organizational performance.

The major difficulties serving to jeopardize effective performance management of expatriates are, first, that a distinctive set of challenges confronts expatriates in adjusting to the host environment, implying an extended 'learning curve' and, second, that culturally specific factors in the host environment may impede individual performance in an unanticipated fashion. Thus, it may be the case that an international transferee to Latin America spends months successfully averting a strike, which, however, gains little recognition by a US headquarters unsympathetic to trade unionism. In these circumstances, effective performance management of expatriates appears to demand adaptation of systems by the MNC. The following are likely to be pertinent considerations in enhancing practice:

■ Review the criteria for expatriate success with reference to the realities of doing business in the host environment.
■ Include cross-cultural and related factors as necessary competences for many occupations (as well as technical factors).
■ Combine parent and local company standards as appropriate.
■ Involve returning expatriates from the country in question in the design and operation of performance management systems.
■ Maximize sources of information (people and materials) relating to the individual expatriate in arriving at judgements concerning his or her performance.

## Repatriation

The final stage of the expatriation cycle is returning to the home environment, or repatriation. While re-entry into the parent location offers potential benefits both to the employing organization and to the expatriate him or herself, in practice there have been difficulties realizing these benefits. From the point of view of the international enterprise, the returning expatriate represents a potentially invaluable knowledge resource, possessing first-hand insight into the realities of doing business in the host environment. Fink et al. (2005) identify five categories of repatriate knowledge, as follows:

- *Market-specific knowledge*: the local political, social and economic system, language and customs.
- *Personal skills*: intercultural knowledge, self-confidence, flexibility, tolerance.
- *Job-related management skills*: communication, project management, problem-solving.
- *Network knowledge*: clients, suppliers, subsidiary personnel and other expatriates.
- *General management capacity*: an enlarged job description, broader job responsibilities, exposure to other parts of the organization.

Sánchez-Vidal et al. (2007) suggest that repatriates have acquired valuable international experience for the company, which could be used for managerial improvement and organizational development. These authors also argue that, if repatriates leave their companies, such indispensable knowledge could be gained by competitors. The international insight of repatriates encompasses not only the formal domain of business activity in the host environment (concerning job-related and contextual facts, procedures, regulative mechanisms, etc.) but also the vital informal dimension (concerning useful contacts both inside and outside organizations, customs and practices on the ground, methods of bypassing unnecessary bureaucracy, etc.). Thus, the possibility exists for the 'recycling' of this knowledge into the international organization, which both lowers the risk of subsequent expatriate failure in the same locality, and generally broadens the organization's international awareness, which broadens marketing and operational potential.

The returning expatriate may disseminate acquired international knowledge into the organization in a number of capacities; for example, by engaging in training programmes for new expatriates or by providing specialist advice to colleagues with an operational interest in the subsidiary. As Dowling et al. (2008) assert, however, drawing on the GMAC/GRS (2002) survey, international enterprises are prone to neglect the potential utility of acquired expatriate knowledge, adopting instead a single-dimensional paradigm of knowledge transfer, from the parent to the host. Sánchez-Vidal et al. (2007) assert that companies have tended to systematically ignore the repatriation phase of international assignments, which implies redundancy of expatriate knowledge on assignment completion.

From the perspective of the individual expatriate, there is likely to be an expectation that positive international experience will be instrumental in future career progression. However, as a series of GMAC surveys have demonstrated (GMAC/GRS, 2002, 2004, 2007):

- A majority of organizations do not provide post-assignment guarantees.
- Returnees with international experience are most likely to leave the company.
- Expatriates anticipate a lack of attractive positions within the employing organization and seek better opportunities elsewhere.

Brewster et al. (2007) find that, counterproductively from the perspective of the employing organization, many exiting expatriates do not radically change their careers, but instead move to close competitors. At the organizational level, Tung (1988) uncovered the following issues that are detrimental to expatriate reintegration at organizational level:

- The 'out-of-sight out-of-mind' syndrome was common.
- Organizational changes made during the period abroad may make the position redundant or peripheral.
- Technical advances in the parent may make skills and knowledge obsolete.

The tribulations confronting returning expatriates are well captured in the following quotations, reported by Adler (2002):

- My colleagues react indifferently to my global assignment ... they view me as doing a job I did in the past.
- The organization has changed. Work habits, norms and procedures have changed and I've lost touch with all that ... I'm a beginner again.
- I came back with so many stories to share, but my friends and family couldn't understand them. It was as if my years overseas were unshareable.

It is therefore of considerable strategic significance that MNCs should attend to the problem of effective repatriation in order to harness the vital knowledge possessed by expatriates and to manage their career aspirations. The principles of adjustment referred to in Chapter 4 (Black et al., 1991) may also be applied to the process of repatriation in order to guide 'good practice' (Sánchez-Vidal et al., 2007). Accordingly, MNCs would be advised to focus on the nature of the job role confronting the international returnee, as well as general lifestyle factors, recognizing the likelihood of a new 'learning curve' being entered on reimmersion in the home environment, and the significance of family-related factors. Accordingly, Brewster et al. (2007) call for more proactive management of the expatriation cycle, with an ultimate eye for effective repatriation, incorporating the following activities:

- pre-departure career discussions;
- a named contact person at the home country organization;
- a mentor at the host location;
- re-entry counselling;
- family repatriation programmes;
- employee debriefings;
- succession planning.

### Activity

In your first managerial role after graduating, you are to be expatriated to China for a three-year period in a general management capacity to facilitate the 'start-up' of a European-owned food and drinks subsidiary. How would you expect the experience you acquire to assist in your future career development? Specify the main competences/areas of expertise and knowledge you would envisage acquiring and share them with the rest of the group.

## Summary

In this chapter the complexities of determining expatriate payment methods have been discussed, with particular reference to the strategic dilemma of whether to adhere to home or host market rates. The main difficulties in managing expatriate performance have been considered, and suggestions made for enhancing the utility of international performance appraisal processes. Finally, the neglected activity of repatriation has been explored, highlighting the value of the returning assignee as a source of international knowledge.

## Expatriate voices from locations with high expatriation failure

**Angola**: difficult living conditions ... difficulty living in a vastly different environment from the home location ...

**Brazil**: unable to adapt culturally ... the medical facilities ... poor infrastructure to do business ...

**Chile**: the business in that country is new; not only did the employee need to adapt to the culture but also handle many issues relating to the business ...

**China**: lifestyle, climate, safety ... unable to adapt culturally ... the medical facilities ... hardship of location takes a toll on the families: families were unable to communicate with locals ...China is so far from headquarters that expats are left on their own without adequate supervision, and they either don't meet expectations or go off and do unproductive things ... environment ... employees are being hired by competitors in the host location; the root cause would be uncompetitive remuneration.. generally performance issues ... usually the wrong person for the position ... difficulties associated with the host site and family ... expectations too high; difficult cultural environment, candidates not selected carefully ... far away; difficulty in closely controlling expatriate success there ... standard of living; inability to adapt to local culture ... political and family reasons ... big intercultural gap ... family not settled ... family health issues ...

**Ethiopia**: difficulty living in a vastly different environment from the host location ...

**France**: intercultural differences ...

**Germany**: schooling ... generally performance issues ... cost of living and culture ... family desire to return to the home country; demands of work and the lifestyle change

**India**: lifestyle, climate, safety ... living conditions ... difficulties associated with the host site and family ... standard of living; inability to adapt to local culture ... did not fit in culturally ... family not settled ...

**Iran**: political instability ...

**Ireland**: the culture ... adaptation to the local organization environment and everyday living in the local environment ...

**Japan**: cross-cultural differences and lack of planning with the head office ... generally performance issues ... inability to find new positions for repatriating expatriates ... adjustment difficulties ... cultural adjustment challenges ... did not support the cultural transition enough ...

**Nigeria**: significant cultural differences, isolation, low quality of life, remoteness from family, harsh weather and conditions (disease, crime etc.) ... security, cost of living, lack of infrastructure, competition regarding compensation, difficulties living in a vastly different environment from the home location ... political instability ... assignees lose professionalism and dedication seen in the home office ...

**Russia**: significant cultural differences, isolation, low quality of life, remoteness from family, harsh weather and conditions (disease, crime, etc.) ... cross-cultural differences and lack of planning from the head office ... living conditions ... poor selection ...

**South Africa**: security concerns, career opportunity at the headquarters location, desire for family (to be) based in the home location after a certain time abroad ...

**United Arab Emirates**: security, cost of living, lack of infrastructure, competition regarding compensation ...

**UK**: cross-cultural difficulties and lack of planning from the head office ... security concerns, career opportunity at the headquarters location, lack of cultural understanding ... usually the wrong person for the position ... expectations of the employee and lack of realization of the importance of cultural differences at work and in personal life ... inability to find new positions for repatriating expatriates ... cost of living and ability of spouse/partner to easily convert their education and experience to a similar role in the UK ...

**USA**: intercultural differences are underestimated; very rural locations ... sheer volume ... trying to renew a visa ... job did not live up to expectations and cost of living ... family desire to return to home country; demands of work and the lifestyle change ... adjustment difficulties ... problems adapting to a new environment ... improper cultural fit ...

*Source*: GMAC/GRS (2007).

## Further reading

**Adler, N.J.** (2002) *International Dimensions of Organizational Behavior* (4th edn.), Boston: South Western, Thomson Learning.

This book is predicated on the notion that sophisticated management responses in the field of organizational behaviour are required to respond effectively to the international dynamics of the business environment. The text embraces issues such as the effect of culture on organizations, cross-cultural team working and negotiation, and managing global careers, including gender and family issues. Stimulating case study material is used for illustrative purposes.

**Brewster, C., Sparrow, P. and Vernon, G.** (2007) *International Human Resource Management* (2nd edn.), London: CIPD.

An international and comparative approach is taken to the formulation of policy areas in international companies, including recruitment, reward, and training and development. The book also draws attention to new developments in IHRM, including organizational capability, outsourcing and talent management, and to the role of the HR department.

## Useful websites

www.expatwomen.com
Information is provided to assist specifically with female expatriation.

www.gmacglobalrelocation.com/survey.html
The Global Relocation Trends Survey issued by GMAC/GRS provides up-to-date and comprehensive data on global relocation.

www.harzing.com
The personal website of Professor Anne-Wil Harzing provides information on online papers and resources on international management, including research-based insights into expatriation.

## References

**Adler, N.J.** (1984) Women do not want international careers and other myths about international management, *California Management Review*, 26(4): 78–89.

**Adler, N.J.** (1987) Pacific Basin managers: a Gaijin, not a woman, *Human Resource Management*, 26(2): 169–192.

**Adler N.J.** (2002) *International Dimensions of Organizational Behavior* (4th edn.), South Western, Thomson Learning.

**Argyris, C.** (1990) *Overcoming Organizational Defences: Facilitating Organizational Learning*, Boston, MA: Allyn & Bacon.

**Argyris, C.** (1994) *On Organizational Learning*, Oxford: Blackwell.

**Barham, K. and Devine, M.** (1991) The quest for the international manager: a survey of global human resource strategies, London: Ashridge Management Guide, Economist Intelligence Unit.

**Black, J.S., Mendenhall, M. and Oddou, G.** (1991) Towards a comprehensive model of international adjustment: an integration of multiple theoretical perspectives, *Academy of Management Review*, 16: 291–317.

**Bonache, J.** (2006) The compensation of expatriates: a review and a future research agenda, in G. Stahl and I. Björkman (eds) *Handbook of Research in International Human Resource Management*, Cheltenham: Edward Elgar.

**Brewster, C.** (1991) *The Management of Expatriates*, London: Kogan Page.

**Brewster, C., Sparrow, P. and Vernon, G.** (2007) *International Human Resource Management* (2nd edn.), London: CIPD.

**Briscoe, D.R. and Schuler, R.S.** (2004) *International Human Resource Management* (2nd edn.), London: Routledge.

**Camiah, N. and Hollinshead, G.** (2003) Assessing the potential for effective cross-cultural working between 'new' Russian managers and western expatriates, *Journal of World Business*, 38(3): 245–261.

**Dowling, P.J. and Welch, D.E.** (2004) *International Human Resource Management: Managing People in a Multinational Context* (4th edn.), London: Thomson Learning.

**Dowling, P.J., Festing, M. and Engle, A.D. Sr.** ( 2008) *International Human Resource Management: Managing People in a Multinational Context* (5th edn.), London: Thomson Learning.

**Dowling, P.J., Schuler, R.S. and Welch, D.** (1994) *International Dimensions of Human Resource Management* (2nd edn.), Belmont, CA: Wadsworth.

**Fenwick, M.S., De Cieri, H. and Welch, D.E.** (1999) Cultural and bureaucratic control in MNEs: the role of expatriate performance management, *Management International Review*, 39(3): 107–24.

**Fink, G., Meierewert, S. and Rohr, U.** (2005) The use of repatriate knowledge in organizations, *Human Resource Planning*, 22(4): 30–36.

**GMAC/GRS**, US National Foreign Trade Council and SHRM Global Forum (2002) Global Relocation Trends, Survey Report, Woodridge, IL.

**GMAC/GRS** (2004) Global Relocation Trends, Survey Report, Woodridge, IL.

**GMAC/GRS** (2007) Global Relocation Trends, Survey Report, Woodridge, IL.

**Harris, H.** (2004) Women's role in international management, in A.W. Harzing and J. Van Ruysseveldt (eds) *International Human Resource Management* (2nd edn.), London: Sage Publications.

**Harris, H. and Brewster, C.** (1999) The coffee-machine system: how international selection really works, *International Journal of Human Resource Management*, 10(3): 488–500.

**Kolb, D.** (1983) *Experiential Learning: Experience as the Source of Learning and Development*, Englewood Cliffs, NJ: Prentice Hall.

**Kupta, B., Everett, A.M. and Cathro, V.** (2008) Home alone and often unprepared: intercultural communication training for expatriated partners in German MNCs, *International Journal of Human Resource Management*, 19(10): 1765–1791.

**Kyriakidou, O.** (2005) Operational aspects of international human resource management, in M. Özbilgin (ed.) *International Human Resource Management: Theory and Practice,* Basingstoke: Palgrave Macmillan.

**Linehan, M.** (2005) Women in international management, in H. Scullion and M. Linehan (eds) *International Human Resource Management: A Critical Text*, Basingstoke: Palgrave Macmillan.

**Lowe, K., Downes, M., and Kroef, K.** (1999) The impact of gender and location on the willingness to accept overseas assignments, *International Journal of Human Resource Management*, 10(2): 223–234.

**Mendenhall, M.E. and Oddou, G.** (1986) Acculturation profiles of expatriate managers: implications for cross-cultural training programmes, *Columbia Journal of World Business*, Winter: 73–79.

**Mendenhall, M., Punnett, B.J. and Ricks, D.** (1995) *Global Management*, Cambridge, MA: Blackwell.

**Pym, D.** (1973) The politics and ritual of appraisal, *Occupational Psychology*, 47: 231–235.

**Revans, R.** (1982) *The Origins and Growth of Action Learning*, Bromley: Chartwell Bratt.

**Reynolds, C.** (2000) *2000 Guide to Global Compensation and Benefits*, San Diego, CA: Harcourt Professional Publishing.

**Rothwell, S.** (1984) Positive action on women's career development: an overview of the issues for individuals and organizations, in C.L. Cooper and M.J. Davidson (eds) *Women in Management: Career Development for Managerial Success*, London: Heinemann.

**Sánchez-Vidal, M.E., Sanz-Valle, R. and Barba-Aragón, M.I.** (2007) The adjustment process of Spanish repatriates: a case study, *International Journal of Human Resource Management*, 18(8): 1396–1417.

**Tung, R.** (1981) Selection and training of personnel for overseas assignments, *Columbia Journal of World Business*, 16(1): 68–78.

**Tung, R.** (1988) Career issues in international assignments, *Academy of Management Executive*, 2(3): 241–344.

**Wills, S. and Barham, K.** (1994) Being an international manager, *European Management Journal*, 12(1): 49–58.

**Woodall, J.** (2006) International management development, in T. Edwards and C. Rees (eds) *International Human Resource Management: Globalization, National Systems and Multinational Companies*, Harlow: FT/Prentice Hall.

# PART 03

# Comparative Themes and Regional Studies

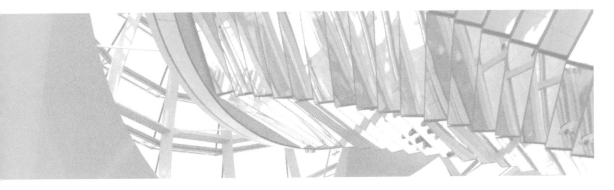

# International labour relations and employee participation

**06**

❖ **LEARNING OBJECTIVES**

❖ To appreciate institutional explanations for regional variations in labour relations structures

❖ To gain insight into variations in trade union structure, membership and objectives between the EU, the USA and Japan

❖ To examine the role and significance of employers' organizations in these global regions

❖ To consider variations in the structure of collective bargaining across these global regions

❖ To comprehend contrasting international philosophies and practices in employee involvement and participation

❖ To gain insight into the rationale for, and effect of, the European Works Council Directive

❖ To appreciate the significance and functions of the International Labour Organization (ILO) and the Organization for Economic Co-operation and Development (OECD)

## Introduction

In Chapter 2 the institutional 'bedrock' for national variations in observed human resource management (HRM) policies and practices was explored. Using the analogy of systems 'hardware', it was asserted that primary institutions, including industrial enterprises, public utilities, financial establishments, educational institutions, trade unions and government/quasi-governmental agencies vary in the extent to which they 'interlock' from society to society. It was argued, following Whitley (1996) and others, that proximity between such institutions, engendering a climate of mutual supportiveness, was consistent with 'investment-oriented' approaches towards the management of the human resource, while 'space' between institutions tended to perpetuate a climate of competition and a 'resource'-oriented view of the potential of human capital. Such an analysis provides an appropriate point of departure for study of international labour relations that is concerned with the modes of interaction between trade unions, employers and government and its representatives in various national and regional settings.

Indeed, 'neo-liberal' and 'neo-corporatist' perspectives delineated in Chapter 2 possess considerable value in comprehending broad variations in the conduct of labour relations across regions.

Following O'Hagen et al. (2004) in the USA, which has been regarded as an exemplar of neo-liberal ideology, over 85 per cent of the workforce is non-unionized, with broad management discretion determining terms and conditions of employment for this substantial grouping. In the minority unionized sector, relations between management and organized workers have traditionally been adversarial and low trust in nature (Poole and Warner, 1998). Canada, the UK, Australia and New Zealand also manifest labour relations characteristics associated with neo-liberalism. By way of contrast, continental European countries, including Germany, the Netherlands and Scandinavia, exemplify neo-corporatist tendencies in the conduct of their labour relations (O'Hagen et al., 2004). Here, an emphasis is placed on the integration of centralized, national-level, trade unions into national economic planning, balancing employment flexibility with the nurturing of internal labour markets, and gaining consensus at enterprise level through well-established mechanisms for employee participation. In a similar vein, but drawing a broader global map, Lipietz (1997) asserts that the industrial world may be divided into core and peripheral zones of industrial regulation. In the core, employers and national administrators seek to gain competitiveness through quality production, founded on robust structures to engender employee involvement (which would involve consensual arrangements with trade unions) and complemented by a strong labour law base. In the periphery, competitiveness is gained through flexible sub-standard employment contracts and the absence of robust systems of employee representation and participation. In the latter, flexible working practices reinforce a 'low road' strategy by attracting foreign direct investment on the basis of flexible and lower cost features.

While the above typologies serve to distinguish regional employment structures at a broad level of generalization, closer scrutiny of global regions reveals variations within institutional 'clusters'. In particular, the more highly regulated, neo-corporatist-influenced continental European bloc is marked by some notable internal diversity. Hyman (2004: 422) identifies three main 'models' of labour relations in western Europe:

1  A 'Germanic' model, in which economic governance is largely private but subject to strong collective institutions; the actors and procedures of industrial relations are significantly influenced by legislation; and in many cases the substance of the employment relationship (pay, working hours, etc.) is subject to significant legal regulation.

2  A 'Nordic' model, in which economic governance is also largely private but modified by an extensive, egalitarian welfare system; an industrial relations system that is not subject to detailed statutory regulation, but which is coordinated by collective organization of employers and trade unions (and facilitated by the state).

3 A 'Mediterranean' model, with (until recently) an extensive nationalized sector and significant state intervention in economic development, significant legal regulation of employment contracts, and institutional incorporation of employers and trade unions into statutory welfare provision.

Multinational corporations (MNCs), in straddling international territories, will therefore need to take account of variations in the 'contours' of labour relations from region to region. The extent to which international companies will adapt to local institutional arrangements or assert labour relations policies and practices emanating from the home country environment is subject to some debate (see, for example, Edwards, 2004), and is related to the extent to which an MNC is adopting an ethnocentric or polycentric orientation (see Chapter 3). However, in terms of actual policy considerations, variations in labour relations structures across regions are likely to impact most profoundly upon the obligation of the MNC to *consult* its workforce on important matters affecting its employment. So, for example, a US-owned MNC establishing a subsidiary in Germany would technically be obliged to establish a works council, comprising management and employee representatives, which would be legally empowered to take decisions on matters such as changes in working hours, training within the enterprise and recruitment methods. Moreover, beyond the national perspective, US corporations operating in Europe would be bound by pan-European consultative and other employment obligations emanating from the 'social agenda' of the European Union (EU). In particular, the European Works Council Directive, adopted by the EU in 1994, requires all 'community scale' companies operating across European boundaries to establish European-level procedures for employee information and consultation on transnational matters.

In this chapter, international variation in the orientation of principal labour relations actors is considered (notably employers and trade unions), as well as the dynamics of labour relations processes (including collective bargaining, employee involvement and participation). Drawing on available data, primary comparisons will be made in labour relations institutional arrangements between Europe (including the new EU accession countries), the USA and Japan, Whitley (2002) describing the latter as a 'highly coordinated' business system, a form of 'micro-corporatism', distinguishing it from 'insider' and 'outsider' capitalist typologies (see Chapter 2). The chapter also attends to global and pan-European regulations in the field of labour relations that are likely to impact on MNCs.

## Trade unions

The most well-known definition of trade unions was coined by Sidney and Beatrice Webb (1920) as 'a continuous association of wage earners for the purpose of maintaining and improving the conditions of their working lives'. In advanced capitalist economies trade unions enjoy the status of free and independent associations that are established by workers in order to defend their interests at the workplace and at a broader political and economic level.

From an international perspective, trade unions may vary according to structure, membership and orientation. Structure refers to the 'architecture' of union organization across enterprises, industries and sectors. In general, union structures may be classified as industrial (i.e. recruiting workers in particular industries), general (i.e. recruiting workers across industries) or occupational (recruiting workers in a particular occupation). A significant variant, which is commonly found in Japan, is enterprise-based unionism (i.e. recruiting workers on a company-specific basis). Unions may affiliate to 'umbrella' confederations at, national level, as is typical in Europe. Also in Europe, the European Trade Union Confederation (ETUC) acts on behalf of trade union confederations at a pan-European level, while there is an increasing incidence of trade union organization across European states in particular sectors (notably the European Metalworkers Federation (EMF)).

Predominant structural configurations across Europe, the USA and Japan are as follows.

## Trade union structure

In, *Europe* a complex pattern of trade union organization is found in the EU, including the new accession countries (see Table 6.1). In Germany and Austria there is a single dominant confederation made up of a relatively small number of predominantly industrial unions.

**Table 6.1 Trade union structures in the 25 EU countries**

| | Confederations | Main divisions between confederations | Main division affiliates | Remarks |
|---|---|---|---|---|
| Austria | ÖGB | | Sector and status | Political factions significant |
| Belgium | AVC–CSC; ABVV–FGTB; ACLVB–CGSLB | Political | Sector and status | ACV–CSV Christian trade union is largest |
| Cyprus | PEO; SEK; DEOK; POAS | Political | Sector | |
| Czech Republic | CMKOS; ASO; KUK; CMS; KOK | Political/ religious/regional/occupational | Sector | CMKOS is the dominant confederation |
| Germany | DGB; CGB; DBB | Macro-sector/religious | Sector | CGB and DBB are small; Verdi and IG Metall are important |
| Denmark | LO; FTF; LH; AC | Occupation | Occupation and sector | |
| Estonia | EAKI; TALO; ETMAKI | Macro-sector/status/profession | Sector | Rural workers in a separate small federation |
| Greece | GSEE; ADEDY | Public/private | Occupation and sector | Public and private unions merging |
| Finland | SAK; STTK; AKAVA | Occupation | Sector | |

| France | CGT; CFDT; CGT–FO; CFTC; CFE–CGC + UNSA and G10–SUD | Political/religious/occupational (status) | Sector | Five 'representative' confederations and two new ones pushing for national recognition |
|---|---|---|---|---|
| Hungary | MSZOSZ; SZEF/ESZT unió; LIGA; MOSZ; ASZSZ | Macro-sector/political | Sector/branch/ profession | SZEF–ESZF unió (started in 2002) is only a cooperation framework not a formal merger |
| Ireland | ICTU | | Occupation and sector | Trade unions with members in Northern Ireland and affiliation with UK unions |
| Italy | CGIL; CISL; UIL and other smaller main organizations | Political/religious | Sector | Autonomous unions and regional unions active |
| Lithuania | LPSK; Soldarumas; LDF | Political/religious | Sector | Independent trade unions active |
| Luxem-bourg | OGB–L; LCBG; CGFP | Political/religious/status/ macro-sector | Sector | Strong autonomous unions in services sector; CGFP important confederation in public sector |
| Latvia | LBAS | | Sector | Restructuring |
| Malta | GWU; CMTU | To some extent private/public | Sector | Weak confederations |
| Netherlands | FNV; CNV; MHP | Political/religious/occupational status | Sector | FNV–Bondgen often as 'super union' in the private sector |
| Poland | OPZZ; NSZZ Solidarnosc; FZZ | Political | Sector, local branch | New third confederation that wants to be politically neutral |

| Portugal | CGTP; UGT | Political | Sector and region | 28 sector confederations and 39 regional branches |
|---|---|---|---|---|
| Spain | CC.00; UGT | Political | Sector | |
| Slovakia | KOZ | | Sector | Small Christian trade union confederation |
| Slovenia | ZSSS; KNSS; Pergam; Konfederacija' 90 | Macro-sector (mainly private/public and industry/services) | | Two new main unions established recently (Alternativa and Solidarity) in the railway sector but not represented in national tripartite social dialogue |
| Sweden | LO; TCO; SACO | Occupational (status) | Sector and occupation | Several mergers occurring |
| United Kingdom | TUC | | Occupation and sector | General unions as TUC affiliates; small independent union sector |

*Source*: Eurofound–Eironline European Industrial Relations Observatory (2007a) *Industrial Relations in EU Member States*, 2000–2004, Dublin. Reproduced with permission from Eurofound–Eironline.

In the UK and Ireland there is also a single confederation at national level, with a significant number of member unions constituting a mixture of industrial, general and occupational unions. In the UK, the architecture of union organization has historically been referred to as 'multi-union', that is, based on a 'bottom-up' form of development in which a number of unions might coexist in a single workplace. 'Multi-unionism' has however been subject to rationalization and reform in recent years.

Multiple trade union confederations, divided mainly on political and religious lines, have been typical in Belgium, France, Italy, Luxembourg, the Netherlands, Portugal and Spain. Such 'umbrella' federations may incorporate numerous constituent sectoral federations. In France and Italy, however, a number of trade unions operate outside the organizational ambit of the national confederations.

In Nordic countries, separate confederations exist for different occupational groups (typically blue-collar, white-collar and professional/academic comprising industrial and occupational unions).

*In the United States*, a single confederation, the American Federation of Labor and Congress of Industrial Organizations (AFL – CIO) – forms the national umbrella organization for 65 industrial and occupational unions.

*In Japan* – the major confederation is the Japanese Trade Union Confederation (Rengo) that organizes over 60 per cent of unionized workers. Rengo acts as the umbrella for enterprise-based unions, which are organized into sectoral federations. A smaller confederation, the National Confederation of Trade Unions (Zenroren), represents around 7 per cent of unionized workers.

A common trend across the EU, Japan and the USA has been towards the merging and rationalization of trade union organizations. For example, in Germany, the United Service Sector Union (Vereinigte Dienstleistungsgewerkschaft, ver.di) was created in 2001, comprising approximately 2.5 million members. In the USA, the number of AFL–CIO affiliates has fallen from 96 in 1985 to approximately 65. In Japan, a slow process of consolidation has occurred among Rengo affiliates.

*Source*: Eurofound–Eironline (European Industrial Relations Observatory) (2001) *Industrial Relations in the EU, Japan and USA*, Dublin. Reproduced with permission from Eurofound–Eironline.

## Trade union membership

A global trend, epitomized by the three leading economies reviewed in this chapter, is a general decline in trade union membership, although levels of union membership and rates of decline are by no means common across national boundaries. Sinclair (2003) suggests a number of factors to explain dwindling participation in trade unions over recent decades. These include:

- the business cycle–including rates of unemployment and inflation;
- compositional changes in employment, including the decline of male manual workers (and increased participation of female workers) and growth in part-time work;
- legal reforms and state policy – the UK provides an example of diminishing legal support for trade union organization and industrial action. Privatization of state-owned industries also typically has an adverse effect on trade union membership;
- employer policies – the USA and the UK provide examples of employers seeking to engage with employees directly (not via third parties). Also, decentralization of mechanisms for determining pay and other conditions closer to workplace level (see page 119 on 'Collective bargaining') tends to be at the expense of union organization.

Union membership is typically calibrated through 'density' statistics that relate to the proportion of those in employment who are union members. Table 6.2 compares union density across western European countries, the USA and Japan.

**Table 6.2 Union density in Europe, the USA and Japan**

| Country | Union density (%) |
|---|---|
| Denmark | 87.5 |
| Finland | 79.0 |
| Sweden | 79.0 |
| Belgium | 69.2 |
| Luxembourg | 50.0 |
| Ireland | 44.5 |
| Austria | 39.8 |
| Italy | 35.4 |
| Greece | 32.5 |
| Portugal | 30.0 |
| Germany | 29.7 |
| UK | 29.0 |
| Netherlands | 27.0 |
| Japan | 20.7 |
| Spain | 15.0 |
| USA | 13.5 |
| France | 9.1 |

*Source*: Eurofound–Eironline (European Industrial Relations Observatory) (2001) *Industrial Relations in the EU, Japan and USA*, Dublin. Reproduced with permission from Eurofound–Eironline.

The following observations relate to Table 6.2:

- The average trade union density in the EU is approximately double that in Japan and more than three times that in the USA.
- Considerable variation is evident across EU countries – from nearly 90 per cent in Denmark to just over 9 per cent in France (although it should be noted, in the French case, that agreements made between employers and unions are extended to non-union members).
- Although not shown in Table 6.2, union membership in the new EU accession countries is generally lower than for western Europe.
- Unionization is higher among men in the USA and in many EU countries with low to medium overall unionization rates (including Austria, Germany, the Netherlands and the UK). However, in the highly unionized Scandinavian countries, female participation rates in trade unions are higher than those for men.

## Trade union objectives

As Table 6.1 suggests, the objectives and orientations of trade unions vary within Europe, and contrasts in trade union character are more widely evident at a global level.

*In Europe*, trade union orientation varies from a relatively instrumental, 'bread-and-butter' approach, placing greatest concern on matters such as pay, working hours and job security (evident in Germany and the UK) to a more overt political (particularly communist) or religious (Catholic or Christian) predisposition (e.g. France and Italy).

*In the USA*, despite the origins of the labour movement in socialism and class consciousness in the latter part of the nineteenth century, the unionized minority of the workforce have accepted an emphasis on 'business unionism'. This refers to an implicit acquiescence with the social and political status quo and a concentration of union leaderships on the improvement of members' pay and welfare benefits (Bennett, 1997).

*In Japan*, enterprise-based unions are closely integrated into the management structures of their companies. While a high level of collusion with enterprise management teams has provided them with access to vital corporate information, the 'insider' status of Japanese trade unions promotes company loyalty and dissuades collective labour from assertive and thoroughgoing action against employer interests (ibid.)

## Employers' organizations

*In Europe*, associations of employers have played a significant role in the conduct of labour relations, and are regarded as social partners alongside trade union representatives. Employer 'voice' is expressed at various levels: EU, European sectoral (i.e. combining industry-specific interests across Europe), national intersectoral (i.e. across industries in a single nation state) and national sectoral (i.e. representing the interests of a single industry).

■  At EU level, 'BusinessEurope', formerly known as the Union of Industrial and Employers Confederations of Europe (UNICE), represents almost all main national intersectoral confederations of private sector employers and business in EU member states. It acts as an employers' organization, engaging in negotiations with the ETUC, and as a trade/industry association, seeking to influence EU decision making in areas of relevance. Minority business interests in Europe are represented by the European Association of Craft and Small and Medium-sized Enterprises (UEAPME) and the European Centre of Enterprises with Public Participation and of General Economic Interest (CEEP).

■  At European sectoral level, 26 dialogue committees exist, involving European level representatives of trade unions and employers. Employers' interests are therefore voiced at a European level in sectors such as agriculture, banking, civil aviation cleaning, commerce, construction, electricity, footwear, hotels and catering, inland navigation, insurance, leather, maritime transport, personal services (hairdressing), postal services, private security, public services, railways, road transport, sea fishing, sugar, telecommunications, textiles and clothing, tobacco and woodworking.

■  At national level, employers' organization varies considerably between member states (see Table 6.3). In Belgium, Denmark, France, Ireland, Italy, the Netherlands, Spain, Sweden and the UK, there is essentially a single umbrella organization, at least for the private sector. In Germany, however, there is a division between the representation of employer and business/trade interests. Regular national intersectoral bargaining with trade unions is part of the remit of central employers' associations in Belgium, Finland, Greece, Ireland and Portugal. Employers associations engage in intersectoral bargaining over specific issues or procedural matters in Denmark, France, Italy, Spain and Sweden. In Austria and Germany, employers' confederations have close collaboration with trade unions in various forums, which leads to the formulation of joint texts or approaches. In the UK, the CBI (Confederation of British Industry) has a minimal bargaining approach or direct engagement with the TUC.

■ At industry level, employers' associations engage in collective bargaining with trade union counterparts over pay and other substantive employment conditions in most EU countries, including Austria, Belgium, Denmark, Finland, France, Germany, Greece, Italy, the Netherlands, Portugal, Spain and Sweden. Exceptional countries are Ireland, Luxembourg and the UK, in which collective bargaining occurs predominantly at company level (although overlaid with intersectoral bargaining in Ireland).

Strong and representative employers' associations are uncommon in the new accession countries.

*In Japan*, a single business federation (Nippon Keidanren) was formed in 2002 following the merger of two constituent associations. Nippon Keidanren does not participate in collective bargaining with trade unions, but is involved with formal tripartite dialogue with government and trade unions. The association also seeks to influence the annual 'spring offensive' (Shunto) bargaining round, in which enterprise unions combine to push for a common wage increase, by issuing guidelines to employers.

*In the USA*, there is no national intersectoral body with a labour relations role. The United States Council for International Business (USCIP) provides an employer voice on international business matters. As collective bargaining and pay determination takes place primarily at enterprise level, few employers' bodies have an active involvement in labour relations matters.

*Source*: Eurofound–Eironline (European Industrial Relations Observatory) (2001) *Industrial Relations in the the EU, Japan and USA*, Dublin. Reproduced with permission from Eurofound–Eironline.

**Table 6.3 Main features of employer organization structure in the 25 EU countries**

| | General | Industry | Construction | Services | SMEs | Social economy | Agriculture | Remarks |
|---|---|---|---|---|---|---|---|---|
| Austria | WKO | VOI | | | | | | Compulsory membership – provincial level important |
| Belgium | FEB/VBO | | | | UCM Unizo | | | Regional organizations involved in tripartite dialogue; FEB/VBO most important in industrial relations |
| Cyprus | OEB; CCCI | | | | | | | Other important organizations at sectoral level |

| | | | | | | | | |
|---|---|---|---|---|---|---|---|---|
| Czech Republic | SPCR; KZPS | | SPS | | AMSP | | | Sectoral organizations in charge of bargining |
| Germany | BDA | | | | | | | |
| Denmark | DA | | | FA | | | SALA | DA re-organizing |
| Estonia | ETTK | | | | | | | |
| Greece | | | SEB | ESEE | GSE–BEE | | | |
| Finland | EK | | | | | | | Important employer organization in public sector; EK is a merger of TT and PT and mainly involved in the bargaining system |
| France | MEDEE | | | | CGP–ME; UPA | Us-geres | | MEDEF is much more important than others |
| Hungary | MGYOSZ | OKISZ; VOSZ; STRAT–OSZ | OKISZ; VOSZ; STRAT–OSZ | KISOSZ | IPOSZ | AFE–OSZ | AMSZ; MOSZ | MGYOSZ is a merger of MMSZ and GYOSZ, and now the leading employer organization; CEHIC acts as the umbrella organization for international representation |
| Ireland | IBEC | | | | | | | |
| Italy | Confindus-tria | | | | Confapi | | | In services sector, partisan and agricultural sector, confederations exist and are structured by political divisions (left and right) |

| Lithuania | LPK | | | | LVDK | | | Cooperative agreement between LPK and LVDK for representation in national and international social dialogue |
|---|---|---|---|---|---|---|---|---|
| Luxem-bourg | UEL | | | | | | | Chamber system with obligatory membership plays a role in tripartite dialogue |
| Latvia | LDDK | | | | | | | Several other smaller associations exist; LDDK is a recognized actor in social dialogue |
| Malta | MEA; COC | FOI | | MHRA | GRTU | | | No umbrella organization exists – attempts in the 1980s failed; federations are based mainly on individual membership |
| Nether-lands | VNO–NCW | | | | MKB | | LTO | Small organization in the agricultural sector; alliance announced between VN0–NCW and MKB |
| Poland | KPP; PKPP; BCC | | | | ZRP | | | KPP is the oldest group with roots in the Chamber of Commerce and formerly state-owned enterprises |

| | | | | | | | | |
|---|---|---|---|---|---|---|---|---|
| Portugal | AEP–AIP | CIP | CIP | CCP; CTP | | | CAP | CIP and CCP are leading federations for industrial relations; AIP and AEP recently created a federation to boost their influence |
| Spain | CEOE | | | | | | | Mixed association of sectoral and territorial organizations and a SME organization associated |
| Slovakia | RUZ; AZZZ | | | | | | | Split up in 2004 |
| Slovenia | GZS; ZDS | | | | OZS; ZD–ODS | | | Compulsory membership of chambers dominates, but this system is under debate |
| Sweden | SN | | | | | SFO; KFO | | SN is the former SAF; SKL is an important local employer confederation in the public sector |
| UK | CBI | | | | | | | |

*Source*: Eurofound-Eironline (European Industrial Relations Observatory) (2007a) *Industrial Relations in EU Member States, 2000–2004*, Dublin. Reproduced with permission from Eurofound–Eironline.

## Collective bargaining

The ILO (1997–2002), in its *Right to Organize and Collective Bargaining Convention*, defines collective bargaining as: 'Voluntary negotiation between employers or employer organizations and worker organizations with a view to the regulation of terms and conditions of employment by collective agreements.' Thus, in countries where collective bargaining is well established, it provides joint institutional machinery for the determination of pay. A critical strategic issue in the organization of collective bargaining is the *level* at which it occurs. In regions with neo-corporatist traditions, including a number of continental European countries, collective bargaining occurs at a relatively *centralized* level, this permitting the orchestration of pay structures by trade unions and their confederations, employers and their organizations, and governmental agencies. Where neo-liberalism holds sway, for example in the USA and the UK, the pronounced tendency is for bargaining over pay to be decentralized to company level. This permits individual company management to relate pay closely to local market circumstances, and to use pay as a mechanism to stimulate the performance of each profit centre. Decentralization of collective bargaining is also likely to lessen the influence of trade unions on pay determination. Table 6.4 indicates predominant levels for wage bargaining in the EU, Japan and the USA.

**Table 6.4 Wage bargaining levels: the EU, Japan and the USA**

|  | Intersectoral level | Sectoral level | Company level |
|---|---|---|---|
| Austria |  | XXX | X |
| Belgium | XXX | X | X |
| Denmark | XX | XX | X |
| Finland | XXX | X | X |
| France |  | X | XXX |
| Germany |  | XXX | X |
| Greece | X | XXX | X |
| Ireland | XXX | X | X |
| Italy |  | XXX | X |
| Japan |  |  | XXX |
| Luxembourg |  | XX | XX |
| Netherlands |  | XXX | X |
| Portugal |  | XXX | X |
| Spain |  | XXX | X |
| Sweden |  | XXX | X |
| UK |  | X | XXX |
| USA |  | X | XXX |

*Notes*:
X = existing level of wage bargaining
XX = important, but not dominant level of wage bargaining
XXX = dominant level of wage bargaining

*Source*: Eurofound–Eironline (European Industrial Relations Observatory) (2001) *Industrial Relations in the EU, Japan and USA*, Dublin. Reproduced with permission of Eurofound-Eironline.

Eurofound–/Eiroline (2001) identify the following key characteristics of bargaining structures in the EU, the USA and Japan:

■ EU member states have widely different systems of collective bargaining, yet a distinctive feature is relatively centralized systems. Nevertheless, a significant trend is towards decentralization; this being pronounced in the UK, France and Germany. Deviations from multi-employer agreements (taking various forms such as hardship or opt-out clauses, 'local pacts' or 'area contracts') have also occurred in Spain, Denmark, Italy and the

Netherlands. In Germany, decentralization has been organized within the framework of sectoral agreements as 'opening clauses' for locally agreed deviations from sectoral standards under specified conditions. In France, decentralization has been stimulated by legislation on working time and a new law on collective bargaining (Eurofound–Eironline, 2007a).

■ For the new accession countries, the company is the dominant bargaining level, with continuing sectoral influence in certain cases. Table 6.6 denotes primary levels of bargaining for the 12 relative newcomers to the EU.

■ In Japan and the USA, the predominant bargaining level for pay and other issues is the individual company (with some exceptions at industry level in the USA). In the USA, trade unions conduct 'pattern bargaining' whereby an agreement is struck in a particular company and then extended to other firms in the sector. In Japan, there is coordination on both trade union and employer sides during the annual 'Shunto' bargaining in springtime. Major manufacturers in leading industries such as electrical goods or cars take the lead in bargaining and are then followed by other larger companies and then small- and medium-sized enterprises (SMEs).

■ Collective bargaining coverage (i.e the proportion of workers having their pay and conditions wholly or partially set by collective agreements) is generally high in the EU, although it ranges from nearly 100 per cent of private sector employees in Austria to around one-third of employees in the UK. In the USA, collective bargaining covers around 15 per cent of the workforce, with pay and conditions for the majority non-union sector being determined by management. In Japan, the 'bargaining sector' relates to around 21 per cent of the labour force, although wage increases agreed in the unionized sector influence general wage levels (see Table 6.5).

It should also be noted that the subject matter for collective negotiations varies from country to country. In the USA, 'business unionism' has placed a major focus on pay and related matters, while in Japan the close relations between enterprise unions and company management provide union exposure to a wider range of strategic issues. There is considerable variation in the bargaining agenda matters in Europe, but, in addition to pay, the following matters tend to have gained significance: working time (France), health and safety at work (Poland), training (Germany), pensions (Ireland and Norway) and age discrimination and diversity/discrimination issues (France) and job security (Cyprus) (Eurofound–Eironline, 2007b).

**Table 6.5 Collective bargaining coverage: Europe, Japan and the USA**

| Austria | 98% |
|---|---|
| France | 90–95% |
| Belgium | 90%+ |
| Sweden | 90%+ |
| Finland | 90% |
| Italy | 90% |
| Netherlands | 88% |
| Portugal | 87% |

| Denmark | 83% |
|---|---|
| Spain | 81% |
| Germany | 67% |
| Luxembourg | 58% |
| UK | 36% |
| Japan* | 21% |
| USA** | 15% |

*Sources*: Eurofound–Eironline (European Industrial Relations Observatory) (2001) *Industrial Relations in the EU, Japan and USA*; Dublin. Reproduced with permission from Eurofound–Eironline.
*Notes*:
*JIS
**USA

**Table 6.6 Bargaining levels in new EU member states**

| Bulgaria | A combination of whole-sector, branch and company agreements, with a strong emphasis on the latter |
|---|---|
| Cyprus | Largely at enterprise level, though with sectoral agreements in some important industries |
| Czech Republic | At both enterprise and multi-employer level |
| Estonia | Mainly at enterprise level |
| Hungary | Private sector bargaining predominantly at enterprise level and mainly in larger firms, though with some multi-employer bargaining. Central agreement provides for basic increases and minimum wages |
| Latvia | Collective bargaining has limited coverage and occurs mainly at company level (especially in larger enterprises, state and local government enterprises and in former state-owned entities) |
| Lithuania | Almost exclusively at company level |
| Malta | Almost exclusively at company level |
| Poland | About one-third of workforce covered, mainly in larger enterprises, with collective agreements covering a single employer predominating and sectoral agreements rare |
| Romania | National collective agreement that provides minimum framework for employment conditions. Also sectoral agreements and a growth in company level agreements |
| Slovakia | Around 40–50% of workforce covered and sector key level |
| Slovenia | Reduction of tripartite centralized agreements and growth of sectoral agreements |

*Source*: adapted from Eurofound–Eironline (European Industrial Relations Observatory) (2007b).

# Employee involvement and participation

Across national borders, corporations have engaged in a variety of methods to actively engage employees in decisions that affect their working lives. In order to understand the rationale underlying a range of international systems for employee involvement and participation, it is instructive to relate these to 'neo-liberal' and 'neo-corporatist' ideologies. In those countries where neo-liberalism influences management thinking (notably the USA and the UK), unfettered corporate responsiveness to 'the market' is likely to be of paramount significance. In consequence, management may recognize the strategic sense in engaging employees with corporate goals and values, and formulating mechanisms to put them in the picture about the competitive position of their enterprise, the rationale for change, and related matters. By way of contrast, in neo-corporatist influenced economies (notably in continental Europe), systems for employee participation tend to be ingrained into prevailing institutional arrangements and are underwritten by the state. Consistent with the 'stakeholder' or 'social partnership' model of corporate governance, systems for employee participation in continental Europe are predicated on the notion that 'consensus'-based forms of management will enhance employee commitment and productivity, and involve the ceding of strategic authority from management to employee representatives.

The existence of a spectrum of approaches towards employee involvement and participation is recognized by a number of authors. Salamon (2001) suggests that 'involvement' schemes can be distinguished from participation on the dimension of purpose, involvement seeking to engender employee commitment to the objectives of the organization, while 'participation' schemes seek to provide employees with the opportunities to take part in organizational decision making. Ramsay (1992) also distinguishes participation schemes that are managerial approaches for seeking employee involvement from those that are labour-oriented and predicated on industrial democratic principles.

Marchington et al. (1992) summarize four different perspectives or models of participation, as follows:

1   the recognized relationship between employee involvement and job satisfaction;
2   the gaining of high levels of employee commitment and enhanced performance through employee involvement;
3   the linking of participation with enhanced cooperation and reduced levels of conflict;
4   the actual transfer of control from management to labour.

In the following section key employee involvement and participation mechanisms are considered in Europe, the USA and Japan. Using the terminology adopted by Salamon (2001), European approaches are perhaps most appropriately referred to as 'participative', while mechanisms in the USA and Japan may be typified as engendering employee 'involvement'.

## Employee participation in Europe

### Works councils

Frequently, as an adjunct to collective bargaining involving trade union representatives, works councils are a fact of industrial life and upheld by law in a number of EU countries (although this form of consultative forum has been rare in the UK). Following Hollinshead and Leat (1995), works councils (or committees) can be joint management–employee bodies, but are more commonly councils of employee representatives only. Works councils may include or exclude external union officials. These consultative forums may be convened at various corporate levels (site, division or corporate), although they are most commonly found at the level of the establishment or site.

Councils are normally legally obliged to *discuss* particular specified matters, and entitled to *take decisions* (effectively giving employees the right of veto) on others (Bennett, 1997).

Bennett (1997) suggests that works councils may exert a powerful countervailing influence on management decisions; for example, being able to delay company mergers in the Netherlands and Germany. Examples of issues that are subject to decision making by works councils are:

- criteria for hiring temporary staff and for selecting workers for redundancy (Belgium);
- profit-sharing agreements (France);
- changes in working hours, training agreements, recruitment and disciplinary procedures (Germany);
- operation of job evaluation schemes, appraisal and grievance procedures, working hours (the Netherlands).

Examples of matters that are subject to *discussion* (Bennett, ibid.) by works councils in various EU countries include:

- financial plans and company structures;
- acquisitions, physical investments and divestments;
- working practices and the introduction of new technology;
- proposed incentive systems and wage payment systems;
- company sales, profits and prices;
- personnel policies (including recruitment methods);
- health and safety at work.

### Worker directors and supervisory boards

In Germany, Belgium, the Netherlands and Denmark there are legal requirements for large companies to establish a two-tier board of directors. Executive boards, constituting company managers, assume responsibility for day-to-day operational matters, while supervisory boards, to which a proportion of worker directors are appointed, oversee the strategic direction of the enterprise. In this way, HR and welfare considerations are incorporated into systems of corporate governance. As Bennett (1997) states, the functions of supervisory boards include:

- the appointment and dismissal of executive management and the determination of their remuneration;
- deciding the overall direction of the enterprise (products, markets, major new investments, etc.);
- matters concerning mergers and takeovers and how the company is to be financed.

## Employee involvement in the USA

In contrast to participation initiatives in Europe, the mechanisms to involve employees in corporate decisions in the USA are solely led by management and are not supported by statute. In a predominantly non-union environment, enterprises have experimented with a range of involvement mechanisms, some of which have been highly sophisticated. Over the past few decades, US corporations have adopted methods such as self-managing teams, problem-solving groups and quality circles (Hollinshead and Leat, 1995). More recent departures in employee communications have been based on high-technology platforms (Internet, e-based and audio-visual systems), which are instrumental in the dissemination of corporate culture and values. Large multinational companies in the information-technology sector have been renowned for flat and open management structures, permitting direct and informal communication between groups of 'knowledge workers'.

In the unionized sector, there have been some notable examples of management and union representatives collaborating through partnership in order to facilitate change in work practices and bring about increased productivity. For example, at the GM/Toyota joint venture at the NUMMI (New United Motor Manufacturing Inc.) plant in Fremont, California, 'Japanese' flexible-style working practices were introduced with the active involvement of the United Auto Workers (UAW).

More generally, the drive towards the 'high-performance workplaces' in manufacturing has been endorsed by management and labour with an emphasis being placed on the importance of training and the devolution of responsibility to 'front-line' workers. Joint union-management training agreements involving the UAW, United Steel Workers, the Service Employees Union, and the Building and Construction Trade Unions, include formal management–labour commitments to upgrade the skills of workers to enhance productivity and job security (Eurofound–Eironline, 2001).

## Employee involvement in Japan

In Japan, there is a high incidence of face-to-face communications and an absence of visible hierarchy. In theory, communications are on an equal basis. Managers spend considerable time on the shop floor and there is an emphasis on open planning in offices. There is no legal regulation of employee involvement mechanisms, or statutory provision for employee interests to be represented at board level, although in core Japanese industries it may be argued that worker interests will be accounted for at board level as directors have traditionally been lifetime employees of the enterprise (Hollinshead and Leat, 1995). The quality circle is commonly thought to have originated in Japan and is consistent with notions of *ring-sei*, or consensus decision making. Quality circles represent a 'bottom-up' form of employee involvement that encourages front-line workers to generate ideas for product and production enhancement through periodic 'brainstorming' activities with immediate co-workers. Group suggestions are then passed to more senior management for scrutiny and possible implementation. Participation in these problem-solving groups is technically voluntary, although undoubtedly workers are strongly encouraged to participate by their employing organizations. Team-based work organization has also become widespread in manufacturing, aiming to engender work flexibility and team ownership of production planning and quality.

### Activity

Imagine you are on the board of directors of a US-owned MNC in the retail sector establishing a subsidiary in Germany. Identify the strategic benefits and drawbacks associated with establishing a works council in the subsidiary.

## Labour relations structures and MNCs

It is clear from this study of the three most advanced global regions that institutional structures for labour relations vary profoundly on a geographical basis. From the perspective of the MNC, a critical strategic question is the extent to which it should seek to *adapt* to labour relations systems in the host environment, or whether there is scope to circumvent local obligations and to assert home country customs and practices. Edwards and Ferner (2002) point to the significance of institutional and cultural aspects of national business systems in shaping and constraining transfer of employment practices from the home environment. These authors also imply that localization of employment practices is potentially a highly political process within the MNC, as international and local managers may seek to facilitate or impede this process according to their vested interests and positions of power. Gunnigle et al. (2002) investigated whether US MNCs are less likely to adopt local HR practices than European companies. It was found that in countries such as the UK and Ireland, where domestic HR and labour relations practices were less codified, US firms were less likely to adapt or to recognize trade unions. However, US firms were more likely to localize practices in, for example, Germany and Sweden, where labour relations were highly regulated and codified. This finding would suggest that US MNCs are likely to establish subsidiaries in less regulated regions that are amenable to non-unionism. If, however, MNCs decide to localize, varying labour relations structures across national barriers may be regarded as imposing a series of strategic constraints or dilemmas, including the following:

■ Should a trade union/trade unions be recognized for bargaining purposes? It should be borne in mind that trade union structures and characteristics vary widely.
■ Should the MNC (if in Europe) associate with employers' organizations for the purpose of bargaining with trade unions?
■ At what level does collective bargaining occur? If at a sectoral or intersectoral level, this may impose restraints on the company's ability to formulate pay policies on an autonomous basis.
■ If operating in continental Europe, should the company establish a works council?

In surveying labour relations structures across global regions, it becomes clear that the obligation of companies to consult workers on matters affecting their working lives assumes a high priority in the European region. Superimposed across national consultative systems is a European-wide directive impacting on MNC operations, which is the subject of the next section.

## European works councils

While various European-based companies have for some time recognized the benefits of establishing pan-European consultative forums (i.e. a meeting chaired by management at European level and inviting the participation of worker delegates from across European regions), such European-wide consultative initiatives were boosted by the adoption of the European Works Council Directive by the EU Council of Ministers in September 1994. According to Leat (2003: 250), the Directive addresses concerns of the European Commission about 'the power of the multinational to take decisions in one member state that affect employees in others without the employees being involved in the decision-making process'. As Leat (ibid.) states, the Directive was in part a response to the increase in MNC activity following the inception of the Single European Market, and it also concerned the ability of MNCs to divert capital investment from one state to another without due consultative process.

The Directive, now applying to all EU members, requires 'community scale' companies (i.e. those with 1,000 or more employees in the EU, and employing 150 or more in at least two EU states) to establish European-level procedures for employee information and consultation on transnational matters, a process triggered by a request from representatives of employees in more than one country. A report by the European Trade Union Confederation (2008) – reviewing progress relating to the Directive some 12 years after its implementation – reports the following:

- Of the estimated 2,204 companies covered by the legislation, some 772 have EWCs in operation. However, many of these are larger, multinational firms, so that the proportion of employees represented by EWCs is more than 60 per cent, or 14 million workers across Europe. An additional 125 EWCs have been set up, but ceased to exist following mergers, takeovers and bankruptcies.
- The majority of companies covered by the Directive employ less than 5,000 workers.
- Among multinationals employing 10,000 people or more, 61 per cent have EWCs.

---

### Case study: The impact of European works councils

## Success stories

EWCs could be counted "success stories" for a number of reasons. The agreement on which they are based might be particularly innovatory or influential, or their operation might have proved particularly satisfactory – for example by helping reach a satisfactory solution to a restructuring crisis.

National reports suggest a number of such success stories, though the evidence is patchy. It could be said that the pioneering pre-Directive agreements of the 1980s in French MNCs such as BSN–Danone were success stories in the sense that they helped to demonstrate that EWCs are not harmful to the economic competitiveness of MNCs. At the level of the EWCs' fit into existing structures, a notable example of a success story is Aer Lingus, the Irish airline. The Aer Lingus EWC is based on a voluntary agreement concluded just before the 22 September 1996 deadline. The EWC was built on to the existing participation, information and consultation structures. A consequence of this is that there are dense participatory structures underpinning the EWC and the people involved also have prior experience of works council-type institutions. Furthermore, a novel feature of the agreement itself was that the company included employees in the UK, USA and Switzerland, who would have been excluded under the strict terms of the Directive.

In terms of operational success stories, the Netherlands seems to be a particularly rich source of examples. The European Works Council (or, more accurately, its coordinating committee) at the Anglo-Dutch Unilever group has been consulted and intervened in two cases of transnational restructuring. With respect to the closure of a Danish subsidiary, it consulted local employees and, in line with their wishes, subsequently advised Unilever management to prolong the period set for closure from a few weeks to several months. Subsequently, Unilever did indeed prolong the term so as to grant the employees involved more time to find a good job elsewhere. In the case of another closure (relocation of production from the Netherlands to Belgium), Unilever agreed to take measures to find alternative employment for the employees involved.

At KNP BT, the Dutch-owned paper and chemicals group, there has been a "demerger" operation over the past two years and two international business units – KNP Leykam and KNP BT Packaging – each with its own EWC have been sold. In both cases, the central management of KNP BT Holding consulted the EWC on the selection of the purchaser (its market position and strategy in relation to guaranteeing employment at KNP). In the case of KNP Leykam, the first to be sold, the EWC is seen to have had a real dialogue with central management and according to management the consultation process showed an effective cooperation between the EWC, the national works councils involved and the Dutch central works council of KNP BT Holding. The Dutch central works council had to advise on the sale and the disinvestment and, as continued employment was guaranteed by the chosen purchaser, it insisted on the continuance of the EWC. When KNP Leykam was sold to the South African multinational Sappi, the Leykam EWC became the European information and consultation structure in the new concern.

Other Dutch success stories cited include: the role of the EWC and Dutch works council at DAF Trucks during its sale to the US multinational, Paccar Inc; the involvement of and cooperation between the EWC and the central works council in the case of the takeover of Banque Brussel Lambert by ING Group; the granting to the Hoogovens EWC of a role in the development of an international human resources strategy; and the reported contribution of the Shell European Forum, during a restructuring process, to a new vision for the development of Shell Europe Oil Products.

The EWC at Schmalbach-Lubeca, a metalworking concern, has been held up as a German success story. A 1996 agreement that put the existing EWC on a formal footing went beyond the Directive in many respects, such as granting the EWC information rights vis-à-vis national management outside formal meetings. The initial phase of the EWC's operation was reportedly marked by some tensions, in particular between German and Dutch employee representatives. A change in the occupancy of the chair of the German group works council, who is also president of the EWC, apparently led to a change in the approach of the whole EWC. Non-German employees were more strongly drawn into the EWC's work, allowing for an improvement in relations between members. The EWC has reportedly become less focused on the joint meeting with management and has developed into an independent body, which has already been able to register a number of successes. For example, a decision by group management to relocate some production from Germany to Italy was partially reversed following intervention by the EWC, with advantages for both the Italian and the German employees (fewer job losses for the latter, and the avoidance of inferior working conditions for the former).

## Failures

EWCs could be counted as failures where they have proved to be ineffective in some way – for example, by failing to influence events or decision-making or by becoming split. Among the relatively few negative experiences reported by Eiro national centres is one from Austria. At the Semperit tyre company, a subsidiary of the German-owned Continental, it is reported that the EWC played no role in conflicts over the relocation of production during 1997 and in fact more or less 'disintegrated' in the conflict.

In France, the Renault-Vilvoorde case presents interesting aspects and can be interpreted as a negative experience with mixed results. The Renault EWC brought a court case claiming that the management's announcement in early 1997 of the planned closure of the Renault plant in Vilvoorde (Belgium) without prior information and consultation of the EWC was unlawful. The ruling issued by the Versailles appeals court quoted the terms of the Community Charter of Fundamental Social Rights of Workers, to which the Directive makes an explicit reference, which states that information must be provided in 'due time'. On this basis, the court considered that any decision 'having a significant effect on the interests of employees' must lead to information and consultation of the EWC. Changing the earlier first instance ruling of the Nanterre court, the Versailles court stipulated that this consultation need not necessarily be prior to the decision, but must at least have 'useful effects', which means that consultation must leave scope for 'observations, contention and criticism', in a way that the initial decision might eventually be modified. Following these facts, in a March 1998 amendment to the existing 1995 EWC agreement, Renault and the signatory trade unions introduced a right of consultation 'in the event of a planned exceptional decision which has transnational consequences and is of a nature such as to affect significantly employees' interests'. In this case, the EWC is consulted 'in due time', so that 'the elements of the discussion can still be taken into account in the decision-making process'. Renault can thus be seen as both a 'failure', in that management did not consult the EWC on the closure of their Belgian plant, and a 'success story' because the EWC coordinated a pioneering Euro strike, won two court cases and obtained a modification of the agreement.

*Source*: Eurofound–Eironline (European Industrial Relations Observatory) (1998) *The Impact of European Works Council*, Dublin. Reproduced with permission from Eurofound–Eironline.

As well as the rate of uptake of EWCs being relatively slow, there is also evidence that, from the employee point of view, they may represent ineffectual 'talking shops'. This view is confirmed by Royle (2000), who examines the operation of the fast food chain McDonald's EWC. Streeck (1997) asserts that 'country of origin' effect has a significant bearing on the form and functions of EWCs (see Table 6.7), which suggests that consultative procedures at pan-European level will be more meaningful in a German-owned MNC, with a track record of stakeholder involvement, than would be the case in a US- or UK-owned counterpart. From a managerial perspective, the EWC Directive has raised concerns about cost and use of time.

**Table 6.7 Impact of EWCs on selected national industrial relations**

| Country | Impact |
|---------|--------|
| France | The Directive fits rather well into the French system – unsurprisingly, as it was largely inspired by the early practice of EWCs in French-based MNCs, which were themselves inspired by the 1982 French legislation on national group-level works council structures (group committees or *comités de groupe*). In the first phase of voluntary EWCs, the nationalization of major industrial companies helped to create a management milieu in favour of EWCs. The transposition process has remained close to existing French provisions – going so far as to make the statutory EWC a joint management–employee body (rather than the employee-only body outlined in the Directive's subsidiary requirements). French employee representatives in the statutory EWC are appointed by trade unions, with the distribution in line with the results of the most recent works council elections. They must be chosen from among elected works council members or union delegates (with direct elections as a fallback method). The model is the same as used for the French group committee. |
| Germany | The impact of EWCs on industrial relations has so far been marginal. Linkages between EWCs and national representation structures and workforces are still in their infancy, and few EWCs seem to regard it as their task to anchor the EWC in these structures and seek to win the acceptance and interest of ordinary employees. In the past, trade unions have tended to concentrate on establishing as many EWCs as possible – they are only now being increasingly faced with the task of advising and training established EWCs, giving them strategic direction and integrating them with other fields of trade union activity. This presupposes that the unions are taking a major step forward in the direction of Europeanization. However, it is also true that Germany's highly developed system of co-determination and 'trustful cooperation' might reduce the status of EWCs and limit their independence. Where the parent company is in Germany, then, this may also lead to a clear leadership of German representatives, which could make the EWC less of a supranational body. In legislative terms, the German representatives on statutory EWCs are appointed by existing works council structures. |
| Ireland | Ireland is a very interesting case, since EWCs seem to be quite an important innovation in the national industrial relations system. Ireland differs from many other European countries because there are no provisions for works council structures at national, regional or local level, while the Irish model of 'partnership' is rather narrow, being largely confined to tripartite negotiation and consultation at a national level. Therefore, EWCs have an important potential in the process of diffusing social partnership from national to local level, though they apply to quite a small number of companies. |
| Italy | EWCs are linked to the existing system of representation via the procedure of appointing employee representatives on statutory EWCs: these are appointed by works council-type 'unitary union representative bodies' and nationally representative trade unions. There is no specific research on the impact of EWCs in Italy, but their limited spread, together with the existing widespread presence of information and consultation rights has resulted in no evident effects on the Italian industrial relations system |

| Netherlands | As in Germany, EWCs have been introduced in a context where co-determination rights are quite highly developed – and include group works council structures. Existing works council structures appoint employee representatives on statutory EWCs (with direct elections as a fallback). Employers' sources have stated that, because EWCs have an essentially different role from that of national works councils, the EWC should not be seen as a natural extension of existing consultation structures. Union sources, however, see employee-side-only EWCs (but not joint bodies) as a natural extension of the national works council structure to the European level. Given the strict traditional separations between bargaining, assigned to trade unions, and co-determination, attributed to works councils, the fact that negotiations for the creation of EWCs are carried out by employee representatives could be considered a minor innovation. |
|---|---|
| Spain | The EWC, both as a legal institution and as a representative body, is seen as fitting very easily and 'naturally' into the Spanish industrial relations system, mirroring quite closely the legal position of Spanish works councils. Existing union delegations play the key role in appointing members of statutory EWCs. EWCs are seemingly having two main effects on Spanish industrial relations. First, there is a significant change in industrial relations culture in that trade unions more fully recognize the importance of the European, and indeed global, field of operations, and are increasingly taking steps to improve their skills in this new area. Second, the move to create EWCs is stimulating, as in the case of Belgium, the setting-up of group-level union committees in companies where previously these did not exist, or, more commonly, facilitating the creation of communication channels between workers in the different plants across the country. |
| Sweden | In the appointment of members of statutory EWCs, priority is given to local trade unions that have signed agreements in force in the company – a provision that harmonizes well with the way that the Swedish system is constructed. Another reason for the lack of evident major effects of EWCs is that EU rules are not as far-reaching as the national ones, as they provide the right to information and consultation only, and not the right to negotiation and influence. |
| UK | Even if the UK was not covered by the Directive until 1997, it is arguably the country where the impact on the national industrial relations system is greatest. The UK relies traditionally on a 'single-channel' system of industrial relations, based on trade union representatives. EWCs have introduced a form of 'dual-channel' representation, as non-union representatives have supplemented trade union-based representation within EWCs. Since in many large UK-based organizations there are no group-wide industrial relations structures, the key level of industrial relations being at site or establishment level, the establishment of EWCs is likely to encourage greater group-wide liaison between employee representatives in such companies. |

*Source:* Eurofound–Eironline (European Industrial Relations Observatory) (*The Impact of European Works Councils*), Dublin. Reproduced with permission from Eurofound–Eironline.

## International labour standards

At a global level, attempts have been made by important agencies to establish a set of internationally agreed norms and standards for the conduct of employee relations. The existence of an international 'safety net' for pay and benefits is intended to prevent unfair competition between nation states on the basis of unacceptably poor labour conditions, and seeks to counteract the worst excesses in flights of international capital and business to developing regions. MNCs, therefore, in formulating ethical standards and practising corporate social responsibility are likely to heed the recommendations of the ILO and the

OECD. As Bennett (1997) asserts, the argument against the existence of international standards is that they can inhibit free markets, diminish competition and create unemployment. Inevitably, some countries will fail to adhere to standards.

## The ILO

The International Labour Organisation (ILO) was founded in 1919 and, since its inception, has embodied the principle of tripartism, bringing together governments, employers and labour organizations to establish minimum employment standards. Indeed, as Ewing (2006) states, the major function of the ILO is the setting of labour standards, whether through conventions or recommendations. The ILO's constitution requires it to:

- encourage the improvement of the conditions of workers;
- discourage particular countries from failing to adopt humane conditions of labour;
- promote the principle that labour should not be regarded as a mere 'commodity or article of commerce';
- support the view that the price of labour be determined by human need and that workers are entitled to a reasonable standard of living.

Fundamental principles espoused by the ILO resolutions are that:

- there should be freedom of association in all member countries;
- workers should have the right to strike;
- specific trade unions should have the right to conduct activities on employers' premises.

Bennett (1997) asserts that a significant constraint confronting the ILO is that governments may not be compelled to accept its standards or adopt its recommendations. In the era of globalization there has also been questioning of the value of labour standards. According to the Director-General: 'Although globalisation obliges us to re-examine the basic concepts and values of standard setting and specify their meaning or relevance, it also instils, in an insidious and more radical way, doubts as to the pre-eminence of these values' (International Labour Organization, 1997, cited in Ewing, 2006: 1).

As Ewing (ibid.) states, international labour standards are ill-suited to deal with multinational corporations as they are addressed primarily to governments.

## The OECD

The Organisation for Economics Co-operation and Development (OECD) was established in 1961 and represents 30 countries. It brings together the governments of countries committed to democracy and the market economy from around the world to:

- support sustainable employment growth;
- boost employment;
- raise living standards;
- maintain financial stability;
- assist with national economic development;
- contribute to growth in world trade.

The OECD also shares expertise and exchanges with more than 100 countries, from Brazil, China and Russia, to the least developed economies in Africa. The OECD has also been one of the largest providers of comparable statistics, as well as economic and social data. It provides a setting in which governments may compare policy experiences, seek answers to common problems, identify good practice and coordinate domestic and international policies. In May 2007, OECD countries agreed to invite Chile, Estonia, Israel, Russia and Slovenia to open discussions for membership and to offer enhanced engagement to Brazil, China, Indonesia, India and South Africa.

---

### Activity

Access the website www.eurofound.europa.eu/eiro/2004/12/study/tn0412101s.htm that provides an authentic overview of current labour relations issues in the European steel industry.
   Consider the following:

- Identify the major challenges confronting the European steel industry.
- How do labour relations in the steel industry vary from country to country?
- Explain how industrial changes are being implemented by 'social dialogue'.
- Would you agree that 'social dialogue' is an appropriate method to modernize the industry? Why/why not?

---

## Summary

This chapter has investigated variations in labour relations structures (including major actors and processes) in the three leading global regions. Heterogeneity in the pattern of global labour relations structures may be attributed to continuing diversity in the institutional hardware, or business systems, lying across international 'fault lines'. Such variations in labour relations structures pose a challenge to MNCs, which may have to modify their approaches to involving employees in corporate decisions, and other labour relations matters, according to their locus of operation.

## Further reading

**Dore, R.** (2000) *Stock-market Capitalism, Welfare Capitalism: Japan and Germany versus the Anglo-Saxons*, Oxford: Oxford University Press.

The text provides an in-depth comparison of the Japanese 'variety of capitalism', and associated labour relations structures, with German and Anglo-American institutional forms and systems of corporate governance. It is contended that the Japanese system is potentially more durable in the era of globalisation.

**Bamber, G.J., Lansbury, R.D. and Wailes, N.** (2004) *International and Comparative Employment Relation* (4th edn.), London: Sage Publications.

This edited volume explores environments, structures and actors in employment in a range of countries, including the USA, Canada, Australia, Italy, France, Germany, Sweden, Japan and Korea. Evaluation is offered of major processes such as arbitration, consultation and employee participation. Developments in multinational enterprises, non-unionism and novel forms of HRM are also considered.

**Morley, M.J., Gunnigle, P. and Collings, D.G.** (**eds**) (2006) *Global Industrial Relations*, London and New York: Routledge.

Variations in regional systems of industrial relations are examined, ranging from North America to India. In-depth analysis is also provided of contemporary developments in the following areas: international trends in unionization, international collective bargaining, industrial conflict and strikes, the impact of multinationals and globalization.

## Useful websites

www.eurofound.europa.eu
The European Foundation for the Improvement of Living and Working Conditions in the European Union provides comprehensive and contemporary reports and surveys on employment relations and related developments in Europe at European-wide, national and sectoral levels.

www.businesseurope.eu
The umbrella group for business interests in Europe.

www.etuc.org
A site devoted to the 'voice' of European workers.

Other websites:
www.emf-fem.org
www.uscib.org
www.uaw.org/solidarity/05/1205/feature04.cfm.
www.ilo.org
oecd.org

## References

**Bennett, R.** (1997) *Employee Relations* (2nd edn.), Harlow: FT/Prentice Hall.

**Edwards, T.** (2004) The transfer of employment practices across borders in multinational companies, in A.W. Harzing and J. Van Ruysseveldt (eds) *International Human Resource Management*, London: Sage Publications.

**Edwards, T. and Ferner, A.** (2002) The renewed 'American challenge': a review of employment practices in US multinationals, *Industrial Relations Journal*, 33(2): 94–111.

**Eurofound–Eironline (European Industrial Relations Observatory)** (1998) *The Impact of European Works Councils*, Dublin.

**Eurofound–Eironline (European Industrial Relations Observatory)** (2001) *Industrial Relations in the EU, Japan and USA*, Dublin.

**Eurofound–Eironline (European Industrial Relations Observatory)** (2007a) *Industrial Relations in EU Member States, 2000–2004*, Dublin.

**Eurofound–Eironline (European Industrial Relations Observatory)** (2007b) *Industrial Relations Developments in Europe, 2006: A Comparative Overview of Industrial Relations*, Dublin.

**European Trade Union Confederation** (2008) *European Works Councils*, Brussels.

**Ewing, K.D.** (2006) International labour standards, in M.J. Morley, P. Gunnigle and D.G. Collings (eds) *Global Industrial Relations*, Oxford: Routledge.

**Gunnigle, P., Murphy, K.R., Cleveland, N.J., Heraty, N. and Morley, M.** (2002) Localisation in human resource management: comparing American and European multinational corporations, *Advances in International Management*, 14: 259–284.

**Hollinshead, G. and Leat, M.** (1995) *Human Resource Management: An International and Comparative Perspective*, London: Pitman Publishing.

**Hyman, R.** (2004) Varieties of capitalism, national industrial relations systems and transnational challenges, in A.W. Harzing and J. Van Ruysseveldt (eds) *International Human Resource Management*, London: Sage Publications.

**International Labour Organization (ILO)** (1997) *The ILO, Standard Setting and Globalisation. Report of the Director-General*, Geneva.

**ILO** (1997–2002) Convention no. 98, 'Concerning the Application of the Right to Organize and Bargain Collectively, Office of the UN High Commissioner for Human Rights, Geneva.

**Leat, M.** (2003) The European Union, in G. Hollinshead, P. Nicholls and S. Tailby (eds) *Employee Relations*, Harlow: FT/Prentice Hall.

**Lipietz, A.** (1997) The post-Fordist world: labour relations, international hierarchy and global ecology, *Review of International Political Economy*, 4(1): 1–41.

**Marchington, M., Goodman, J., Wilkinson, A. and Ackers, P.** (1992) *New Developments in Employee Involvement*, Employment Department Research Series, No. 2, London: HMSO.

**O'Hagen, E., Gunnigle, P. and Morley, M.** (2004) Issues in the management of industrial relations in international firms, in H. Scullion and M. Linehan (eds) *International Human Resource Management: A Critical Text*, Basingstoke: Palgrave Macmillan.

**Poole, M. and Warner, M.** (1998) *The IEBM Handbook of Human Resource Management*, London: International Thomson Business Press.

**Ramsay, H.** (1992) Commitment and involvement, in B. Towers (ed.) *The Handbook of Human Resource Management*, Oxford: Blackwell.

**Royle, T.** (2000) *Working for McDonald's in Europe: The Unequal Struggle*, London and New York: Routledge.

**Salamon, M.** (2001) *Industrial Relations Theory and Practice* (4th edn.), Harlow: FT/Prentice Hall.

**Sinclair, J.** (2003) Employee representation: trade unions, in G. Hollinshead, P. Nicholls and S. Tailby (eds) *Employee Relations* (2nd edn.), Harlow: FT/Prentice Hall.

**Streeck, W.** (1997) Neither European nor Works Council: a reply to Paul Knutsen, *Economic and Industrial Democracy*, 18(2): 325–37.

**Webb, S. and Webb, B.** (1920) *The History of Trade Unionism*, London: Longman.

**Whitley, R.** (1996) The social construction of economic actors, in R. Whitley and P.H. Kristensen (eds) *The Changing European Firm: Limits to Convergence*, London: Routledge.

**Whitley, R.** (2002) Business systems, in A. Sorge (ed.) *Organization*, London: Thomson Learning.

# The Americas: the USA and Mexico

**07**

## ❖ LEARNING OBJECTIVES

❖ To explore the North American Free Trade Agreement (NAFTA) and its economic effects in the region

❖ To gain insight into the economic, political and cultural contexts for HRM in the USA and Mexico

❖ To explore key features of HRM practices (relating to recruitment, training and pay) in the USA and Mexico

## Introduction

In this chapter, we consider the contrasting institutional and cultural contexts and manifestations of HR practice, in two of the members of NAFTA, the USA and Mexico. It is instructive to focus on these countries as, despite geographic proximity and economic interdependence, they have trodden very different paths to 'modernity'. The USA, renowned for its ethnic diversity, has emerged as an economic super-power, as well as the source of modern ideas in many walks of international life, over a relatively brief historical period. On the other hand, Mexico has been steeped in Hispanic traditions for a period of considerable longevity and has been counted amongst the world's less advanced nations, placing considerable economic dependence on agriculture and heavy industry. While freedom of trade catalysed by NAFTA has bound these countries as economic partners, there is also evidence that underlying differences in business and cultural systems have rendered some fissures in the relationship. For example, considerable controversy has been generated through the relocation of manual jobs from the USA to Mexico to take advantage of relatively low labour costs in the latter. Lines of contestation in this development have concerned not only the 'haemorrhaging' of North American manual jobs, but also the poverty of working conditions in Mexican factories. It is also pertinent to note, in the context of an increase in the number of strategic alliances and joint ventures between North and South American partners, culturally determined variations in the mindsets of counterparts from 'across the border' may hamper, as well as potentially enrich, international team working. In the following sections we turn to the USA and Mexico in turn.

## The USA

The USA has been regarded as the global exemplar of 'neo-liberal' economic and employment policy, manifesting a business system that places the highest premium on shareholder values, managerial freedom and corporate competitiveness. Features of neo-liberalism that have been upheld in the US context have been: first, low levels of government regulation (or 'small' government) and low rates of taxation; second, a strong orientation towards private, as opposed to public, ownership of business, and towards small businesses; third, a history of anti-union sentiment across much of industry and a current prevalence of non-unionized enterprises; and, fourth, an orientation towards mobility of labour, both within and across companies.

Despite the apparent prevalence of neo-liberalist thinking, the US government does maintain an important role in national economic management and recent radical statutory interventions into banking and finance in the context of an economic crisis have led to serious questioning of economic and political 'articles of faith'. Examples of past governmental intervention into economic and social matters include: price control, counteracting monopolies through anti-trust law, monetary and fiscal policy, and social regulations to improve public safety and welfare. The federal government owns the postal system, the Amtrak railway system and the Nuclear Regulatory Commission. Controversially, and apparently in contradiction of its own advocacy of international market liberalism, the Bush (G.W.) administration acted to protect the US steel industry from global competitive forces in the 1990s and has protected agriculture from low-cost competition from developing countries.

The historic growth and success of the US economy has been built not only on a wealth of natural resources, and particularly minerals, but also on an expanding and highly productive workforce. The US labour force is characterized by ethnic diversity, embodying immigrant populations including (East and West) Europeans, African Americans, Latin Americans and Asians. While the US economy has been vaunted as leading the world, it has been prone to recession in recent years, 'a shallow' economic downturn occurring in the early 2000s, and a more serious financial crisis in the later part of the decade related to trade deficit and consumer borrowing.

While economic and managerial 'freedom' has represented the ideological catalyst driving the US economy to world-leading status, it is clear also that the pervasive influence of 'the market' has carried with it detrimental social effects. In the USA, the gap between 'winners' and 'losers' is evident both at societal and corporate levels. The United Nations Development Programme (2006) report on income equality ranks the US as tied for 73rd out of 126 countries, the richest 10 per cent in the country earning approximately 16 times more than the poorest 10 per cent. It has been estimated that the salaries of chief executive officers (CEOs) is now around 300 times the earnings of the average US worker (Berliner, 2008). In the era of globalization and rapid technological change, job displacement has become commonplace in the USA, which has had most detrimental effect on unskilled workers as their activities are shifted to lower-cost global regions, but also now affecting more highly educated and semi-skilled employees (Yellen, 2006).

The US economy is strongly international in orientation, as a provider and recipient of foreign direct investment (FDI). As Hodgetts and Luthans (2003) point out, US MNCs are dispersed widely throughout the world; General Motors and Ford, for example, commanding dominant market positions in Europe. The USA also possesses a large international market share in high-technology telecommunications, petroleum and consumer goods, US-owned corporations expanding their interests into Asia, Eastern Europe, the Middle East and beyond.

## The North American Free Trade Agreement (NAFTA)

While the USA and Canada have been major trading partners for many years, Mexico joined NAFTA in 1994 following an economic growth spurt in the early 1990s. North America now constitutes one of the three largest trading blocs in the world, with a combined purchasing power of around $11 trillion (Hodgetts and Luthans, 2006). The key developments associated with NAFTA have been:

- the elimination of tariffs as well as import and export quotas;
- the opening of government procurement markets to all three national members;
- an increase in the ability to make investments in each other's country;
- an increase in the ease of travel between the countries;
- the removal of restrictions on agricultural products, auto parts and energy goods.

Wild et al. (2006) report that since NAFTA took effect, trade between the three nations has increased markedly, with the largest gains being between the USA and Mexico. These authors assert that the US now exports more to Mexico than it does to Britain, Germany and France combined, and that, in 1997, Mexico became the second-largest export market for the USA for the first time ever. As relatively low-cost producers, and enjoying close geographic proximity to the USA and therefore beneficial transportation costs, Mexican businesses are now able to take advantage of US markets by replacing goods previously imported from Asia (Hodgetts and Luthans, 2003). In consequence US-owned companies including Hewlett Packard, IBM and Delphi Automotive Systems have established productive utilities in Mexico, while MNCs from overseas, including Volkswagen, Nissan and Daimler Chrysler, have established operations to take advantage of this market location (ibid.).

While NAFTA has provided a powerful stimulant to trade in the North American regions, it has also prompted ambivalent responses among critical commentators. Considerable attention has been given to the Maquiladoras in northern Mexico, which is a zone of export assembly plants for the USA, and in respect of which the Mexican government has all but waived taxes and customs fees. Over one million Mexicans work in over 3,000 manufacturing plants, and it has been asserted that some of these have offended international labour standards by employing mainly young women on low rates of pay, imposing long hours of work and breaching acceptable health and safety standards. It has also been claimed that the Maquiladoras and other low-cost production sites in Mexico have caused environmental damage by polluting air and water. Since the inception of NAFTA in 1994, there is some evidence that employment and environmental standards have been enhanced in Mexico.

A related concern has been the alleged displacement of unskilled jobs from the USA to Mexico, the AFL–CIO trade union confederation suggesting that 750,000 jobs and job opportunities have been forfeited by the USA by NAFTA (Wild et al., 2006). On the other hand, the US Trade Representative Office claims that exports to Mexico and Canada support 2.9 million US jobs, while Packard Electric has suggested that without its Maquiladoras operations, it would have relocated production from North America to South East Asia (Hodgetts and Luthans, 2003).

## Welfare capitalism and non-unionism

Kochan et al. (1986) explain that there is a deep-seated managerial antipathy towards trade unions in the USA. A notorious incident in US labour relations history centred upon the Ford Motor Company at its River Rouge Plant in Detroit in 1937, where two union organizers were physically assaulted by the company's 'Service Department' (Clayton,1997) engaged to spy on, and expel, trade unionists. The use of violence and intimidation has blighted the history of North American labour relations; a further example occurring in Virginia in 1989, where 'asset protection teams' and 350 state troopers broke a strike of coal miners at the Pittston Company (ibid.). The durability of American, non- or anti-unionism has been confirmed by a number of surveys (e.g. Buckley and Enderwick, 1985; Dunning, 1998) and some well-known US MNCs, for example McDonald's and IBM, have resisted unionization for decades (Ferner et al., 2005).

As an alternative to forceful opposition to trade unionism, a long-established movement has been 'welfare capitalism' which involves the adoption of 'enlightened' employer initiatives that serve to forestall unionization. According to Claydon (1997), welfare capitalism has typically involved careful selection of employees, favourable rates of pay, fringe benefits such as canteens and social facilities, and employee stock ownership schemes. The engendering of 'high commitment' among employees, associated with the avoidance of unions, has also been achieved through the establishment of sophisticated workplace communication systems, 'flat' organizational structures, and powerful and binding corporate cultures, with associated training and socialization into the values of the enterprise. Exemplars of the 'high road' approach to the management of human resources include IBM, Hewlett Packard, Motorola and Delta Airlines. Indeed, the tradition of welfare capitalism in the USA may be closely associated with the 'birth' of softer conceptions of HRM in the mid-1980s (e.g. Beer et al., 1984) predicated on 'high-commitment' structures and values.

## Cultural orientation and the USA

In Hofstedian terms, the most notable cultural predisposition in the USA is its strong orientation towards individualism, which reflects self-reliance, competitiveness, looking after family members and loose bonds with others. The notion of individualism is clearly manifested in the *American Dream,* which romanticizes individual possibilities of rising from the 'log cabin to the Whitehouse' on the basis of personal endeavour and force of personality. Jackson (2002) suggests, however, that powerful individualistic tendencies are sometimes tempered by the requirement for people to 'huddle' into groupings for projects of mutual interest, which rather resembles the tactics in US football games. Tayeb (2005) suggests that North American employees may indeed display solidarity and express collective sentiment at times of national crisis, such as in the recent traumas following the terrorist attacks of 11 September 2001 and Hurricane Katrina (Ferris et al., 2007). According to Hofstede (1994), the USA also scores relatively highly on masculinity, and impatience towards rules and bureaucracy is reflected in a low uncertainty avoidance score, and a preference towards equality and democratic organizational principles implicit in a low power distance score (see Table 7.1).

**Table 7.1 Major US national cultural characteristics and management practices (Tayeb, 2005)**

| National culture |
|---|
| ■ Highly individualistic, self-focused, preference to act as individuals rather than as members of a group , yet can be collectivist in the face of a common threat |
| ■ Small power distance: egalitarian, tend not to treat people differently even when there are great differences in age or social standing |
| ■ Masculine: ambitious, competitive, goal oriented, achievers |
| ■ Low uncertainty avoidance, risk-takers, entrepreneurial |
| ■ Low context: directness, expressive in communication, do not talk around things, tend to say exactly what they mean |
| ■ Open, friendly, informal |
| ■ Ethnocentric: believe their culture and values are superior to all others |
| ■ Future oriented: strong belief that present ways of doing things inevitably are replaced by even better ways |
| ■ Readiness to change: try new things, a predisposition to believe that new is good |
| ■ 'Can do' attitude |

| HRM and other employee-related values and practices |
|---|
| ■ Participative leadership style |
| ■ Superiors are approachable |
| ■ Subordinates are willing to question authority |
| ■ Status based on how well people perform their functions |
| ■ Performance-oriented |
| ■ Promotion and reward based on merit as opposed to status, hierarchy or gender |
| ■ Live more easily with uncertainty, sceptical about rules and regulations |
| ■ Value punctuality and keep appointments and calendars |
| ■ Much more concerned with their own careers and personal success than about the welfare of the organization or the group |
| ■ Value success and profit |
| ■ Acceptance of conflict |
| ■ System-driven: conviction that all problems can be solved, system and energy will overcome any obstacle |
| ■ Proactive: take initiative, aim high |
| ■ Result-oriented |
| ■ Professional: educated and well trained |
| ■ Strong devotion to managerial prerogative |

- Hire and fire policies
- Communication skills, informal, direct, explicit, often aggressive
- Emphasis on entrepreneurship and innovation
- Legalist approach to contracts
- Informality yet a preference for written rules and procedures
- Dislike of trade unions
- Preference for HRM over unionization

## HRM in the USA

It is widely accepted that the current conception of HRM was 'born in the USA' (Communal and Brewster, 2004), seminal contributions to theory and practice in the discipline being made by management theorists at Harvard Business School (Beer et al., 1984) and at the universities of Michigan and Columbia (Fombrun et al., 1984). Formative conceptions of HRM undoubtedly drew on previous influential contributions to management thinking emanating from the USA, notably, scientific management, human relations and human capital theory. Hollinshead and Leat (1995), Beaumont (1982) and others point out that the 'birth' of HRM in the early 1980s was not accidental, but was stimulated by the onset of an important set of environmental and product market conditions, including increasing international competition, 'positive lessons' in people management learned from Japan, declining trade union membership and power, the relative growth of the 'white-collar' service sector of employment, increasing employment of women and the growth of part-time work, the widespread use of computerized technology and credibility problems confronting 'traditional' personnel management.

Thus, it may be argued that HRM policies and practices are strongly 'embedded' in the US business system. Communal and Brewster (2004) state that underlying the philosophy of HRM are assumptions of managerial freedom and enterprise autonomy; these preconditions not necessarily being transferable to other global business environments, most notably the more highly regulated terrain of continental Europe. Consideration of prevalent practices in HRM is therefore founded on the notion that US management teams have discretion in formulation and experimentation with HR strategies, and are minimally constrained by statutory influence.

Thus, the field of *recruitment and staffing* remains conditioned by the 'employment at will' doctrine upheld by the courts in 1908. This implies a considerable reliance on external labour markets for filling vacancies, and offers little job tenure to new recruits. While there has been an emphasis on 'traditional' methods for recruitment purposes (including job descriptions, interviews, psychometric tests and assessment centres), an increasing emphasis is being placed on Internet-based sourcing of new recruits, which permits two-way communication and interaction between the potential applicant and the company. Despite the general climate of non-intervention by the state in employment matters, an important and perhaps contradictory force is the powerful anti-discriminatory, or affirmative action, legislation on grounds including sex, race, ethnic orientation, age, sexual orientation and disability. Indeed, individual (as opposed to collective) rights are subject to vehement protection throughout US employment, as manifested, for example, in protection against sexual harassment. This lends a litigious and contractual orientation to work relations, and compels employers to ensure reliability and validity in procedures for hiring, firing, pay, promotion and training.

Turning to *remuneration and pay*, around 88 per cent of the US workforce belongs to non-union enterprises. Accordingly, employers have considerable latitude to formulate payment strategies, taking into account labour market rates, internal corporate relativities and the need for performance orientation. Indeed, variable pay according to performance management measures applying to individual employees is common in the USA. Increasingly, non-wage benefits are included in the payment package, and employers contribute towards social security, healthcare and pensions. In the unionized sector, there is a tradition of antagonistic as well as, more recently, 'partnership'-based approaches to collective bargaining. Generally, collective agreements have the force of law, and striking is prohibited during the lifetime of a collective agreement.

*Training* is viewed as a high priority area by many US companies, with an emphasis on job-related factors in a high-technology environment and with a need for customer-focused behaviours. At managerial level, there is a strong psychological underpinning in much development activity, critical competences relating to leadership and team working, as well as in dealing with high levels of change and stress.

More generally, there has been a significant increase in 'flexible' forms of employment in the USA, involving not only part-time work, but practices such as teleworking and telecommuting. Indeed, it has been estimated (Eurofound–Eironline, 2001), drawing on statistics produced by the International Telework Association and Council, that around 28 million workers (or one-fifth of the US workforce) are engaged from home, at telework centres, or 'on the road'. A further two million workers (1.5 per cent) are called to work only as needed. In the wake of the attacks on the World Trade Center on 11 September 2001 and Hurricane Katrina, a growing emphasis is being placed on health and safety matters at work, and managing employee trauma resulting from 'environmental' occurrences (Ferris et al., 2007).

## Mexico

### Introduction

The 'United States of Mexico' covers a total area of approximately two million square kilometres and borders in the north with the USA. Mexico's natural resources are petroleum, silver, copper, gold, lead, zinc, natural gas and timber. The population is over 100 million, with an annual growth rate of 1.7 per cent. The predominant religion is Catholicism (embracing 89 per cent of the population), with 6 per cent subscribing to Protestantism and 5 per cent to other faiths. For three centuries, from 1526, Mexico was ruled by Spain. In 1826, the country became independent and was transformed into a republic, being governed by the National Action Party (PAN) until 1929. Although the Mexican constitution stipulates that presidential elections are to be held every six years, the Communist-oriented Institutional Revolutionary Party (PRI) maintained power from 1928 to 2000, allegedly through the 'careful management' of elections (Fowler, 2002). Since July 2000, it is argued that Mexico has moved significantly towards democracy through the election of Vicente Fox of the National Action Party (Arias-Galicia, 2005). The country's political structure embodies 31 states and one federal district (Mexico City), each state retaining a degree of self-government. The political system comprises two legislative houses, the Senate and the Lower House, although central government has demonstrated political ineffectiveness in recent years, having failed to implement economic reforms concerning privatization of state-owned industries and the liberalization of energy.

The Mexican economy is highly diverse, bordering a super-power in the north and the relatively weak economies of Guatemala and Belize in the south east. It is bordered by two grand oceans for exporting and importing to the West and East. There is evidence that parts of the Mexican economy are now burgeoning as firms such as the glass maker, Vitro, gain international strength and reach (Taylor and Napier, 2005), while more arid regions in the centre and south possess the characteristics of developing economies. Mexico has gained global competitive strength through its three main industries of oil, tourism and automobile technologies. The country is the fifth-largest producer of oil in the world, producing 3.8 million barrels per day. It is the eighth most visited country in the world, bringing in over 20 million visitors each year. Mexico's contribution to automobile manufacture differs from its Latin American neighbours as there is significant concentration on the 'higher end' functions of research and development and production of complex components rather than routine assembly of parts. Ford, General Motors and Chrysler have operated in Mexico since the 1930s, with Volkswagen, Nissan, Honda, BMW and Mercedes-Benz locating more recently on Mexican soil.

Mexico's GDP per capita is $10,600. The country's gross national income and income per capita are the highest in Latin America, at $754 billion and $7,310, respectively, making Mexico an upper-middle-income economy. However, these statistics may be regarded as somewhat misleading, as much of the growth and prosperity has occurred in the northern part of the country bordering on the USA. Here, well-developed cities are in evidence and a modern economic infrastructure is in place, with employment prospects in banking, high technology and the like.

By way of contrast, in the central and southern regions, despite economic improvement in the new millennium, a poverty rate of around 30 per cent is still apparent, with agricultural activity dominating employment.

The Mexican economy is strongly oriented towards importing and exporting, with around 90 per cent of trade occurring under free trade agreements. Under the free trade umbrella of NAFTA, around 90 per cent of Mexico's exports are to the USA and Canada; these two countries also provide around 55 per cent of its imports. Trade is also increasing within the Latin American bloc, as Mexico has expressed an interest in joining Mercosur, a regional trade agreement between Brazil, Argentina, Uruguay and Paraguay. From 1993 to 2002, trade between Mexico and the USA increased by 183 per cent, while the equivalent trading statistic with Chile was 285 per cent, Honduras 420 per cent and Costa Rica 528 per cent. Other notable trading partners include Israel, Switzerland and Bolivia.

## Cultural orientation and Mexico

Arias-Galicia (2005: 183), drawing on Kras (1988), makes the following observations concerning Mexican cultural features:

> 66  family is the first priority, which means that many firms are family companies; fear of losing face is paramount; confrontation is to be avoided; dress and

grooming are status symbols; title and position are more important than money; truth is tempered by diplomacy; leisure is considered essential for a full life; autocracy is often exercised in firms; there is basically a theoretical mindset instead of a practical one; promotions are based on loyalty to superiors; deadlines are flexible; planning is aimed at short-term vision instead of the long term; and competition is avoided since harmony is most valued. **"**

Arias-Galicia (2005), referring to Hofstede (1994), identifies the following primary cultural predispositions:

1 *Individualism–collectivism*: Mexicans prefer to work in an environment characterized by close social relations in which group members care for and support each other. Loyalty to the group is a prevailing value. Family ties are strong.
2 *Power distance*: Mexicans follow the superior's orders because she or he is entitled to be obeyed. These views are reinforced by the existing labour law that states: 'Perform work under the Patrón's orders (or his/her representative), to whose authority the worker is subordinate in all matters referring to work.' In many firms, however, empowerment programmes have been very successful. Self-managed work teams are gaining in popularity in many industries, profiting from the collectivistic orientation of Mexican workers.
3 *Femininity–masculinity*: Mexico scores highly on the feminine approach, which values warm interpersonal relations, quality of life and interest in others' matters.

Diaz-Guerrero (1995), however, has found significant shifts in the values of young Mexicans over the period of one decade. Inglehart (1997), following the assertion of Hofstede (see Chapter 2), identifies a general shift towards individualism in a number of economically advancing countries, including Mexico.

## HRM in Mexico

Employment is subject to a relatively high degree of legal regulation in Mexico. Labour laws are based on the Mexican Constitution (1917) and the Mexican Federal Labour Law, which regulates labour contracts, minimum wages, employee benefits and trade union activity. Other significant legal provisions impacting on employment are contained in the Social Security Law and the Worker Housing Institute Law. The following constitute key legally prescribed benefits (Arias-Galicia, 2005), which may be subject to enhancement at individual company level:

■   A 48-hour working week. Workers should have at least one paid day off work each week.
■   A six-day paid vacation after one year of work, and subsequently a sliding scale of holiday entitlements according to length of service.
■   Twelve-week maternity leave.
■   Five per cent of salaries (including fringe benefits and overtime) should be paid by companies to an institute (INFONAVIT) to provide workers with loans to buy houses or renew housing.
■   The legal age for working is normally 16 years.
■   An annual bonus equivalent to at least 15 working days is payable to workers.

- Retirement wages are provided by the social security system, based on salary earned, age of retirement and years worked.

In the field of *recruitment and selection,* as many Latin American companies have strong family traditions (Davila and Elvira, 2005), there has been a strong tendency to recruit family members and close relatives, although this is subject to change (Hoshino, 2004). In seeking to attract applicants, various methods may be used, depending on the size of the organization, including posters on factory doors, mass media, 'word of mouth', 'head-hunters' and employment fairs organized by employers (Arias-Galicia, 2005). In selecting candidates for employment, personality characteristics such as potential for cooperative and courteous behaviour and organizational loyalty are given a high priority; common selection methods include interviews and psychometric tests (ibid.). Although anti-discriminatory laws exist, there is still evidence of a 'glass ceiling' confronting women in employment (ibid.). The Labour Ministry (*Secretaria del Trabajo y Previsión Social*) provides a service to put unemployed people in contact with employers (ibid.).

Turning to *training and development,* a distinction may be drawn between 'for-the-job' and 'on-the-job' training. In respect of the first category, training is provided by the educational system, from basic schooling to higher education. Unfortunately, evidence remains that around 10 per cent of the population has not attended school, with illiteracy remaining a serious social problem. At the higher level, the National College for Professional and Technical Education (CONALEP) has played a major role in technical and professional training over the past 20 years (Galindo, 2003). Two specific training schemes have been developed by the Ministry of Labour in coordination with employers' organizations and the public employment services. The Comprehensive Quality and Modernisation Programme (CIMO) is devoted to providing technical and financial support for short-term training in micro-, small- and medium-sized enterprises. The Training Scholarship Programme for Unemployed Workers (PROBECAT) distributes short-term grants combined with training courses to unemployed and displaced workers (ibid.). An extension of this programme has been targeted at literacy skills and providing adult vocational education to various groups (particularly migrant workers in the informal sector) as a first step towards elementary vocational training. Despite, however, the efforts of training agencies in the state and private sectors, the proportion of the population obtaining 'for-the-job' training remains small. Regarding the second category, training at work is considered to be a social benefit in Mexico and the labour law stipulates training as an employment right. A number of major companies have a pre-employment school, offering 'scholarships' to promising potential recruits to attend, particularly in the technical area (Arias-Galicia, ibid). In general, in keeping with the 'theoretical' Mexican cultural predisposition, results of training are not systematically evaluated or subject to cost–benefit analysis.

In the field of *pay and remuneration,* the aforementioned Federal Labour Law regulates many aspects of pay, employment conditions and fringe benefits. Collective bargaining between management and trade unions is customary in large organizations, with unions being legally entitled to demand a wage increase every year and new working conditions every two years. It is not customary in Mexico to distinguish between wages and salaries; all types of remuneration being referred to as '*salarios*' or '*sueldos*' (ibid.). A significant issue in employment remains the safety of workers, with the culture of *machismo* militating against the wearing of safety helmets and the taking of other protective measures despite employer insistence. Similarly, the maintenance of safe and clean conditions in small shops and similar premises has also been a cause for concern (ibid.).

---

### *Activity*

You are on the management team of a US-owned MNC in the glass manufacturing sector planning to establish a joint venture with a Mexican partner. Using available evidence, consider the potential benefits and drawbacks associated with this, with particular reference to North American and Mexican institutional and cultural factors.

---

## Summary

This chapter has explored the archetypal 'neo-liberal' economic and political system in evidence in the USA, exploring how HRM concepts and practices are predicated on the notion of managerial freedom and organizational autonomy. While the economic relationship between the USA and Mexico has recently intensified as a result of NAFTA, it is evident that Mexico continues to manifest a distinctive cultural and contrasting 'Latin American' approach to HRM, in a broader context of national fragmentation between developed and developing internal regions.

## Further reading

**Werner, E. (ed.)** (2007) *Managing Human Resources in North America*, London and New York: Routledge.

The text provides contemporary insight into North American policies and practices in HRM, as well as their broader context. Issues for consideration include staffing and developing the multinational workforce, sexual harassment training, retaining new mothers, ethics, the travelling employee, health and safety and outsourcing.

**Kochan, T.A., Katz, H.C. and McKersie, R.B.** (1986) *The Transformation of American Industrial Relations*, New York: Basic Books.

A highly authoritative and historically informed analysis of actors and structures in the distinctive North American industrial relations system, capturing moves in the late 1970s and 1980s from 'collectivism' to 'individualism'. The book was produced at a time when 'neo-liberalist' principles were gathering pace.

**Davila, A. and Elvira, M.M.** (2005) *Managing Human Resources in Latin America*, London and New York: Routledge.

The distinctive cultural and economic context for HRM in Latin America is explored, followed by an in-depth analysis of HR characteristics and contemporary policy areas in Argentina, Brazil, Central America and Panama, Chile, Columbia, Mexico, Peru, Uruguay and Venezuela. Emergent directions for HRM research in Latin America are also postulated.

## Useful websites

www.nafta-sec-alena.org
The site of the NAFTA secretariat, including US, Canadian and Mexican sections. Procedural and legal information pertaining to NAFTA is offered.

www.ustr.gov
The site of the United States Trade Representative. Pertinent material is offered on US trading policy, with access to press releases, news items and policy documentation.

Other websites:
www.state.gov/r/pa/ei/bgn/35749.htm
www.pbs.org/pov/pov2006/maquilapolis

## References

**Arias-Galicia, L.F.** (2005) Human resource management in Mexico, in M.M. Elvira and A. Davila (eds) *Managing Human Resources in Latin America: An Agenda for International Leaders*, London and New York: Routledge.

**Beaumont, P.** (1982) The US human resource management literature: a review, in G. Salamon (ed.) *Human Resource Strategies,* London: Sage Publications.

**Beer, M., Spector, B., Lawrence, P.R., Quinn Mills, D. and Walton, R.E.** (1984) *Managing Human Assets*, New York: Macmillan.

**Berliner, U.** (2008) Haves and have-nots: income inequality in America: NPR. Washington.

**Buckley, P. and Enderwick, P.** (1985) *The Industrial Relations Practices of Foreign-owned Firms in Britain*, London: Macmillan.

**Clayton, T.** (1997) Human resource management and the USA, in I. Beardwell and L. Holden (eds) *Human Resource Management: A Contemporary Perspective,* London: Pitman Publishing.

**Communal, C. and Brewster, C.** (2004) HRM in Europe, in A.W. Harzing and J.V. Ruysseveldt (eds) *International Human Resource Management* (2nd edn.), London: Sage Publications.

**Davila, A. and Elvira, M.M.** (2005) *Managing Human Resources in Latin America*, London and New York: Routledge.

**Diaz-Guerrero, R.** (1995) *Psicologia del Mexicano* (Psychology of the Mexican), Mexico: Trillas.

**Dunning, J.** (1998) *American Investment in British Manufacturing,* revised and updated edition, London and New York: Routledge.

**Eurofound–Eironline** (2001) Industrial relations in the EU, Japan and USA, Dublin.

**Ferner, A., Almond, P., Colling, T. and Edwards, T.** (2005) Policies on union representation in US multinationals in the UK: between micro-politics and macro-institutions, *British Journal of Industrial Relations,* 43(4): 703–28.

**Ferris, G.R., Hochwater, W.A. and Matherley, T.A.** (2007) HRM after 9/11 and Katrina, in S. Warner (ed.) *Managing Human Resources in North America,* London and New York: Routledge.

**Fombrun, C., Tichy, N.M. and Devanna, M.A.** (1984) *Strategic Human Resource Management,* Montreal: Wiley.

**Fowler, W.** (2002) *Latin America 1800–2000: Modern History for Modern Languages,* London: Arnold.

**Galindo, L.I.** (2003) Mexico, in M. Zamko and M. Ngui (eds) *The Handbook of Human Resource Policies and Practices in Asia-Pacific Economies,* Vol. 2, Northampton: Edward Elgar.

**Hodgetts, R.M. and Luthans, F.** (2003) *International Management: Culture, Strategy and Behavior* (5th edn.), New York: McGraw-Hill.

**Hofstede, G.** (1994) *Cultures and Organizations: Software of the Mind,* London: HarperCollins.

**Hollinshead, G. and Leat, M.** (1995) *Human Resource Management: An International and Comparative Perspective,* London: Pitman Publishing.

**Hoshino, T.** (2004) Family business in Mexico: responses to human resource and management succession, discussion papers, Institute of Developing Economies, Japan External Trade Organisation.

**Inglehart, R.** (1997) *Modernisation and Postmodernisation: Cultural, Economic and Political Change in 43 Societies,* Princeton, NJ: Princeton University Press.

**Jackson, T.** (2002) *International Human Resource Management: A Cross-cultural Approach,* London: Sage Publications.

**Kochan, T.A., Katz, H.C. and McKersie, R.B.** (1986) *The Transformation of American Industrial Relations,* New York: Basic Books.

**Kras, E.S.** (1988) *Management in Two Cultures: Bridging the Gap between US and Mexican Managers,* Yarmouth, ME: Intercultural Press.

**ayeb, M.H.** (2005) *International Human Resource Management: A Multinational Company Perspective,* Oxford: Oxford University Press.

**Taylor, S. and Napier, N.K.** (2005) International HRM in the twenty-first century: crossing boundaries, building connections, in H. Scullion and M. Linehan (eds) *International Human Resource Management: A Critical Text,* Basingstoke and New York: Palgrave Macmillan.

**United Nations Development Programme** (2006) *Human Development Report*, Basingstoke and New York: Palgrave Macmillan.

**Wild, J.W., Wild, K.L. and Han, J.C.Y.** (2006) *International Business: The Challenges of Globalization* (3rd edn.), Upper Saddle River, NJ: Pearson Prentice Hall.

**Yellen, J.L.** (2006) Income inequality in the United States, President's speech to the Center for the Study of Democracy, Federal Reserve Bank of San Francisco.

# CHAPTER

## 08

# Human resource management and Europe

❖ **LEARNING OBJECTIVES**

❖ To understand the institutional context for Human Resource Management (HRM) in Europe

❖ To rehearse the arguments for and against social regulation in Europe

❖ To investigate the context for, and HR practices associated with, the 'Rhineland model' of social partnership, as manifested in Germany

❖ To explore varying European national contexts for HRM/employment

❖ To explore the process of socio-economic transition in east European countries, and current HR challenges

## Introduction

The continent of Europe undoubtedly embodies considerable diversity in the policy and practice of HRM; this being magnified by the accession of the post-socialist states in May 2004. Yet, for those 'western' nations occupying continental European territory (including France, Germany, the Netherlands, Scandinavia and the 'Latin' countries), 'insider' or 'coordinated' institutional arrangements (see Chapter 2), based on notions of 'social partnership', have powerfully conditioned modes of managing the employment relationship. While high levels of governmental regulation into the economy and employment in Europe are subject to modernization and reform in the context of global competitive forces, Communal and Brewster (2004) identify the following predominant structural factors impinging on HRM in Europe:

■ the regulation of recruitment, dismissal and employment contracts;
■ legislative requirements on pay;

- public funding of labour market programmes (including training, retraining, job transition support, job creation for youth and long-term unemployed);
- quasi-legal nature of industrial relations, including the right to trade union representation, co-determination (worker participation) arrangements in some countries and works councils at shop-floor level;
- regulation of minimum social and employment standards at a pan-European level as a result of European Union (EU) policy making;
- a relatively high degree of public ownership (by international standards) and 'interlocking'/family-oriented patterns of corporate governance;
- high levels of trade union membership and collective bargaining over pay and other employment conditions.

Indeed, HRM across Europe is subject to the overarching influence of EU regulations, important dimensions of which are freedom of movement of labour and the Charter of Fundamental Rights for Workers (see p. 154). The Charter provides for minimum standards in social and employment matters, including remuneration, training, health and safety at work and employee consultation to apply to all members states, although, in practice, national regimes vary in the extent to which the basic floor of rights is exceeded. In general, continental European institutional contexts that embody the principles of social partnership (coordinated market economies; CMEs) will be amenable to the Charter and will implement its provisions in a 'maximum' fashion, while more liberal market-oriented economies in Europe will be disposed towards minimal implementation of European-wide standards in the pursuit of flexibility and cost-effectiveness (Holden, 1997).

Adapting the arguments of McIlroy (1995), the following critical observations may be made in relation to the continued application of a robust European social dimension, the two sides of the debate broadly reflecting employer and employee interests.

The 'deregulatory' case (for minimization of social regulation):

- Labour markets should be allowed to operate in a flexible way without 'rigidities'. National and international competition can only be achieved through 'lifting the burden' on business.
- The Social Chapter aims to improve standards to the level of the most profitable employers and harmonize labour market rules according to the model of the most regulated countries. The results are higher costs for employers, higher process for consumers and fewer jobs for workers.
- When workers do not have a job, employee protection rights represent a barrier to being hired. The foundation of social policy should be the right of individual employers and employees to enter into contracts freely.
- Free competition should involve competition over the price of labour. The Social Chapter will not protect EU workers from competition from developing countries.

The 'regulatory' argument (for minimum, or above minimum, standards):

- The Social Chapter represents only a set of *minimum* standards, or a basic floor of rights, placing minimal obligations on employers. Furthermore, as a result of the EU principle of *subsidiarity*, individual countries possess some latitude as to how to implement policy areas emanating from the chapter.
- European countries should not compete with other global competitors (e.g. in Asia or Latin America) merely on grounds of cost. Welfare legislation can play a role in forcing

employers to become more efficient and innovative. Reducing standards and allowing high unemployment favours wage-cutting and survival of the 'least fit'. An employment environment that emphasizes welfare and participation rather than fear and insecurity can generate higher morale and higher productivity.

- The more regulated countries in Europe have experienced longer-term competitiveness, employers not seeing employee rights as a significant burden. Employment regulation in continental European countries has been consistent with taking the 'high road' to global competition, combining investment in and training of employees with high levels of commitment and flexibility.

- The more impoverished parts of Europe, in which low pay and poor conditions persist, *require* social protection, from a moral and political standpoint.

## Case Study: European Union milestones

### The Treaty of Rome (March 1957)

The six founding European states: Belgium, France, Germany, Italy, Luxembourg and the Netherlands.

'The Community shall have as its task, by establishing a common market and progressively approximating the economic policies of member states, to promote throughout the Community a harmonious development of economic activities, a continuous and balanced expansion, an increase in stability, an accelerated saving in standard of living and a closer relation between the states belonging to it.'

### The Single European Market (January 1993)

Objectives: to remove all remaining physical, technical and fiscal barriers between the member states in order to achieve the four freedoms of movement:

- free movement of goods
- free movement of people
- free movement of services
- free movement of capital

To abolish systematic controls at the borders between the member states through:

- the removal of physical barriers
- the removal of technical barriers
- the removal of fiscal barriers
- the liberalization of internal competition through strict competition policies

Current members: the six founding countries plus Austria, Bulgaria, Cyprus, Czech Republic, Denmark, Estonia, Finland, Greece, Hungary, Ireland, Lativa, Lithuania, Malta, Poland, Portugal, Romania, Slovakia, Slovenia, Spain, Sweden and the United Kingdom.

### The Maastricht Treaty (in force November 1993)

Aims and objectives:

- to promote economic and social progress that is balanced and sustainable, in particular through the creation of an area without internal frontiers, through the strengthening of economic and social cohesion and through the establishment of economic and monetary union, ultimately including a single currency
- to assert the European identity on the international scene, in particular through the implementation of a common foreign and security policy, including the eventual framing of a common defence policy that might in time lead to a common defence
- to strengthen the protection of the rights and interests of the nationals of member states through the introduction of a citizenship of the Union
- to develop close cooperation on justice and home affairs
- to maintain the *acquis communautaire* and build on it with a view to considering to what extent the policies and forms of cooperation introduced by the Treaty may need to be revised with the aim of ensuring the effectiveness of the mechanisms and the institutions of the Community

## The Community Charter of Fundamental Rights for Workers (the Social Charter)

(Social policy formed a separate protocol to Maastricht Treaty as UK rejected provisions until 1997.)
   Aims:

- to combat unemployment and reduce the inequality of its impact
- to ensure growth and greater job opportunities, and to reject all forms of discrimination or exclusion
- to promote improvements in living and working conditions
- to increase the economic and social cohesion of member states

Set of rights:

- freedom of movement
- employment and remuneration
- improvement of living and working conditions
- social protection
- freedom of association
- vocational training
- equal treatment of men and women
- information, consultation and participation of workers
- health, protection and safety in the workplace
- protection of children and adolescents
- elderly persons
- disabled persons

**The Lisbon Treaty (agreed by EU leaders, December 2003)** amends current and previous treaties without replicating them and aims to engender democracy, efficiency, solidarity, security and a global voice. At the time of writing, the future of the Lisbon Treaty is uncertain as it was rejected by Irish voters on 12 June 2008 and, under EU rules, it cannot enter if any of the 27 members fail to ratify it. Opponents of the Treaty argue that it is part of a federalist EU agenda that threatens national sovereignty.

**Eastern bloc enlargements (2004 and 2007)** – the EU now comprises 370 million citizens compared to the US population of 252 million.
  *Source*: El Kahal (1998).

Accordingly, commentators have argued (Gooderham et al., 2004) that a distinctive 'model' of HRM may be in evidence in Europe, contingent on the following features:

- Constraints on management 'freedom' to formulate and implement HR policies due to statutory, employers' organization and trade union influence over these policies. In other words, in contrast to the US, European HR managers' ability to use HR policies and practices in a strategic fashion is mediated by 'external' institutional groupings.
- 'Insider' patterns of corporate governance (see Chapter 2) that 'incorporate' HR considerations into the institutional dynamics of corporate decision making. In other words, HR considerations may be accommodated through the 'stakeholder' or 'social partnership' approach to economic and enterprise decision making rather than exclusively through a specialist and dedicated HR department. This is well captured by the following quotation:

> ❝ The evidence from Europe is not only that the strategy process is more complicated than is often assumed in the textbooks, but that it may well work in different ways and through different systems involving different people. Thus, the strategic implications of a management decision in Germany or the Netherlands will be subject to the involvement or scrutiny of powerful works council representatives or the worker directors on the supervisory board.
>
> (Gooderham et al., 2004: 15) ❞

While the 'European model' of HRM can be viewed as distinct from US conceptions, it is clear also that patterns of convergence in observed manifestations of employment policy and practice are occurring. The following are significant explanatory factors:

- Within Europe, certain national systems vary from 'the norm' and are asserting 'neo-liberal' tendencies in employment/HR practice. This observation would apply particularly to the UK and the new East European accession countries. Illustrative practices would relate to flexibility in employment practices, non-unionism and variability/individualization of pay.
- Throughout Europe, even in the more regulated countries, the need to 'deregulate' in order to match global competition from, for example, India and China, is serving to modify 'insider' or 'coordinated' institutional systems through engendering greater employment and labour market flexibility.

A pressing agenda across Europe, orchestrated by the EU, has been the need to encourage flexibility in working practices in the face of growing international competitive pressures, while retaining the European 'traditions' of job security, high skill and employee commitment to the production of quality goods and services. The concept of 'flexicurity' originated in Denmark and has been defined as 'an integrated strategy to enhance, at the same time, flexibility and security in Europe' (Europa/EU, 2008). Its aim is to develop employment and social welfare policies that simultaneously enable employers to have greater flexibility in how they deploy workers while enabling employees to have greater security if they are out of work and to move easily between jobs. Major components of flexicurity policies are as follows: flexible contractual arrangements, comprehensive lifelong learning strategies, effective active labour market policies and modern social security systems. Its benefits may be stated as follows:

- Greater contractual flexibility enables all employees to be redeployed rapidly and as needed.
- Employers are encouraged to recruit new employees, including young people, women and ethnic minorities.
- Undesirable employment arrangements are counteracted, such as temporary contracts.
- The modernization of social security systems is encouraged to offset the negative impact on workers of movement between jobs.
- Investment in skills and learning is stimulated to enable employees to adapt quickly to innovation and change while enhancing their employability.

While it can be argued that the concept of flexicurity rests comfortably in coordinated market economies (CMEs; see Chapter 2) – for example, in Scandinavia, which has relatively high degrees of expenditure on social welfare and labour market programmes – its transposition to liberal market economies (LMEs) – for example, Britain – may be viewed as problematic. In the latter settings, social security tends to be offered as a 'last resort' (Sapir, 2005) and has demonstrated limitations in assisting in the rapid redeployment and retraining of displaced workers so that they can re-enter the labour market with little career disruption. In LMEs, a 'deregulatory' approach tends to have been taken to social protection, predicated on the removal of 'rigidities' in the labour market and 'lifting the burden' on business. In practice, it appears that various 'pathways' are being followed to introducing flexicurity in Europe, which are conditioned by prevailing institutional and structural systems in various regions (Dewttinck et al., 2006). In France, for example, a primary measure taken has been the implementation of a 35-hour working week, while in the Netherlands there has been a rapid increase in part-time working.

In the next part of this chapter, the 'Rhineland' model of social partnership is explored, which represents the exemplary manifestation of neo-corporatist (CME) philosophy and practice in Europe (Albert, 1991; Streeck, 1992). In the face of global competition, the 'Rhineland' model is now subject to reform and deregulative tendencies.

## Germany

### The context for HRM

Germany is Europe's largest economy, its core being constituted by manufacturing and related service industries, and it possessing a strong export orientation. Undoubtedly, the 'New Germany' has faced some stern economic tests over its limited period of existence; many of these caused by the need to catalyse economic reform in the former GDR and to subsidize high levels of unemployment. Yet Germany's capacity to adjust to economic adversity has occurred through the country's determination to survive and grow through a process of consensus. This may be illustrated by considering the transformation of Volkswagen in the early 1990s. The company needed not only to reduce costs but also to increase productivity. Adopting the slogan 'Costs instead of heads', Volkswagen reduced working time by 20 per cent for all employees while cutting wages by the same amount and introducing a new system of team working. These shifts in conditions of employment occurred with the full and active consent of employee representatives. This is not an isolated example, and it demonstrates the German predisposition to protect jobs wherever possible. The commitment to *internal labour markets* flows from a long-established German tradition of all 'sitting in one boat'. As Wachter and Stengelhofen (1995: 89) state: 'Cartels, close ties between banks and industry, and the exchange of know-how between firms have always been a dominant feature of German capitalism.' This has been coupled with social legislation pioneered in the late nineteenth century to integrate all elements of society while, pre-emptively, warding off the threat of revolutionary socialism.

## A closer look at HRM

In describing HRM in Germany, it is necessary to commence with the important caveat that it has been difficult to find a precise and accurate translation of this term originating in the USA. Such linguistic difficulties reflect German scepticism surrounding the term and the distinctive roots of the equivalent function in Germany. Following from the above, we should note that much of the benign intent of HRM in Anglo-American cultures has already been delivered through the close institutional ties in Germany and the entrenched employment philosophy of nurturing internal markets and harnessing the skills of workers. Important aspects of pay, the (limited) movement of labour from enterprise to enterprise, and the organization of training are typically determined outside companies through legal regulation or collective bargaining. This means that, in contrast to practice in many concerns in the USA and the UK, personnel practitioners in Germany do not have direct access to the 'HR policy levers'. Instead, there is a legalistic feel to the personnel function, with attention being given to the administration of wide-ranging employment legislation as well as corporate regulation. Key areas of concern are *Kundigungsschutz* (protection against dismissal) and *Einstufung* (allocation of workers to jobs).

By virtue of the *Betriebsverfassungsgesetz* (Works Constitution Act), important decisions on matters such as pay, working hours, appraisal and lay-offs normally need to be formally presented to works councils for their agreement. Additionally, legislation on co-determination permits employee representation at a supervisory board level in major enterprises. Consequently, personnel practitioners need to adopt a consultative style and much time will be spent fine-tuning policy areas that are acceptable to works council representatives and other interested parties. The emphasis placed on nurturing internal labour markets also points to distinctive priority areas for German personnel specialists. First, there has been a need to devote considerable time and attention to internal promotion, succession planning, identifying training needs and administering training programmes. Second, it is necessary to attend to the effective design of work to ensure that the high skill base of employees is effectively motivated and deployed. The function itself tends to be occupied by lawyers, economists and social scientists and the professional association for personnel management (DGFP) comprises 1,300 members. Unlike its British counterpart (the CIPD), the DGFP does not collaborate extensively with educational providers to deliver a professional programme.

The following major features of employment practice in Germany are considered:

- *Pay* – agreements between the representatives of employers and employees at industry level continue to determine basic pay and merit increases, as well as terms and conditions such as the duration of the working week, paid breaks, holiday entitlements, bonuses, overtime rates, sickness provision and termination of the work contract. At the level of the plant, works councils are frequently involved in the application of industry-wide rates. Individual employers have greater discretion in the setting of managerial salaries and the provision of incentive payments. In the former West Germany, the generous benefits accruing to employees have been well known. Not only have these included generous basic rates of pay, but also such attractive fringe benefits as subsidized meals, free dental treatment and visits to health spas. Turning to the area of equal opportunities, legislation exists to promote equal pay between men and women, yet inequalities persist. Parents are allowed to return to work up to three years after the birth of a child, and many companies allow unpaid breaks of up to seven years.

- *Staffing* – features of the German labour market are that it is large (drawing on the highest population in Europe, at around 80 million) and diverse. In the 1960s, skill shortages were encountered in a climate of virtually full employment and consequently foreign workers (particularly Turks) were drafted in. The country suffers disproportionately from the 'demographic time bomb' with 'greying' of the labour force being evident whilst birth rates decline. The State retains a monopoly on the placement of labour through the Federal Department of Employment and a placement service operates in larger firms. Companies do, however, publicize job vacancies in appropriate media. Methods of selection are similar to those widely practiced in the UK, including application forms, CVs and references, psychological tests and assessment centres. Significantly, recruitment and selection decisions require the agreement of works councils in companies employing more than 20 staff. Representatives need to consent to each new appointment and are permitted to see all relevant documentation such as job descriptions and application forms.

- *Training and development* – Virtually all medium- and large-sized firms in Germany participate in the country's dual system of initial vocational training. Programmes generally last for three years and combine training in firms with off-the-job instruction in vocational schools. The national apprenticeship system provides national curricula for nearly 400 vocational qualifications, but also general courses, including languages and sport.

## Germany at a glance

*Context*

- Consists of 16 federal states known as 'Bundesländer'
- Population of 8.2 million (including 7.3 million foreigners)
- One of the lowest birth rates in the world/thus 'greying' of the population
- Ranked third economy in the world (GDP over 2000bn Euro)
- Integrated into the global economy and highly dependent upon foreign trade
- Cost of living higher than the rest of EU, including a high expenditure on health
- Hourly labour costs higher than the European average. Considerable emphasis placed on skill/human resources
- Main political parties Christian Democrats (CDU), Social Democrats (SPD), Free Democrats (FDP) and the Greens (Die Grünen). Currently CDU/SPD coalition in power under the leadership of Chancellor Angela Merkel
- Core of economy in manufacturing and related services, including transportation equipment, non-electrical machinery and chemicals

*Cultural predispositions*

- Power distance – orientation towards egalitarianism
- Highly individualistic
- Relatively high masculinity
- Relatively low orientation towards uncertainty avoidance – preference for planning

*The role of HRM*

- Institutionally determined through the 'Rhineland' model
- Tends to be occupied by lawyers, economists and social scientists
- Professional association (DGFP) comprises 1,300 members
- Considerable time devoted to internal promotion, succession planning, identifying training needs, administering training programmes and work design
- Administration of legislation and collective agreements vital

*Pay*

- Industry-level agreements between employers' associations and trade unions provide for basic rates, working week, holiday entitlements, overtime, sickness and termination. Augmented at establishment/workplace level – moves towards individualized/variable/performance-related pay
- Still unequal pay on grounds of gender/ethnicity despite legislation
- No legal provision for minimum pay (although incorporated into industry agreements)

*Recruitment/staffing*

- Large/diverse labour force
- Emphasis on nurturing internal labour markets
- State involved in the placement of labour through the Federal Department of Employment
- Companies advertise jobs and use application forms, interviews, psychological tests, etc.
- Decisions require agreement of works councils in companies employing more than 20 staff

*Training*

- Virtually all medium/large firms participate in dual system of initial vocational training. Programmes generally last for three years and combine training in firms with off-the-job instructions in vocational schools. National apprenticeship system provides national curricula for nearly 400 vocational qualifications, including sport and languages.

## The effects of reunification

Following the dismantling of the Berlin Wall in November 1989 and the demise of the communist regime in the former GDR that it symbolized, optimism was felt in all walks of life, including employment. Yet, in the climate of euphoria immediately following this seismic political event, it was easy to underestimate the difficulties in reforming the former GDR economy. This was characterized by technological backwardness, productivity levels at one-third of the West, stagnation, poor infrastructure, low wages, 'brain drain' to the point of haemorrhage, chronic overstaffing and environmental pollution. In these circumstances, it was perhaps hardly surprising that the creation of the New Germany comprised, in most walks of life, a takeover of its estranged and impoverished blood relation by the powerful West. In effect, the entire West German State and constitutional system was extended into the East, including the institutional infrastructure previously described in the field of employment. Accordingly, at a stroke, taciturn trade unions in the former GDR had their independence from the State technically restored and gained freedom of association with the right to organize. Similarly, the right of 'co-determination' was extended, including the establishment of West German-style works councils at company level. Ambitiously, in March 1991, IG Metall, the engineering trade union, together with former East German managers and West German employers, agreed that harmonization of western and eastern wage levels should occur by 1994; a target that proved to be unachievable.

Turning to the personnel occupation itself, in the previous era the personnel function had concentrated on two main areas:

- *Kaderarbeit*: the selection and induction of the managerial elite. This process was influenced more by political attitudes and affiliations than by professional knowledge. Managers were also typically party officials, and personnel managers undertook surveillance activity at work on behalf of the Party.
- *Sozialpolitik*: this involved the provision of occupational health and welfare, training and education, social integration of the disadvantaged, company housing, subsidized meals, childcare, kindergarten and holiday camps. Women were encouraged to work in the communist era and so provision for equal opportunity had been relatively well established.

Following the 'turn' (as the act of reunification is colloquially described by Germans themselves), personnel management in the East found itself at the brunt of implementing highly unpopular decisions, some of which carried extreme social costs. Large-scale redundancies were inevitable, subjecting swathes of workers to the blight (and previously unknown experience) of unemployment. Power relations in industry were also restructured along more familiar western lines, effectively undermining the position of the 'glorified' worker while empowering a new managerial cadre. Finally, the new breed of personnel practitioners, along with other managerial colleagues, needed to consider how their function 'added value' to the competitive position of the enterprise, rather than merely implementing decisions flowing from their political masters. This called for a considerable shift in the managerial mindset towards strategic thinking, and suggested a pressing management development need.

## Setting up site in Germany

German borders are open to international investment and foreign-owned multinational corporations now enjoy a considerable presence on German soil. To what extent do these companies need to adapt their HR practices when operating subsidiaries? In a study of 26 US- or UK-owned subsidiaries in the banking and chemical sectors, Muller (1998) finds that a degree of latitude exists in the German system for these companies to transpose elements of HR 'best practice' as it is known in the USA or the UK. So, for example, some of the companies were able to introduce sophisticated communication methods to either supplement or even replace works councils. One held regular communication meetings during working hours and conducted regular attitude surveys. Such companies viewed works councils as being cumbersome and inhibiting change. Other foreign investors circumvented multi-employer pay bargaining and set pay above or below going rates. There was also some experimentation with performance-related pay. In the field of training and development, not all subsidiaries subscribed to the 'dual system', some preferring to recruit and dispense with staff according to company demands rather than to nurture internal labour markets.

Nevertheless, it should be pointed out that, although a number of the corporations achieved some scope for autonomous action in HRM, the major elements of the regulatory system remained in place. Significantly, US 'non-union' enterprises were bound to establish mechanisms for employee consultation when operating on German soil. In recent years, foreign direct investors; for example – General Motors in Eisenach – have found that the former GDR provides considerable institutional latitude for the implementation of flexible working practices, with a climate of new-found managerial freedom tending to breach the established consensus-oriented German approach. In the East, trade unions have less of a stronghold and works councils tend to be less potent mechanisms for employee consultation at workplace level.

There has been realization by German industrialists and politicians that the 'social market model' may be too rigid, and that expensive labour market costs need to be controlled. A major fear is that, in the era of globalization, businesses will be tempted to relocate into lower cost bases in Europe or beyond, particularly in Asia. Bosch is among the companies seeking to reap the harvests of more deregulated climes, having established productive facilities in South Wales and Spain. In this context, there are signs that a reformed 'Rhineland' model is emerging comprising the following features:

- heavier reliance on cheaper manufacturing bases, with more goods to be made outside Germany;
- greater flexibility with labour costs, work rules and social requirements;
- more diversified production to meet customer demands and less reliance on expensive, highly engineered products;
- moving into newer, higher added-value technologies.

The reformist agenda in Germany has been manifested at a political level through two significant initiatives in recent years. *Agenda 2010* was introduced in 2003 to improve economic growth and to reduce unemployment. Three main areas were to be the focus of reform: the economy, the social security system, and Germany's position in world markets. In pursuit of the agenda, steps were to be taken to reduce taxation, and to reduce the fiscal burden of health-care costs, pensions and unemployment benefits. The *Harz concept* constituted a legislative package introduced between 2003 and 2005, which provided for the creation of 'mini-jobs' (paying no more than 400 Euro per month, with no social security obligation and a flat rate tax of 25 per cent, financial aid for unemployed persons who found mini-companies (so called Ich-AGs), improved placement services and the creation of temporary work agencies to help unemployed persons and to lay off workers (relating specifically to persons over 52), reform of the benefit payment system to reduce the number of long-term unemployed, and the creation of not-for-profit jobs to supplement welfare payments (Human Resource Overview, 2006). It should be noted that such reforms have been accompanied by structural changes in Germany's system of employment relations, as considered in Chapter 6, notably the decentralization of arrangements for determination of pay and other conditions to the level of the enterprise.

Undoubtedly, the German 'social model' continues to demonstrate great durability in Germany. Yet signs of 'neo-liberalism' in HR practices are suggesting a degree of convergence with the more market-oriented systems of the USA and the UK.

---

### Activity

In small groups, formulate a political, economic, social and technological (PEST) analysis, accessing available information via web and other sources, for a US company establishing a subsidiary in Germany.

---

## European national 'clusters'

Following from the institutional analysis in Chapter 2, we should note that 'varieties of capitalism' co-exist in the continent of Europe. Accordingly, while coordinated and liberal market economies may be represented as prevalent institutional typologies, a third variant may also be identified, in which regulation is entrusted to the State, and in which, according to Van Ruysseveldt and Visser (1996: 27), 'organized interest groups are weak, unbalanced, volatile, and dominated by politics and the state'. In such economies, systems for collective bargaining are poorly institutionalized and there is a tendency towards overt and politically vehement expression of industrial conflict and protestation. The latter 'statist' paradigm may most appropriately be applied to France and also, to a lesser extent, to Italy and Spain.

In this section a series of national 'snapshots' are provided to demonstrate diversity in European institutions, cultures and organizations. The section includes representatives of various institutional typologies, including Denmark (coordinated market economy orientation), the UK (liberal market economy orientation) and France and Italy (statist orientation).

## European country 'snapshots'

## A Nordic/coordinated market economy – Denmark

*Context*

- Situated in northern Europe and one of the three Scandinavian countries.
- 5.5 million inhabitants – 4 million in urban areas.
- English almost universally spoken.
- Currency is Krona.
- Standard of living is among the highest in the world. Ranked the fifth most competitive nation worldwide by IMD (2009) world competitiveness – also highly ranked by the World Bank and Economist Intelligence Unit.
- Relatively high salaries, but also high cost of living.
- Ranked as least corrupt country in the world by Transparency International.

- Among highest educated populations in the world – 32 per cent of 24–64 year olds completing higher education compared to Organization for Economic Co-operation and Development (OECD) average of 24 per cent.
- High service orientation – 75 per cent of workers engaged in services and 25 per cent in industry.
- A strong export orientation, accounting for 20 per cent of GDP – particularly from agriculture and manufacturing.
- A strong emphasis on small- and medium-sized enterprises (SMEs) – three-quarters of firms employing less than 50 workers, including textiles and furniture industries.
- Household-name companies include Lego, Bang and Olufsen, and Carlsberg.
- The oldest kingdom in Europe, with unbroken line of kings and queens since 930s.
- Governments have mainly had minority status. Today's *Folketinget* consists of more than four parties, including Social Democrats, Social Liberal Party, Conservative Party and Socialist Workers Party.

## Culture

- Low power distance, high femininity, high individualism, low uncertainty avoidance.

## Related features

- Emphasis in informality in modes of dress and modes of interaction.
- Preference for egalitarianism.
- 'Jante Law' – 'Don't think that you are anything special or different from us'.
- 85 per cent of the population belong to the Evangelical Lutheran Church.
- Strong work ethic with emphasis on punctuality, but time made for leisure – work/life balance.
- Relatively high levels of equality between men and women – availability of lifestyle choices for women.
- Preference for airy/hygienic environments.

## Distinctive HR/employment practices

- Allocation of resources through organized negotiations between trade unions, employers associations and governments – not by individual market agents or legislation.
- Well-organized trade unions engage in centralized and firm-level bargaining over pay. Institutional isolation of industrial conflict through historical compromises for over 100 years.
- Training and educational systems negotiated at national level, offering nationally negotiated coordinated training programmes – offering skill upgrading throughout careers.
- Emphasis on longer-term growth/investment as finance capital tends to be derived from pension funds and collectively negotiated investment schemes rather than stock markets.
- Employers' organizations participate in active labour market programmes to support long-term unemployed.
- Comparative egalitarianism in payment relativities; for example, Editor 33,528 DK, Journalist 25,806 DK – difference 7452 DK (890€); Doctor 31,978 DK, Nurse 18,090 DK – difference 1334 DK (1552€).

### The concept of 'flexicurity'

■ Danish employees enjoy quite low levels of employment protection by European standards – employer's right to 'hire and fire'.

■ Generous employment policies, health insurance and other welfare benefits provide 'social safety net'.

■ Set of active labour market policies to help workers to obtain new skills and offer encouragement in locating job opportunities.

### Challenges

■ Relatively high rates of exclusion from the labour market (up to one-third), including migrant workers.

■ Relatively high mortality rates, stress-related illnesses and lifestyle problems of economically active workers supporting the welfare state.

*Sources:* Evans, P., Pucik, V. Barsoux, J.K. Engsbye, M. (2003) *Den globale udfordringrammestruktur for International Human Resource Management*, Copenhagen: Jyllands Postens Ervervsbogsklub.

Rogaczewska, A.P., Larsen, H.H. Nordhaug, Doving, E. Gjelsvik, M. (2004) 'Denmark and Norway: siblings or cousins?' in C. Brewster, W. Mayhrhofer, M. Morley (eds.) *Human Resource Management in Europe: Evidence of Convergence*, Oxford, Butterworth-Heinnemann.

Pedersen, O.K. 'The Secret Behind a Negotiated Economy' (2006) in C. MacCarthy and W. Schmidt, (eds.) *Denmark Limited – Global by Design*, Copenhagen, Gads Forlag.

## A liberal market economy – The UK

### Context

■ Includes England (50 million population), Wales (3 million), Northern Ireland (over half a million), Scotland (5 million).

■ Diverse cultural identity (including Indians, Pakistanis, Bangladeshis, Chinese, African, Arabs).

■ Fourth-largest economy in world.

■ London and New York largest financial centres.

■ 'Private enterprise' model dominant – privatization of state-owned industries during period of 'Thatcherism'.

■ Until recently, a long period of economic growth enjoyed, inflation between 2 and 3 per cent, unemployment between 4 and 5 per cent.

■ Dominant service sector, accounting for 74 per cent of GDP, strengths in financial services.

■ Political scene has been significantly dominated by Labour and Conservative parties.

■ One of the biggest donors and recipients of foreign direct investment.

■ One of the four most populated countries in the EU.

■ Parliamentary monarchy, unwritten constitution.

■ Average persons per household 2.4, 38 per cent single parent/one-person households.

## Cultural factors

■ Low power distance, high individualism, high masculinity, low uncertainty avoidance.

## Distinctive HR/employment factors

■ Key contextual factors include the decline in trade union membership (below around 30 per cent of workforce), ageing of the population, increased workforce participation of women although unequal pay still apparent, skills shortages, high levels of immigration, social disparities.

■ The HR function is a growing area of strategic significance, Chartered Institute of Personnel and Development (CIPD) is the largest professional body for HR specialists (internationally), trend has been towards 'outsourcing' HR, a major preoccupation of HR has been 'downsizing'.

■ In the field of recruitment, there has been considerable emphasis on external labour markets and little statutory influence on employer policies. 'Online' recruitment is becoming more common, as is the use of recruitment consultants.

■ There has been evidence of chronic underinvestment in training compared to European counterparts (around 3–10 per cent of annual wage bill); nevertheless, growing strategic attention has been devoted to 'softer' customer-oriented skills; senior managers receive most training.

■ Employers have considerable latitude to formulate pay policies with minimal state intervention. There has been a decline in collective bargaining and decentralization of pay determination. Hourly labour costs among lowest in Europe. Considerable disparities in pay in terms of managerial/manual divide and gender/race. Around three-quarters of organizations use variable/performance-related pay. Performance appraisal linked to pay in around one-third of organizations. Overtime accounts for around 15 per cent of gross average earnings for male manual workers.

■ Other issues/developments – long working hours persist in European terms, a significant growth/use of part-time/flexible working.

## Challenges

■ A key historical challenge has been to engender high levels of skill and employee commitment; this being linked to productivity.

*Sources*: Atterbury, S., Brewster, C., Communcaal, C., Cross, C., Gunnigle, P., Morley, M. (2004) 'The UK and Ireland: traditions and transitions in HRM' in C. Brewster, W. Mayhrhofer, M. Morley (eds.) *Human Resource Management in Europe; Evidence of Convergence*, Oxford, Butterworth-Heinneman.

EIU Country Profile (2006)_ United Kingdom.

Office for National Statistics 'Patterns of Pay; Results of the Annual Survey of Hours and Earnings, 1997 to 2006' *Economic and Labour Market Review* 1(2), February 2007.

## Employer survey highlights labour market concerns

The Confederation of British Industry's latest employment trends survey, published in September 2008, provides data on employer views and policies on a range of key industrial relations topics, including domestic and EU legislation. The survey reveals positive employer responses to developments such as the right to request flexible working and postponed retirement, but employers continue to express concern at the cumulative impact of employment regulation.

In September 2008, the Confederation of British Industry (CBI) published the results of its annual employment trends survey conducted in conjunction with the Pertemps recruitment agency. The survey, carried out in May 2008, analyses the responses of over 500 employers across all sectors of the economy, 12% of which were public sector employers. In terms of company size, 7% of respondents employed 5,000 or more staff, 32% employed 500–4,999 workers, 20% employed 200–499 workers, 25% employed 50–199 workers and 17% employed fewer than 50 staff. This article gives an overview of the report's main findings relating to industrial relations.

### Impact of employment regulation

Almost two-thirds (64%) of respondents saw the cumulative burden of employment regulation as a threat to labour market flexibility, and 67% felt it would continue to threaten flexibility and competitiveness in the future.

### Working time

Companies reported that an average of 29% of employees had signed an individual 'opt-out' from the 48-hour limit on weekly working hours, compared to 32% of staff in the 2007 survey. Employers with 50–199 employees had the largest proportion of opted-out employees (33%). However, the proportion of employees who in practice regularly worked more than 48 hours a week was lower in 2008 (11%) than in 2007 (13%). Use of the opt-out by employees varies across economic sectors and is particularly prevalent in low-paying sectors. More than half (56%) of transport employees and almost half (49%) of construction workers have signed an opt-out.

In total, 40% of employers believe that the potential withdrawal of the individual opt-out would have a significant or severe detrimental impact on their organisation.

### Temporary agency workers

Temporary agency workers constitute, on average, 3% of employers' workforces – but with some notable sectoral variation. Skilled sectors are significant users of temporary agency workers, including energy and water supply (7%), manufacturing (5%) and science, high-tech and information technology (5%).

The CBI survey showed that 70% of companies were concerned that the draft EU directive on temporary agency work – prior to revisions agreed in June 2008 – would impose increased costs and 63% believed that it would reduce flexibility. As a result, 59% of companies stated that they would reduce their use of temporary agency

▶

workers. However, the survey found that 60% of all temporary agency work assignments lasted less than three months. Most of these will be covered by the extended 12-week qualifying period for equal treatment with directly-employed staff that is currently incorporated in the draft directive.

## National minimum wage

Companies were asked about the likely impact of the GBP 5.73 (€7.36 as at 15 October 2008) national minimum wage (NMW), effective from 1 October 2008. A quarter of respondents indicated that the increase would have an impact on them – the same as for the previous year's increase. Of these workers, almost half (48%) stated that the increase would mean a basic pay rise to ensure compliance, but with no knock-on impact on differentials (down from 66% in the previous year's survey), and slightly fewer (44%) revealed that the increment would also have a knock-on impact on pay differentials further up the pay scale (up from 32% last year). Almost a third of respondents (32%) indicated that the move would lead to increased prices. Concern over the impact of the increased NMW was reported to be greatest in the hospitality sector, where 60% of companies are affected, followed by retail (52%), transport and distribution (37%) and manufacturing (32%).

## Flexible working

As in previous years, part-time work was the most common flexible working practice, used by 89% of respondents, followed by job sharing (54%), teleworking (46%), flexitime (43%), career breaks or sabbaticals (35%), term-time working (29%), annualized hours (26%) and compressed hours (21%).

With regard to the operation of the statutory right for employees to request flexible working arrangements, 95% of requests from parents had reportedly been accepted by employers – some 65% of these were accepted formally, 17% informally and 13% resulted in a compromise – while 5% of the requests were declined. A similar proportion of requests from carers for adults (96%) had reportedly been accepted by employers; of these, some 62% were accepted formally, 22% informally and 10% on a compromise basis–while 4% of requests were declined.

Almost half (47%) of the employers surveyed revealed that they offer the right to request flexible working to all employees, not just those groups covered by the statutory provisions. Some 69% of respondents indicated that the right to request flexible working arrangements had had a positive impact on employee relations, and 63% of respondents reported a positive impact on recruitment and retention. However, about one in five employers (22%) reported a negative effect on labour costs, and 15% highlighted the negative impact on productivity and customer service.

## Flexible retirement

According to the survey, almost a third (31%) of employees reaching retirement age requested the postponement of their retirement, and 81% of requests were granted by their employer. Employers offer a range of options for flexible retirement, including continuing full-time employment (71%), part-time employment (66%), receiving a pension and continuing to work (41%) and phased retirement. However, only 20% of employers allow staff to continue accruing pension benefits.

## Employment tribunal cases

Nearly two-fifths (39%) of employers had faced an employment tribunal (ET) claim in the last year. In 29% of cases, ET claims were subsequently withdrawn by the applicant. Over a quarter of cases (26%) were reportedly settled 'out of court' by employers despite legal advice that the tribunal would rule in their favour, and 23% were settled after advice that the company was unlikely to win. Less than a fifth (17%) of cases went to an ET hearing and were won by the employer. Only 3% were fought by employers at a hearing and lost.

Close to half of respondents (44%) believed that weak and vexatious claims had increased over the past year, while 47% reported no change and 9% reported a decline in such claims.

## Working with trade unions

Some 38% of respondents recognized trade unions for collective bargaining. Respondents were asked what they thought were the main reasons for the decline of trade unions in private sector workplaces. Almost half of respondents (45%) chose 'resistance to change', 28% felt that trade unions were 'out of touch with the workforce', 12% attributed the decline to 'globalization' and 17% to unions being too 'confrontational'.

Asked about their expectations in respect of their relationships with trade unions over the next 12 months, employers were broadly neutral. Almost half of respondents (49%) expected a 'balanced' relationship with both national officials and workplace union representatives. The latter were seen as more likely (37%) to be 'cooperative' than were national officials (29%) and less likely to be 'adversarial' (15% and 22%, respectively). More employers (29%) expected adversarial relationships with local union officials.

## Workforce diversity

Some 43% of employers responding to the survey reported having a formal diversity policy, while 19% had no formal diversity policy but did have equality practices in place. A quarter of employers surveyed reported that they had taken positive action in relation to, for example, recruitment, advertising and training, to achieve a more diverse workforce; 19% had an action plan on diversity and monitored progress. Larger companies were more likely to report formal diversity policies and to take positive action than smaller ones.

About three-fifths of respondents (59%) reported that the main obstacle to achieving a more diverse workforce was a lack of applicants from among disadvantaged groups, and 18% cited the 'lack of a clear business case' for diversity.

## Equal pay audits

Almost a third (32%) of employers surveyed had conducted an equal pay audit in the past three years (compared to 28% in 2007), 9% of respondents planned to do so in the next year and 26% were considering conducting one but had not yet drawn up any firm plans. As in 2007, at least a third of employers had 'never considered conducting an equal pay audit'. Large employers with 5,000 or more employees were more likely, at 55% (up from 46% in 2007), to have conducted an equal pay audit than smaller companies.

## Commentary

The CBI's employment trends survey, now in its eleventh year, provides an annual barometer of current employment practices among UK companies and of managerial opinion on key policy issues. Notable aspects of the survey include the reported increase in companies undertaking equal pay audits, the incidence of flexible retirement and the finding that most temporary agency work assignments in the UK will be unaffected by the draft EU agency workers directive now that the legislation includes a 12-week qualifying period. However, as the Trades Union Congress (TUC) pointed out in a press statement, the survey is not representative of all UK companies. Most respondents were from large and medium-sized companies whereas the majority of UK businesses employ fewer than 50 staff. The TUC commented: 'This is a survey of Britain's better employers and therefore looks through rose-tinted glasses at today's world of work.' In September 2008, the TUC published its own survey of what UK workers think about their experience of work. This found that, while most workers were generally satisfied with their jobs, substantial minorities reported problems relating to pay, workloads, stress and working hours.

*Source*: Eurofound–Eironline (2008). Reproduced with permission from Eurofound–Eironline.

## Mediterranean/'statist'-influenced economies: France and Italy

## France

*Context*

- President Nicolas Sarkozy (Leader of French Conservative Party, UMP) – established cross-party 'slimline' government, including nearly half female representatives – a reformist agenda adopted – holds executive power with Prime Minister Francois Fillon
- France possesses a mixed cultural identity and is a colonial power
- A pivotal EU member
- Population of 60 million
- Economy fifth-largest in the world
- 70% of trading with European partners
- Previous manufacturing orientation now reversed – the vast majority of jobs now in service sector – leading agricultural producer in EU
- Relatively high cost of living
- Government ownership of railway, electricity, aircraft, telecommunications
- Labour force highly productive, yet relatively high rates of unemployment – major skills in machinery, vehicles, chemicals, plastic, aircraft manufacture

- 35-hour week adopted in 2000
- Two-thirds of women now employed but largest gender pay gap amongst European neighbours
- Around 10% of workforce are immigrants
- Average retirement age under 60
- Problem of ageing population
- Public sector highly unionized
- 6% of population live below poverty line
- Most visited country in the world

### Culture

- Rich culture – strong sense of national identity
- In Hofstedian terms, high power distance, relatively high on femininity, high uncertainty avoidance, relatively high on individualism

### HR factors

- High incidence of HR representation on company boards
- Oral tradition of policy making
- Hierarchical mode of managing and communicating
- Written documentation often preferred to e-mail

### Employment relations

- Traditionally low membership, although agreements made by unions and employers extended to non-union members
- Trade union functions carries out by national welfare system
- Works councils, workplace health and safety committees, workforce and trade union delegates established and supported by law
- Compulsory collective bargaining each year over wages and working time
- Only agreements with representative unions are legally effective – CFTC, CGT, CFDT, FO and CG

### Recruitment

- Internal systems used for senior and middle managers
- Grandes écoles provide for highly skilled junior managers – engineering and business schools
- Emphasis on application forms, one to one interviews, some use of graphology and references

### Pay

- Legislation supplemented by regional collective bargaining; adjustments may be made at company/establishment level
- Extensive welfare system covering health insurance and unemployment
- Wage individualization becoming more common

## Training

- Professional training in France highly regulated by legislation
- Statutory obligation of employers of more than ten employees to devote at least 1.5% of wage bill to company training system
- Companies need to provide a 'training plan' and individuals possess a 'right to training'
- Many companies exceed basic requirements

## Other HR issues

- The need to make training 'portable' from company to company
- Moves towards 'flexibility' in traditional forms of work – particularly towards part-time work
- Dealing with unemployment/marginalized parts of the labour force

*Source*: Buyens et. al. (2004).

# Italy

## Context

- History of coalition governments. Crisis in January 2008 after Prime Minister Romano Prodi lost confidence vote. Centre Right returned to power under Silvio Berlusconi
- Less homogenous than other European nations – re-unified in 1971
- Latin and Catholic traditions
- Economic and social divisions between entrepreneurial North and agricultural South. Lombardia second-richest region in EU in terms of per capita income. 35% youth unemployment in South and 20% total unemployment
- High population density – 57 million inhabitants
- High unemployment compared to EU neighbours, particularly female unemployment
- 3.2 average number of people per household
- High life expectancy – 76.1 for men, 82.6 for women
- GDP tends to lag EU partners tenth-largest economy in the world
- Major trading partners Germany, France, UK, Spain and US
- Similar per capita output to France and UK
- Tight fiscal policy in recent years – country has benefited from lower interest and inflation rates – public debt reduced but structural reforms still needed – high tax burdens and labour market rigidities
- Massive programme of privatization over past 15 years, including banks, telecom, motorways, etc.
- Large public sector – health care, childcare, education – although modest influence of commercial forces in recent years
- 234 million in employment – majority of jobs in service sector – 32% in public sector
- Relatively low average labour costs – high levels of manual and technical skills
- A high proportion of small- and medium-sized enterprises (SMEs) – usually organized around larger local enterprise
- Prices close to EU average – very high cost of water, electricity, health care and housing
- Generous pension scheme – allowing retirement at 55/56 – structural reform being considered

### Culture

- Rich cultural traditions – strong Italian identity – quality of life orientation
- In Hofstedian terms – relatively high power distance, relatively high individualism – also communitarianism, relatively high masculinity and uncertainty avoidance
- 'High context' tendencies – importance of blood relations and extended family

### Business system

- Tradition of small, family-owned, entrepreneurial companies managed by patriarchal families. Reform in this area due to global influences, consultants' advice, new generation. Large companies, e.g. Fiat, have also been subject to family control
- Large public sector also subject to modernization

### HR policies and practices

- A small majority of companies have HR representation on the board of directors
- Significant trade union involvement in employment policy formulation – now decreasing
- The need for modernization and reform generally recognized, particularly concerning employee flexibility and commitment

### Recruitment and selection

- Mutual responsibility of HR and line managers
- Emphasis on internal recruitment of managers
- Loyalty and reliability recognized
- Standard recruitment methods common – particularly one to one interviews – some evidence of informality, oral traditions, nepotism

### Pay

- Centralized influence of national trade union confederations in industrial/sector-level pay determination
- Minimum rates and other conditions established by law
- Government also involved at central level – agreements extended to non-union members
- Enhancements made at company level – also work/life balance issues considered and moves towards variable/performance-related pay
- Pay higher in public than in private sector – low skilled workers earn more in public sector, high skilled more in private sector

### Training and development

- 'Learning organisation' concept popular
- Around 1% of average salaries spent on training
- Actual training provision lagging behind European neighbours
- Recent increases in training for manual staff
- Performance appraisal widespread, although some scepticism as to its utility

### Other HR considerations

■ Little movement towards participative management, management by objectives, etc. Managerial patronage still common

■ Flexible work patterns not widespread, although some growth in part-time working

*Source*: Papalexandris and Gjelsvik (2004).

In the final part of this chapter, the focus is placed on the transitional economies in Central and Eastern Europe, which may be characterized as 'post-socialist' while manifesting neo-liberal tendencies.

## HRM and eastern Europe

## Introduction

Definitions of Central and Eastern Europe (CEE) may vary but typically include the Czech Republic, Slovakia, Hungary, Poland, Albania, Bulgaria, Romania and the countries constituting the former Yugoslavia, as well as the former German Democratic Republic (GDR). Soviet influence was pervasive in the post-war economic development of these countries, which occurred along the lines of the 'command economy' (Turnock, 1997). Important features of this came to include the introduction of five-year plans that provided for growth and structural change, also ensuring that industrial projects were supported by the necessary buildings, raw materials and labour (Wilczynski, 1977). Provision for international trade occurred through the Council for Mutual Economic Aid (CMEA or COMECON), whose members were the USSR, Bulgaria, Czechoslovakia, Hungary, Poland, Romania, the GDR, Mongolia and Vietnam, with Albania withdrawing in 1981. A founding purpose of COMECON was to deliver a Soviet-oriented economic bloc but which, nevertheless, retained national economic divisions and regional specialization. For industrial organizations, prominent features were 'gigantomania' or a preference for large, centrally-planned concerns, high levels of monopolization, the technical provision of full employment, and the existence of politically reliable management. A broad distinction has been drawn between the 'northern' East European countries, comprising the Czech Republic, the former GDR, Hungary and Poland, and the 'southern' region, which includes Albania, Bulgaria, Romania, Bosnia-Herzegovina, Croatia, Macedonia, Slovenia and Serbia. It may be argued that the northern region has achieved more advanced economic development, these countries tending to constitute the 'first wave' of EU accession countries in 2004.

As a number of the former 'iron curtain' countries are now members of the EU (Bulgaria, Czech Republic, Estonia, Hungary, Latvia, Lithuania, Poland, Romania, Slovakia, Slovenia), it is tempting to conclude that the transition of Central and Eastern Europe from planned to market economies has run its course. Closer scrutiny of the post-socialist societies in Europe would reveal, however, that it is premature to suggest that free market orientation has 'triumphed' in the region as political structures remain in a state of institutional flux, and significant social fragmentation has occurred, leaving the 'losers' in transition with a sense of nostalgia for the previous communist era (Verdery, 1996). In this section the nuances of the transformation process are considered, as are emerging HRM challenges.

The study of HRM in CEE is at a formative stage, yet a number of trajectories can currently be discerned. Morley et al. (2009) note that HRM issues have inevitably been associated with the context of economic transition and radical transformation (e.g. Meardi, 2006; Tung and Lazarova, 2006) and the employment effects of moving from centralized planning systems associated with state-owned industries to privatized enterprise structures. A second strand of study, notably Soulsby and Clark (2006), has questioned the dominance placed on macro-level change in the CEE region , and has encouraged a shifting of focus to the level of the enterprise, and the socially embedded behaviours of managerial and other actors at workplace level. Such an approach would imply that the emergent study of HRM in CEE should account for humanistic, as well as institutional, considerations.

As a number of CEE countries have joined the EU, academic attention has shifted to the convergence of employment/HR practices in eastern and western enterprises (Cyr and Svcheider, 1996 Mia and Suutari, 2004). In the context of the increase in West–East joint ventures, attention has also been given to international staff mobility and knowledge diffusion. Convergence of HR paradigms across West and East has also been prompted by the extension of EU equal opportunities legislation to post-socialist members, although the enforcement of laws designed to counter discrimination in the East, including the use of child labour, remains variable (Morley et al., 2009).

## Challenges for the management of people

During the socialist period, the role of personnel management and priority areas in terms of policy and practice were conditioned by the prevailing political, economic and ideological climate. In the context of centralized power structures and planned approaches to economic management, the personnel role was predominantly an administrative one, as decisions on key areas such as staffing and pay were taken by central authorities. At least part of the personnel role also involved the monitoring of communist party allegiance. Typically, personnel administration would be subdivided into separate departments: labour and wages, training and development, administrative services and records, employee care and benefits administration, and health and safety. The ideological imperative of maintaining full employment, implemented by the central authorities, had a number of manifestations. Recruitment at an organisational level was rendered superfluous, as were constraints on dismissing staff. These bolstered worker power at establishment level and the sanctions that accompany western patterns of managerial control were absent. The system whereby jobs were found for people, rather than people finding jobs, clearly had a detrimental effect on labour productivity. Although skill was an important factor in promotion, party allegiance had an important bearing on individual career progression and support through training provision. In the absence of legitimate conflicting interest groups within organizations, the role of union representatives was confined largely to dealing with individual grievances and welfare matters. Enterprises themselves, in a paternalistic fashion, catered for many aspects of workers' lives beyond the immediate sphere of their employment, from housing provision to childcare (see the 'Eden Weisser case study' in Chapter 3).

In the post-communist era, the activities of personnel management cannot be isolated from broader societal influences. A 'shock therapy' taken towards privatization of the state sectors in a number of CEE economies has been associated with radical downsizing programmes, associated high levels of unemployment, the growth of the informal economy, and a polarization of economic fortunes at work and in society (Stiglitz, 2002). The stigma of unemployment is exacerbated by the societal value that construed the lack of a job as 'parasitism'. The position of female employees has also become more precarious with the withdrawal of state facilities designed by the communist regime to force women into the labour market. Yet, in general, the labour force in CEE is a highly skilled one and the downward pressure of high unemployment on wage levels means that there is a strong incentive for MNCs wishing to set up 'greenfield' sites or operate joint ventures. In such concerns, new and flexible working practices may be introduced with workforce compliance.

It is evident, then, that a range of challenges confront newly professionalizing HR managers who, for example, in the Czech Republic and Bulgaria are forming specialist clubs or associations. First, in the new competitive climate, there is a growing need for effective management of staff engagement and deployment and for measures to appraise staff performance. The need to motivate employees while controlling labour costs is promoting variability of pay for individuals and differentiation of reward within enterprises. Deregulation of labour markets is stimulating mobility of staff between enterprises, as well as the growth of more flexible forms of labour utilization, including part-time work. The pace of change in CEE has created significant training and development needs. Managers themselves need to be equipped in psychological and technical senses to operate in competitive environments, with a paramount need to engage in strategic thinking (Hollinshead and Michailova, 2001). The EU-sponsored PHARE programme has engaged in the transfer of managerial knowledge from 'west' to 'east', as part of a general 'institution-building' initiative, to bolster the aptitudes of post-socialist managerial groupings (ibid.).

For workers, similar problems of adjustment should not be underestimated, as well as the need for practical skills development to deal with changing working practices and technological developments. The influx of foreign-owned concerns is leading to 'internationalization' of HR practice, associated with radical change from secure and rigid organizational administration of employment towards 'neo-liberal'-inspired managerial approaches. This includes the diffusion of modern 'western' techniques and technologies, such as 'high-performance' workplaces and just-in-time production. Frequently, such developments occur in non-union environments. In benchmarking performance of international subsidiaries, operations in CEE are increasingly setting the standards for cost-effectiveness. Where collective bargaining is a predominant method of determining pay and conditions, trade union representatives as well as HR practitioners are experiencing a 'learning curve' in negotiating pay through self-determining means rather than having it imposed by the State.

---

### Activity

In small groups, identify the major challenges confronting HR managers in a post-socialist country of your choice, as that country is exposed to international competitive pressures.

## Summary

This chapter has explored the relatively highly regulated context for HR policy and practice in Europe. Placing a focus on the 'Rhineland' model, it has explored manifestations of HRM in Europe's leading economy, as well as pressures for reform in the face of global competition. It has also revealed considerable diversity in national contexts and business/HR systems. Study of HR challenges in the transitional economies of eastern Europe reveals that the region remains one of considerable diversity, ambiguity and dynamism.

## Further reading

**Brewster, C., Mayhrofer, W. and Morley, M.** (eds) (2004) *Human Resource Management in Europe: Evidence of Convergence*, Oxford: Butterworth-Heinemann.

This edited book is based on the data derived from CRANET-E – the world's largest longitudinal and comparative HRM survey. Invaluable and empirically informed insights are provided into distinctive HR policies and practices in a range of European national contexts, implying the need for strategic adaptation for companies operating across European regions. The book also provides a theoretical introduction to the meaning and applicability of the concept of HRM in Europe, and considers whether divergence or convergence is occurring in observed manifestations of employment and organizational practice.

**Holt Larsen, H. and Mayhrofer, W.** (eds) (2006) *Managing Human Resources in Europe*, London and New York: Routledge.

Analysis is provided of contemporary themes in HRM in Europe supported by national examples and case study materials. Examples of topics for analysis are the EU and HRM, 'flexicurity', European employment relations and multinational corporations. A broad view is taken of international organizations in Europe, including small- and medium-sized enterprises and not-for-profit organizations.

**Morley, M., Herarty, N. and Michailova, S.** (eds) (2009) *Managing Human Resources in Central and Eastern Europe*, London and New York: Routledge.

This text investigates the transitional context for HRM in the 'post-socialist' European region. Key legislative and labour market reforms are investigated, as well as key trends in HRM policy and practice. Country-by-country analysis embraces Estonia, Lithuania, Poland, the Czech Republic, Slovakia, Hungary, Slovenia, Bulgaria and Russia.

## Useful websites

www.eurofound.europa.eu/eiro/2008/country/germany.htm
Sector-specific and contemporary developments in German employment relations and related matters are provided.

www.europa.eu/lisbon_treaty/index_en.htm
A detailed exposition of the Lisbon Treaty and related national issues.

www.europa.eu/pol/socio/index_en.htm
The various areas of EU social policy are presented, with links to summaries of legislation and policy in areas such as equal opportunities, health and safety at work, free movement, job creation and social dialogue.

## References

**Albert, M.** (1991) *Capitalisme Contre Capitalisme*, Paris: editions de Seuil.

**Atterbury, S., Brewster, C., Communal, C., Cross, C., Gunnigle, P. and Morley, M.** (2004) The UK and Ireland: traditions and transitions in HRM, in C. Brewster, W. Mayhrhofer and M. Morley (eds) *Human Resource Management in Europe: Evidence of Convergence*, Oxford: Butterworth-Heinemann.

**Brewster, C., Mayhrofer, W. and Morley, M.** (**eds**) (2004) *Human Resource Management in Europe: Evidence of Convergence?*, Oxford: Butterworth-Heinnemann.

**Buyens, D., Dany, F., Dewettinck, K. and Quinadin, B.** (2004) France and Belgium: language, culture and differences in HR practices, in C. Brewster, W. Mayhrhofer, M. and Morley (eds) *Human Resource Management in Europe: Evidence of Convergence*, Oxford: Butterworth-Heinemann.

**Communal, C. and Brewster, C.** (2004) HRM in Europe, in A.W. Harzing and J.Van Ruysseveldt (eds) *International Human Resource Management* (2nd edn.), London: Sage Publications.

**Cyr, D.J. and Scheider, S.C.** (1996) Implications for learning: human resource management in East–West joint ventures, *Organization Studies*, 17(2): 207–226.

**Dewetttinck, K., Buyens, D., Auger, C., Dany, F. and Wilthagen, T.** (2006) Deregulation: HRM and the flexibility–security nexus, in H. Holt Larsen and W. Mayhrofer (eds) *Managing Human Resources in Europe*, London and New York: Routledge.

**EIU Country Profile** (2006) United Kingdom.

**El Kahal, S.** (1998) *Business in Europe*, Maidenhead: McGraw-Hill.

**Eurofound–Eironline** (2008) Employer survey highlights market concerns, Mark Hall, IRRU, Warwick, 24 November.

**Europa/EU** (2008) Press release memo/07/256, 27 June, Brussels: Bevan Foundation.

**Evans, P., Pucik, V., Barsoux, J.L. and Engsbye, M.** (2003) *Den globale udfordring-rammestruktur for International Human Resource Management,* Copenhagen: Jyllands Postens Ervervsbogsklub.

**Gooderham, P., Morley, M., Brewster, C. and Mayfhofer, W.** (2004) Human resource management: a universal concept?, in C. Brewster, W. Mayhrofer and M. Morley (eds) *Human Resource Management in Europe: Evidence of Convergence?,* Oxford: Butterworth-Heinemann.

**Holden, L.** (1997) Human resource management in Europe, in I. Beardwell and L. Holden (eds) *Human Resource Management: A Contemporary Perspective,* London: Pitman Publishing.

**Hollinshead, G. and Michailova, S.** (2001) Blockbusters or bridge-builders? The role of western trainers in developing new entrepreneurialism in eastern Europe,' *Management Learning,* 32(4): 419–436.

**Human Resource Overview** (2006) Country Commerce Report, Germany.

**IMD World Competitive Yearbook** (2009).

**McIlroy, J.** (1995) *Trade Unions in Britain Today* (2nd edn.), Manchester: Manchester University Press.

**Meardi, G.** (2006) Multinationals' heaven? Worker responses to multinational companies in eastern Europe, *International Journal of Human Resource Management,* 17(8): 1366–78.

**Mia, E. and Suutari, V.** (2004) HRM in foreign affiliates: a multiple case study among Estonian affiliates of Finnish companies, *Journal for East European Management Studies,* 9(4): 345–366.

**Morley, H., Heraty, N. and Michailova, S. (eds)** (2009) *Managing Human Resources in Central and Eastern Europe,* Oxford and New York: Routledge.

**Muller M.** (1998) Human resource and industrial relations practices of UK and US multinationals in Germany, *International Journal of Human Resource Management,* 9: 4.

**Office for National Statistics** (2007) Patterns of pay: results of the annual survey of hours and earnings, 1997 to 2006, *Economic and Labour Market Review,* 1(2): 25–31.

**Papalexandris, N. and Gjelsvik, E.** (2004) Italy, Greece and Cyprus, HRM in the south eastern Mediterranean corner of the EU, in C. Brewster, W. Mayhrofer and M. Morley (eds) *Human Resource Management in Europe: Evidence of Convergence,* Oxford: Butterworth-Heinemann.

**Pedersen, O.K.** (2006) The secret behind a negotiated economy, in C. MacCarthy and W. Schmidt (eds) *Denmark Limited: Global by Design,* Copenhagen: Gads Forlag.

**Rogaczewska, A.P., Larsen, H.H., Nordhaug, O., Doving, E. and Gjelsvik, M.** (2004) Denmark and Norway: siblings or cousins?, in C. Brewster, W. Mayhrofer and M. Morley (eds) *Human Resource Management in Europe: Evidence of Convergence,* Oxford: Butterworth-Heinemann.

**Sapir, A.** (2005) Globalisation and the reform of European social models, *Bruegel Policy Brief,* Brussels.

**Soulsby, A. and Clark, E.** (2006) Changing patterns of employment in post-socialist organizations in Central and Eastern Europe: management action in a transitional context, *International Journal of Human Resource Management,* 17(8): 1398–1410.

**Stiglitz, J.E.** (2002) *Globalisation and its Discontents,* London: Penguin Politics.

**Streeck, W.** (1992) *Social Institutions and Economic Performance: Studies of Industrial Relations in Advanced Capitalist Economies,* London: Sage Publications.

**Tung, R.L. and Lazarova, M.** (2006) Brain drain versus brain gain: an exploratory study of ex-host country nationals in Central and Eastern Europe, *International Journal of Human Resource Management,* 17(11): 1853–1872.

**Turnock, D.** (1997) *The East European Economy in Context: Communism and Transition,* London and New York: Routledge.

**Van Ruysseveldt, J. and Visser, J.** (1996) *Industrial Relations in Europe: Traditions and Transitions,* London, Thousand Oaks and New Delhi: Sage Publications.

**Verdery, K.** (1996) *What was Socialism and What Comes Next?,* Princeton, NJ: Princeton University Press.

**Wachter, H. and Stengelhofen, T.** (1995) *Germany,* in I. Brunstein (ed.) *Human Resource Management in Western Europe,* Berlin and New York: de Gruyter.

**Wilczynski, J.** (1977) *The Economics of Socialism,* London: Allen & Unwin.

# CHAPTER 09

# Human resource management in East Asia

## ❖ LEARNING OBJECTIVES

- ❖ To expose the distinctive cultural and institutional features of Human Resource Management (HRM) in East Asia

- ❖ To identify essential features of working/HRM practices in Japan

- ❖ To investigate contexts and practices relating to HRM in China, and to consider problems and issues in establishing a joint venture in the region

## Introduction

Over the past 40 years, East Asia has enjoyed rapid economic development. In the 1980s and early 1990s, Japan was regarded as a 'miracle' economy on the global stage and, more recently, China has emerged as a potential superpower. As Zhu and Warner (2004) explain, economic success in the region has often been explained in culturalist terms, notably through Confucian and Daoist teachings, and the influence of *Bing Fa*, or war strategies.

According to Zhu and Warner (pp. 199–200), such philosophies have impacted on HRM in East Asia in the following ways:

- The establishment of the fundamental version of *ren* (heartedness/benevolence) within the organization. Under such influence, the concept of 'workplace is family' is widespread amongst Chinese organizations. It requires organization/management to look after the interests of fellow employees, while employees have high commitment to the organization, and is reflected in practices such as job security and self-discipline.

- Collectivism and interdependent relational value. It is a well-defined principle within Confucianism that an individual is not an isolated entity. Therefore, the concept of family life as the basic in the society is emulated in the work setting, as are the broader societal values that ensure that social harmony and behavioural ritual are preserved (Scarborough, 1998; Whiteley et al., 2000; Yao, 1998). HRM practices such as team work, sharing values and information, and group-oriented incentive schemes are based on the foundation of collectivism.

- The doctrine of harmony and the balance between *yin* and *yang*: the effort to achieve harmonization of the workplace and maintain a dynamic reversion that perpetually counterbalances all propensities towards one extreme or the other puts the organization in a stable and sustained position. The concept of *yin* and *yang* provides a mindset for coping with the environment in an adaptive and flexible way.

- *Bing Fa* and the philosophy of war strategy leads to strategic thinking and strategic management: the ever-changing nature of internal and external factors forces human beings to adopt strategic thinking in order to survive in the short and long term. The outcome of combining different philosophies such as *Bing Fa* provides the general guidance for strategic thinking that helps organizations to form business strategies.

- The virtues and qualities of leadership emphasized by Confucianism have been adopted by current management thinking in the area of leadership: managerial leadership requires the qualities of wisdom, trust, sincerity, benevolence, courage and strictness to carry out policies (Chu, 1995). If managers lack these qualities, they will experience a shortage of support from employees, and the consequence will be low productivity and discontent.

## HRM in Japan

### Contextual and cultural factors

Japan is highly industrialized, a free market economy and the world's third largest economy by purchasing power parity. After the Second World War, Japanese economic policies were influenced by Marxist ideas and US regulations. Between the 1960s and 1990s, the Japanese economy experienced an unprecedented boom, catalysed by factors including increased public spending, loyal and highly skilled workers and the protection of the Japanese 'island' economy from foreign competitors. Major industries in Japan include banking, insurance, real estate, retailing, transportation, construction and telecommunications. The country is also home to leading multinational corporations (MNCs), particularly in the technology and machinery industries. Japan has been particularly affected by the 'demographic time bomb'; around 13 per cent of its population being under 15 years of age, 65 per cent between 15 and 64 years and 21 per cent being 65 or over (Japan in Figures, 2007).

Japan may be categorized as a constitutional monarchy. Since the emperor has no governmental power, Japan is led by the Prime Minister, who is elected by the two chambers of the Japanese Parliament and the Cabinet of Ministers. The Japanese Parliament (Diet) is divided into two chambers: the House of Representatives (lower house) and the House of Councillors (upper house).

In keeping with Confucian philosophy, which emphasizes the five virtues of mutual love, virtuousness, consciousness, honesty and reciprocation, group belonging is a primary facet of Japanese society. Emotional self-control, or *enryo,* refers to the tendency to refrain from expressing opinions that contradict the majority. The belief in group behaviour and interpersonal harmony is also reflected in *nemawashi* (consensus building) and *ringi* (shared decision making). Schneider and Silverman (2000) emphasize the division of Japanese values into 'material' and 'non-material', the latter including values, beliefs, language and symbols.

## Core cultural concepts in Japan

These five cultural concepts have strong implications for how Japanese companies do business. Nevertheless, the cultural patterns found in particular industries, regions, economic classes and corporations themselves vary substantially. Preferred cultural practices have also changed in response to globalization and the economic downturn in the 1990s.

## Core concepts: relationships

### Cultivating long-term relationships

- Other-centred, work-centred (rather than me-centred)
- Lifelong relationships are a person's main resource – inter-dependence and reciprocity
- Benefits: loyalty, security, belonging, being cared for. Drawbacks: onerous obligations and social constraints
- Pressure to blend in, harmonize, cooperate and conform
- Ethics based on relationship and context rather than fixed principles
- Attentive to the nuances of the situation, subtle cues, accommodating the needs and views of others

### Knowing one's place: role and rank

- Every person is either senior or junior
- Language and interaction always reflect relative rank
- A mature person fulfils role faithfully: sincerity, respect, training, character, self-control
- The polite fiction 'I am humble, you are honoured' is the fundamental message behind polite language and etiquette
- It is important to know when to reveal *honne* (one's true feeling or opinion) and when to maintain *tatemae* (one's role – appropriate face to the world)

### Keeping face

- Appearances matter greatly
- Lifelong relationships require careful maintenance – no option to 'move on'
- Fear of standing out, not fitting in, being laughed at or scolded
- Your reputation affects the reputation of your family and colleagues
- Difficult issues are communicated through indirect, non-verbal subtext – it is easier to deny or shift direction
- People give each other private space (physical distance from gaze and touch, home space), which makes it easier to maintain public face

▶

*Following form*

- There is a correct way to do almost everything
- There is a correct phrase or thought to convey for many situations
- How work is done often matters more than what is accomplished
- Practise the form and understanding will eventually come

*Working, diligence and details*

- The appearance of diligence requires a serious facial expression, alert body posture, no evidence of own needs or reactions
- Patient thoroughness, especially in preparation, is valued over speed or creativity
- Put in long hours
- Focus on work content – little 'small talk'
- Thorough documentation allows context to speak for itself – avoids participants appearing confrontational or opinionated

*Source*: Adapted from Beer (1997–2003).

## The Japanese business system

These cultural predispositions correspond with Whitley's (2002) institutional framing of the 'highly coordinated' business system that epitomized Japan, involving high levels of employer–employee interdependence and the incorporation of the workforce into the enterprise. A distinctive institutional feature of Japanese organizational life is the *keiretsu*, which represents a large, integrated group of companies cooperating and working closely with each other to provide goods and services to end users. Members may be bound together by cross-ownership, long-term business dealings, interlocking directorates and social ties (Hodgetts and Luthans, 2003: 320).

Keiretsus have been defined as being either *horizontal*, that is, comprising networks of related producers or service providers, or *vertical*, that is, the integration of members of the supply chain and buyers into a network fostered by the 'mother' company – although this dichotomy has been argued to be rather over simplified in practice, as companies have straddled both categories (McGuire and Dow, 2009). The Japanese economy has been dominated by six major horizontal *keiretsus*, three of which (Mitsui, Mitsubishi and Sumitomo) are descendants of pre-war *zaibatsu* originating from feudal social bonds. The three others (Dai Ichi Kango, Fuyo and Sanyo) have developed around major banks during the post-war period (ibid.). In 2000, Sumitomo and Mitsui merged to become the Sumitomo Mitsui Banking Corporation and, in 2001, Sanwa was incorporated into the Bank of Tokyo Mitsubishi group. The number of horizontally-based *keiretsu* therefore now stands at four. As MacGuire and Dow (2009) assert, there are four interrelated benefits of membership of this form of *keiretsu*: (1) access to stable financing (as banks may be part of the grouping); (2) insulation from market pressures (as stronger members will sustain weaker counterparts during market or economic downturns); (3) risk reduction (as a result of risk sharing among members); and (4) mutual assistance.

Vertical *keiretsu* have been particularly evident in automobile manufacturing, for example those centring on Toyota and Honda. Vertical groupings emerged during the 1950s, enabling

Japanese firms to expand production in a context of scarce financing. In such *keiretsus* ,core firms possess a relatively high degree of equity holding in affiliates, this being consistent with high levels of control of the latter by the former, fostering longer-term contracts and the encouragement of suppliers to work towards high quality and low cost (ibid.). The arrangement also creates more binding relationships between core companies and affiliates whose supplies are critical to the firm (Ahmadjian, 1997). From the point of view of suppliers, *keiretsu* membership offers a stable market for their products, offers the possibility of technical, managerial or financial assistance from core companies, and it may encourage innovation (Suzuki, 1993).

## The 'pillars' of Japanese employment

Within the prevailing institutional and cultural context, primary features of the Japanese employment system were heralded for the achievement of Japanese 'miracle' economic status in the 1970s and 1980s, followed by a serious downturn in the 1990s. As Hollinshead and Leat (1995) describe, until the beginning of the First World War, there was a fluid labour market in Japan. It was recognized that excessive labour mobility could be at the expense of national competitiveness and so a dual structure was established. Core employees, concentrated in *keiretsu,* were assumed to have lifetime employment and were surrounded by more malleable and dispensable, peripheral employment in satellite firms or subcontractors. In general, female workers have found themselves in the periphery. Labour mobility in *keiretsu* occurs within the parameters of the corporate structure, and three principal elements characterize the Japanese employment system:

- *Lifetime employment*: those in the core labour force are assumed to stay with the same employer for their working lives; a strong emphasis being placed on internal labour markets.
- *Seniority-based wage system*: incremental pay according to time served.
- *Enterprise unionism*: collaborative relations without external interference between management and union representatives.

Primary features of Japanese HRM are as follows.

### Recruitment

- Selection is vital as the expectation is that core employees will remain until retirement. Major companies recruit directly from educational establishments.
- Careful screening ensures that candidates endorse company values. Entrance ceremonies may involve extensive induction programmes, including team activities.

### Remuneration

- Many Japanese companies have seniority-based wage systems. This encourages employees to stay with companies and contributes towards predictability in wage costs.
- A range of other benefits is frequently available to core employees, which may include subsidized housing, holiday homes, company schools and shops, assistance in cases of accidents and death.

### Training and development

■ The assumption of lifetime employment is positive as far as training is concerned. A view of employees as assets, rather than costs, means that employers are willing to train and develop human resources at their own expense. There is collaboration between schools/universities and companies, and the education system incorporates a strong vocational orientation. General disciplines incorporate the philosophy of the 'company man'.

■ A major aim of training and development under the internal labour market is to provide employees who are readily transferable between jobs. Multi-skilling is therefore a fundamental ingredient of training programmes and job rotation a prerequisite for promotion.

### Other important HRM features

■ Just-in-time production is a group of related practices aimed at ensuring that the exact quantity and quality of raw materials, parts and subassemblies are delivered 'just-in-time' for the next stage of the production process, which relieves the accumulation of idle stock.

■ The concept of 'internal customers' is applied to those at progressive stages of the production process.

■ Flexible and responsive forms of work organization are based on the pivotal concept of the team, or cellular work group, as an adjunct of just-in-time.

■ There is a high incidence of 'face-to-face' communications and an absence of visible hierarchy. In theory, communications are on an equal basis. Managers spend considerable time on the shop floor, and there is an emphasis on open planning in offices and the shop floor.

■ Quality circles have been common, in which small groups of workers 'brainstorm' ideas for improving quality and productivity in their work areas. Such suggestions may then be taken up by management.

■ The *ringi* system of decision making involves large-sized company boards, frequently comprising seniority-based (male) employees, officially approving corporate decisions so they gain the fullest possible approval.

■ *Kaizen*, or continuous improvement, is emphasized, in which all staff constantly consider methods of improving quality and efficiency.

---

**A typical career path for a salaryman**

This 'ideal' is now fracturing under the pressures of Japan's recession, but is still the model for managerial workers.

1 **Companies hire once a year and once a lifetime.** During the recruitment season, companies select from the current year's 'crop' of graduates. Teachers, friends and other connections will assist in finding prospective employers, and rigorous entrance requirements may be confronted.

2 **Employment begins on 1 April.** For career-track employees, there will be several months of orientation and training. New recruits learn the company way, learning how to bow and speak. The new cohort begins to socialize – members will belong

▶

to this group for their entire career. The new recruit is assigned his (typically men) first job. More experienced workers will assist the new recruit so that he (or she) will learn a job through constant example or mentoring.

3  **Job rotations.** Every March, the personnel department determines job assignments for all staff for the forthcoming year. Promising young employees will be given stints in a range of positions and divisions so that they can obtain a broad overview of the company's business.

4  **Kacho.** Members of a cohort are promoted to first-line supervisor position at the same time, at around the age of 30, because it is uncomfortable to supervise seniors in terms of age. The kacho oversees daily work and may also engage in educational and certification classes.

5  **Tanshin-Funin**. Several times during a salaryman's career, he may be transferred to a branch or overseas, often with very short notice. Once his children reach senior school age, usually the family stays behind and he commutes home occasionally.

6  **Madogiwa (by the window)**. Failures are 'put out to pasture' by getting a desk next to the window and removed from critical functions.

7  **Bucho.** Department head – around age 40.

8  **Senior Management.** Members of the cohort who have not reached the senior position will be given vague titles or positions in subsidiaries.

9  **Retirement.** 55–65 for most, much later for those who reach board and senior positions. Usually the company can place retirees in less strenuous jobs with affiliated companies at a great cut in salary and prestige.

10  **'Silver years'.** Corporate retirees in their 50s to 70s are often healthy and well off and ready for new adventures, hobbies and travelling.

*Source*: Adapted from Beer, (1997–2003).

While these practices and philosophies have been associated with world leading business performance through engendering maximum organizational responsiveness to customer demands, they have been criticized for binding employees' 'hearts and minds' to their employing organizations in an excessive fashion, for coercing employee engagement in 'participative' practices and through intensification of working conditions (Delbridge and Turnbull, 1992). Such employment practices have been related to high levels of suicide and alcoholism and other social malaises.

As Hollinshead and Leat (1995) point out, Japanese working practices have exerted a significant influence on organization and management across national borders. Lean and efficient production systems and cellular group working have been established in Japanese concerns and local companies emulating them in countries such as the USA, Australia, the UK and eastern Germany. The influence of 'Japanization' received considerable attention from managers and academics in the 1980s, and powerfully informed the emerging 'philosophy' of HRM (ibid.).

In recent years, with growing international influence in the Japanese economy, there is evidence that the above practices are subject to reform and modernization. Most notably, as McGuire and Dow (2009) assert, the corporate bonds constituting horizontal *keiretsu* are loosening, or are being severed, following recession and regulatory reform. The pressure towards North American-type performance outcomes, associated with a move towards 'arm's length' systems of corporate governance maximizing shareholder value, has meant that 'zombie' or underperforming firms have been vulnerable. It has been argued that such firms have perverted efficient resource allocation in Japan, which renders the costs of *keiretsu* membership in excess of the benefits (Hoshi, 2006). Similarly, in vertical *keiretsu* arrangements, suppliers of core companies have forfeited long-term bonds of trust characterizing their past relationship, and are now instead obliged to compete with domestic and international rivals on grounds of cost and quality.

Associated with such institutional reform, 'modernization' is occurring in HR and related policies and practices as follows: a move towards individualized and performance-related pay, increased mobility of professional staff between enterprises, the 'flattening' of corporate hierarchies, women and younger workers breaching the patriarchal 'glass ceiling' and gaining promotion to senior levels, the streamlining of corporate decision-making processes and company boards, instability in previously secure jobs – particularly 'company men' and early retirement (Beardwell, 1997).

As an example of company-level reform, the MNC Canon has implemented a performance-related payment system since 2002, creating significant differentials among the workforce. Recently, Honda, Fujitsu and Sony have followed suit.

While Japan has transformed from a feudalistic to a state-led capitalist and, more recently, a capitalist market economy, China may still be regarded a 'socialist market economy' having experienced a long period of communist rule in the current century. In the remainder of this chapter, HRM developments in China are considered as this nation emerges as a potential industrial super-power.

## HRM in the People's Republic of China

### Background

The status of the People's Republic of China as the 'sleeping giant' on the global economic stage is well captured by some headline statistics:

- One in four of the world population lives in China, or approximately 1.2 billion people.
- It has the second-largest consumer market in Asia after Japan.
- There is a workforce of over 700 million, split almost equally between industry and agriculture.
- Real GDP growth has, until recently, been in the region of 8 per cent, with an annual growth in industrial production at around 9 per cent.

Yet, although the potential of China to become a top-flight global economic player is beyond doubt, it remains something of a 'strange relation' within the international trading community. While other reforming countries – for example, in Eastern Europe – have moved rapidly towards liberal market structures, China has taken a much more cautious and gradual approach to reform. This has meant that the guiding principles of Confucianism, as well as the legacy of communism, continue to exert a strong influence on ways of doing business in China.

Now described as a 'socialist market' economy, the opening of its trade doors to the West in 1979, in the Deng Xiaoping era, has been combined more successfully with measures for social stability than in most other transitional economies. Authoritarian yet paternalistic state intervention over the past couple of decades has enhanced the diet of the population, professional health care, housing and life expectancy (which is now 71 years). Yet the economic, as well as social, achievements of China should not be underestimated. Now a member of the World Trade Organization (WTO), the World Bank has hailed the country as a potential 'economic super-power'.

In understanding the 'essence' of China, it is first necessary to reflect on the principles of Confucianism, instilled approximately two thousand years ago. The teachings of Confucius concerned societal bonds and notions of hierarchy, stressing in particular three primary expressions of loyalty: (1) loyalty to the ruler; (2) filial loyalty; and (3) fidelity to the wife or husband. It was out of such binding social ties that *guānxi* emerged, a phenomenon still alive and well today, which essentially refers to clan-like networks based on exchange of favours and services. The significance of these informal interdependencies should not be underestimated, as they have served to lubricate and streamline more bureaucratic interactions.

Turning to more recent history, following 'Maoist' liberation in 1949, it was communist ideology that began to exert a conditioning effect on Chinese culture and values. Through the period of industrialization, driven to some extent by Soviet economic aid, there was experimentation with central planning and Soviet-style egalitarian employment principles. A central tenet of socialist-style economic structures were the large state-owned enterprises, based mainly in the large cities such as Beijing, Shanghai and Shenyang and producing around 80 per cent of industrial output in the late 1970s. However, in contrast to its Soviet mentor, China has been treading a path of modernization and reform since as early as 1979, entering into trade arrangements with overseas partners, decentralizing the monolithic structures of state-owned enterprises and engaging in a programme of enterprise privatization.

## Staple HRM practices

Although the winds of change are now blowing perceptibly through Chinese employment structures, the powerful cultural legacies defined above continue to hold sway in the domain of people management. At an attitudinal level, particularly in the dwindling state-owned sector, employees continue to place both emotional and practical dependency on their organizations. This state of mind, and the set of HR interdependencies associated with it, has been prosaically described as the 'iron rice bowl'. Associated principles include:

- *A job for life*: embodying the Marxist glorification of the worker, this essentially places the political imperative of full employment (although often merely technical) before the need for enterprise flexibility. Familiar western HR practices are meaningless in this setting as little attention needs to be given to recruiting staff on grounds of 'merit', to configuring organizational and working patterns according to the demands placed on enterprises, or to discharging staff on the grounds of poor performance.

- *Eating out of one big pot*: epitomizing Marxist as well as more traditional communitarian values, this manifests itself in egalitarian payment structures that have no relationship to performance. Orthodox western notions of motivation and career progression have limited utility in this context.

- *Cradle to grave welfare*: in traditional Chinese society the function and responsibility of enterprises has been considerably more extensive than as mere employer. They have acted in a paternalistic fashion in all walks of Chinese life, including education, health and housing. This means that labour markets have been highly segmented, there being considerable restrictions on employment mobility from enterprise to enterprise.

- *Passive trade unionism*: workers in all state-owned enterprises were members of the only trade union, the All-China Federation of Trade Unions (ACFTU). Possessing over 100 million members at its zenith, this union was organized on Soviet principles, acting as a 'transmission belt' for Party and enterprise management. Such a role meant that it was unable to actively oppose enterprise decisions, or represent worker interests in a truly independent fashion. Instead, the union role has been confined to enhancing worker productivity, providing training, assisting with welfare provision and promoting spare-time cultural activities.
- *Hierarchically-based enterprises*: reflecting Confucian notions of subservience as well as the Marxist orientation towards centralization of power, Chinese enterprises have been subject to 'one-man management' with little or no delegation of strategic authority to subordinates. This principle clearly flies in the face of much western management orthodoxy, suggesting a cultural chasm in preferred management styles.

Associated with *guānxi* are other Confucian-inspired social phenomena that inculcate patterns of behaviour at work. These include *renqing,* which means maintaining 'face' by returning favours, and *mianzi,* which relates to reciprocal behaviour in relationship-building. *Chang bei* stresses respect for elders and seniority, which explains access to senior corporate positions on the basis of 'acquired wisdom' as opposed to western notions of performance. We should note also that Chinese society remains highly patriarchal, which reflects the Confucian principle of female servitude.

## Westernization and modernization

Since Deng removed the restrictive barriers surrounding the Chinese economy in 1979, the practices outlined above are beginning to look increasingly archaic, constituting a diminishing feature in a broader mosaic of practices. According to the *Economist* (2000), the non-state-owned sector (comprising urban collectives, town and village industries, privately-owned enterprises, joint ventures and wholly foreign-funded firms) now accounts for the majority of China's industrial output and employs more workers than state-owned enterprises. Three hundred out of the top 500 US corporations have invested in China, injecting $35 billion (£24.4 billion), with further commitments of more than $33 billion. China has already become the US's fourth-largest trading partner. Although household-name MNCs are rapidly gaining footholds in the People's Republic, including GE, Motorola and AOL, small- and medium-sized Western concerns are entering into joint venture arrangements in their wake. The increasing flow of foreign direct investment into the People's Republic (foreign-funded firms now producing a quarter of exports) promises not only economic regeneration, but also modernization of the HR policies and practices, with quantum leaps towards the use of more sophisticated recruitment tools (including references and testing), employment contracts and performance-related pay. There is also some evidence of the freeing-up of Chinese labour markets, with barriers on staff mobility from enterprise to enterprise being loosened. A new labour law introduced in 1995 reflects the modernization of HR systems and structures in China and signals a breach of long-held traditions and values. Provisions include:

- Workers having the right to choose jobs, and to receive payment, holidays, workplace protection and training.
- No employment of children under the age of 16.
- Equal opportunities on the grounds of sex, race, nationality and religion.

- Minimum wage levels.
- Contracts between employer and employee setting out pay, conditions, tasks and termination arrangements.
- Permission for enterprises on the brink of bankruptcy to discharge staff providing consultation with the trade union has occurred.
- Average working week of 44 hours with one day off.
- An eight-hour working day.
- Maternity leave and health provisions for female workers.
- Dispute committees in the workplace, to include employer and worker representatives.

## The high or low road to reform?

Undoubtedly, the near miraculous transition of the Chinese economy owed a great deal to the preparedness of low-paid workers to achieve very high levels of industrial productivity. China has demonstrated remarkable productive capacity for commodities such as shoes, clothes, toys, electronic products and data processing machines (see Table 9.1). The 'bargain basement' productive status of the People's Republic has ruffled feathers in Japan, where labour costs are considerably higher and employment regulation tighter. The allegations of Chinese unscrupulousness in breaking the Asian model came to a head in a legal battle over the sale of DVD players. *Nihon Keizai Shimbun*, Japan's most influential business daily newspaper, has reported slumping US sales for Sony and Matsushita as Chinese competitors 'sell cheap knock offs without paying patent fees'.

Naomi Klein (2001) also graphically demonstrates the bleak side of 'hell for leather' Chinese business practice in her best-selling anti-global treatise, *No Logo*. In a profile of 'sweatshops' she identifies a number of household, name US manufacturers outsourcing to factories in the People's Republic, including Wal-Mart, Kmart and Nike. In a flagrant breach of the new legal provisions above, conditions include wages of around $2 an hour, up to 80 working hours a week, forced overtime, corporal punishment and arbitrary fining of pregnant women.

In contrast, a number of western companies are now taking a far more benign and investment-oriented view of human resource capability in the People's Republic. A recent *Business Week* (2003) reports on the rapid increase in natural science and engineering college graduates over the decade from 1989 to 1999, from 127,000 to 322,000, with 41,000 now possessing Masters' qualifications or doctorates. The expanding pool of 'knowledge' workers in the region has proved attractive to Intel, Philips and Microsoft, who draw on indigenous strengths in hardware design and embedded software. In the finance sector, HSBC has moved its credit and loan processing activity to the People's Republic. Indeed, the recent liberalization of financial services is bound to attract more fully-fledged western institutional presence on the Chinese high street (with Prudential being an early mover in this direction). Yet, despite the recent growth spurt of Chinese businesses towards a more obvious manifestation of 'western'-type maturity, there are still significant deficits in the field of human and intellectual capital. Most glaringly, although China has accumulated reserves of 'productive' and even 'knowledge' talent, it is still sorely lacking in the relatively intangible area of managerial or entrepreneurial acumen.

As in other post-socialist societies, a vacuum in managerial competence accompanied the demise of communist edifices, as the epoch of central planning had engendered administrative rather than entrepreneurial skills. Sorely needed now are capabilities in change management, strategic planning and international vision. Also pressing is the need for Chinese enterprises to adopt globally recognized standards of corporate governance, as the drive to produce at an unbeatable cost has involved procedural and ethical corner-cutting. In the short term, learning from 'the West' is likely to be the most expeditious avenue for reform, most notably through the conduits of the new joint ventures spawning in the People's Republic.

**Table 9.1 China facts**

| | |
|---|---|
| ■ Percent of the world's umbrellas made in China | 70 |
| ■ Percent of the world's buttons made in China | 60 |
| ■ Percent of U.S. shoes made in China | 72 |
| ■ Percent of U.S. kitchen appliances made in China | 50 |
| ■ Percent of U.S. artificial Christmas trees made in China | 85 |
| ■ Percent of U.S. toys made in China | 80 |
| ■ Percent of Chinese goods sent to the U.S. that end up on Wal-Mart's shelves | 9 |
| ■ Percent of the unsafe toys recalled in the U.S. in 2007, including Thomas the Tank Engine, that were made in China | 100 |
| ■ Number of months a Chinese factory worker would need to work to earn the cost of a Thomas the Tank Engine train set | 9 |

Source: National Geographic (2006).

## Problems and issues in joint venture management

Although the prospect of gaining a foothold in a massive emerging marketplace is a tantalizing one for many western businesses, the realities of physical location on Chinese territory remain unpredictable and even unfathomable. Although state-owned enterprises are in demise, the concepts and practices associated with them continue to exert a strong normative effect on the Chinese mindset. Industrial practices in the People's Republic still constitute a mosaic of old and new, which means that embryonic joint ventures quite often find themselves locating on shifting sands. Sergeant and Frenkel (1998) have identified a number of practical problems confronting Chinese international joint ventures in the field of HRM, which are adapted below:

■ *Recruitment*: high turnover, poaching of skilled staff, nepotism and overhiring, difficulties in transferring staff from more regulated and paternalistic state-owned enterprises.
■ *Reward systems*: discrepancies/inequities between (higher paying) joint ventures and indigenous concerns. The need to incorporate social benefits in pay packages. Difficulties in introducing differentials to reflect individual skills/performance as this disrupts interpersonal harmony and social relations based on *guanxi*.
■ *Employee retention*: difficulties in holding on to skilled staff, although compensation and other motivational tools can now be used to assist.
■ *Work performance and employee management*: lack of personal initiative taken by Chinese staff (including managers) and inadequate attention to product/service quality. Problems in exiting poor performers.

- *Management–employee relations*: poorly established systems for collective bargaining, although new laws may help consolidate the position of independent unionism.

It is salutary to note that around two-thirds of joint ventures in the People's Republic fail, and this is largely attributable to inadequate understanding of the distinctive facets of Chinese culture by inward investors. If the success rate of joint ventures is to be enhanced, then clearly the issue of expatriate adjustment needs to be given more attention by academics and practitioners alike. Pioneering westerners in the inhospitable 'Land of the Dragon' will need to devote more attention to gaining Chinese language proficiency than has been the case in the past, as well as acquiring greater insight into the nuances of Chinese culture. This not only involves 'hard' information on institutional arrangements, financial systems, and so on, but also sensitivity towards, and empathy with, particularistic social phenomena such as *guānxi*. Unless westerners are somehow able to tap into pre-established networks, they will continue to be regarded as outsiders, and restricted to the formalized, bureaucratic rituals that remain at the periphery of much real business activity.

As mentioned above, expatriate managers will also need to mentor their Chinese counterparts in joint ventures and transfer appropriate areas of western 'knowledge'. Not only will new Chinese managers need to be put in the picture about 'state-of-the-art' western technologies, financial methods, and so on, but also they will need to be coaxed to relinquish their post-socialist comfort zones and become more comfortable with risk orientation. As is the case with other transforming economies, it is likely to be the younger generation of Chinese managers, most of whom now speak English, who possess most intuitive understanding in dealing with westerners. It is likely to be incumbent on western HR professionals operating on Chinese soil to formulate finely-tuned HR policies that stimulate the commitment of individual employees to the quality of the product and goals of the enterprise through appropriate motivational techniques, while recognizing the precious status of group orientation and social stability at an organizational level among indigenous workforces. The challenge and complexity of this cross-cultural balancing act should not be underestimated as it implies an unprecedented fusion of western individualist and materialist values with the Confucian orientation towards reciprocation and social harmony. We conclude by providing recommendations to assist western corporations active in China:

1  Assist fuller integration of expatriates into the Chinese community.
   Useful policies are likely to include selecting expatriates on the basis of previous knowledge of Chinese language and culture, cross-cultural sensitivity training (for expatriate families also, if appropriate) and possibly longer-term placements. Proactive corporate policies to assist with accommodation could pay dividends.
2  Modify in-organization barriers between westerners and Chinese managers.
   This could enhance the pooling of local and international knowledge. Useful policies are likely to include the engineering of real and virtual cross-cultural groupings, establishing equal opportunities to ensure excellent Chinese staff can gravitate to senior positions, promoting mentoring systems between westerners and Chinese managers and enhancing the Chinese knowledge base through transfer and internship in the West.
3  Manage the interface between the organization and its environment.
   It is important that western-owned concerns eventually become accepted as part of the fabric of the new Chinese business environment and learn from it. Useful policies are likely to be the management of business ethics and legal regulation, prioritizing social

responsibility in matters such as urban regeneration, environmental protection, training and job creation. Western-owned companies could take the lead in establishing new business networks.

---

*Activity*

Compare and contrast evolving HR/employment practices in the 'capitalist market economy' of Japan and the 'socialist market economy' of China.

---

## Summary

This chapter has investigated the influence of time-honoured cultural values and philosophical teachings on HRM practices in East Asia. An overview has been provided of the distinctive nature of organizational and working practices in the region, with variations being apparent between the 'socialist market' economy of China, and the more fully-fledged capitalistic Japanese context. In each country, HR/employment practices are in a state of flux as these national systems adapt to the competitive volatilities of the new global economic order.

## Further reading

**Budhwar, P.S. (ed.)** (2004) *Managing Human Resources in Asia-Pacific*, London and New York: Routledge.

This book provides systematic analysis of the context for HRM in a range of Asia-Pacific countries, including China, South Korea, Japan, Hong Kong, Taiwan, India, Thailand, Vietnam, Malaysia, Singapore and Australia. The dynamics and growth in each of these countries is explored, as well as the challenges confronted by HR professionals. The transfer of practices to multinational affiliates in Asia is considered, and the agenda for future research and policy.

**Sako, M. and Sato, H. (eds)** (1997) *Japanese Management and Labour in Transition*, London and New York: Routledge.

A cogent analysis of the 'pillars' of the Japanese employment system is presented, as well as reforms necessitated by the 'bursting of the Japanese economic bubble'.

**Child, J. (1994) *Management in China in the Age of Reform*, Cambridge: Cambridge University Press.**

A comprehensive and insightful commentary is offered on changes in the role and ethos of management in China over the period of gradual reform from communism to socialist market orientation since the late 1970s.

## Useful websites

ec.europa.eu/external_relations

This site provides news and information on the EU's external relations with various global regional governments and other parties, including East Asia. Detailed contextual information on regions and indigenous countries is provided.

www.aseansec.org

The principles and objectives of the Association of South East Asian trading nations are presented.

## References

**Ahmadjian, C.** (1997) Japanese auto parts supply networks and the governance of inter-firm exchange, working paper, Graduate School of Business, Columbia University, New York.

**Beardwell, I.** (1997) Human resource management and Japan, in I. Beardwell and L. Holden (eds) *Human Resource Management: A Contemporary Perspective* (2nd edn.), London: Pitman Publishing.

**Beer, J.E.** (1997–2003) www.culture-at-work.com/japancores.html.

*Business Week* (*2003*) *The new global job shift, 3 February, pp. 1–3.*

**Chu, C.N.** (1995) *The Asian Mind Game: A Westerner's Survival Manual* Crow's Nest, Australia: Stealth Productions Australia.

**Delbridge, R. and Turnbull, P.** (1992) Human resource maximisation: the management of labour under just-in-time manufacturing systems, in P. Blyton and P. Turnbull (eds) *Reassessing Human Resource Management*, London: Sage Publications.

*Economist, The* (2000) *A Survey of China*, pp. 1–16.

**Hodgetts, R.M. and Luthans, F.** (2003) *International Management: Culture, Strategy and Behavior* (5th edn.), New York: McGraw-Hill.

**Hollinshead, G. and Leat, M.** (1995) *Human Resource Management: An International and Comparative Perspective*, London: Pitman Publishing.

**Hoshi, T.** (2006) Economics of the living dead, *Japanese Economic Review*, 57(1): 30–49.

**Japan in Figures** (2007) Foreign Press Centre, Japan.

**Klein, N.** (2001) *No Logo*, New York: HarperCollins.

**McGuire, J. and Dow, S.** (2009) Japanese *keiretsu*: past, present, future, *Asia Pacific Journal of Management,* 26: 233–251.

*National Geographic* (2008) China – inside the Dragon – factory to the world, Special Issue, p. 170.

**Scarborough, J.** (1998) Comparing Chinese and western cultural roots, *Business Horizons*, November 15–24.

**Schneider, L. and Silverman, A.** (2000) *A Global Sociology: Introducing Four Contemporary Societies*, New York: McGraw-Hill.

**Sergeant, A. and Frenkel, S.** (1998) Managing people in China: perceptions of expatriate managers, *Journal of World Business*, 39(1): 19–34.

***Sunday Times*** (2002) Enter the Yankee Dragon, 17 February.

**Suzuki, K.** (1993) R&D spillovers and technology transfers among and within vertical *keiretsu* groups – evidence from the Japanese electrical machinery industry, *International Journal of Industrial Organization*, 11(4): 573–92.

**Whiteley, A., Cheung, S. and Zhang, S.Q.** (2000) *Human Resource Strategies in China*, Singapore: World Scientific.

**Whitley, R.** (2002) Business systems, in A. Sorge (ed.) *Organization*, London: Thomson Learning.

**Yao, O.** (1988) Chinese cultural values: their dimensions and marketing implications, *European Journal of Marketing*, 22(5): 44–57.

**Zhu, Y. and Warner, M.** (2004) HRM in Asia, in A.W. Harzing and J. Van Ruysseveldt (eds) *International Human Resource Management* (2nd edn.), London: Sage Publications.

# CHAPTER 10

# Human resource management in developing countries

❖ **LEARNING OBJECTIVES**

❖ To define developing countries and to distinguish between developing and emerging countries

❖ To consider varying degrees of integration of developing/emerging economies into global economic structures and reasons for relative backwardness; for example, in Africa

❖ To examine traditional and modern facets of human resource (HR) in developing/emerging countries

❖ To provide an overview of context and emerging HR policies and practice in India

## Introduction: context

Hoogvelt (2001) suggests that the core/peripheral model associated with colonial and post-colonial eras has given way to a three-tier structure of concentric circles, as follows:

■ The elites of all continents and nations, albeit more prevalent in developed countries. Within this core exist the 20 per cent of the world population that is bankable, and the 'knowledge workers', whose skills are transferable across national and regional boundaries.

■ A larger layer of between 20 and 30 per cent of the world population labouring in insecure forms of employment, subject to elimination of jobs by machines and the driving down of wages and conditions to the lowest common denominator. This grouping tends to be tied to specific geographic areas.

■ The remainder of the world population, who are effectively excluded from the global system. This group perform neither a productive function nor present a potential consumer market, and are beyond the ambit of aid programmes.

We should emphasize that the hierarchical division of labour as stated cuts across national and regional boundaries, so that the first two categories in particular may be found in both developed and developing countries. Following Reich (1991), however, it may be predicted that the growth of the second category will undermine the security of the first, such that the move of market-oriented production to South America, Indonesia, India, China and South East Asia will bring over a billion workers in developing countries into global economic structures, earning less than $3 a day, over the next two decades or so (Kennedy, 1996). It is likely that this development will exert a significant downward pressure on wages in developed countries, relative security attaching to in-person services (such as salespeople, hairstylists, waiters and waitresses) who are bound to stay close to customers, and whose functions cannot be relocated (Reich, 1991).

The term 'developing country' as used, for example, by the United Nations, embraces a wide range of countries that are heavily dependent on primary production and normally lack an advanced industrial infrastructure, including education, health, communications and transport facilities (Punnett, 2006). According to Jackson (2004a), this definition would include all African countries, Latin America, many parts of South East Asia and Polynesia, and Central Asia including many former Soviet Republics, and may be stretched to incorporate some transitional economies in central and eastern Europe, the newly industrialized economies of East Asia, and much of the Middle East. It is recognized that an advanced stratum of 'developing' or 'transitional' economies now represent a type of emergent 'super league' as they have integrated most fully into global economic structures, the latter category including Russia, China, India and Brazil (Verbeke, 2009).

Punnett (2004) identifies the following characteristics of developing countries:

- People are concerned with basic needs, or, in the least poor of these countries, with achieving economic stability.
- Infrastructure is limited. Roads, railways, ports and other facilities are non-existent in some locations and are only adequate in the less poor countries.
- Social services are limited. Education, health and other social services do not exist in some locations and are only adequate in the less poor countries.
- Resources are scarce, and projects need to be clearly justified to warrant funding.

In keeping with *neo-liberal* economic orthodoxy, as embodied in the 'Washington Consensus', prominent global agencies such as the World Trade Organization (WTO) have exhorted developing countries to advance by 'opening up' to international trade (Stiglitz, 2002). The neo-liberal view therefore advocates economic development through integration of emerging economies into global structures, facilitated by trade liberalization and foreign direct investment (FDI) (Bird, 2004). Indeed, neo-liberal ideology has been converted into real-world policy and practice through the application of 'structural adjustment programmes' to virtually all developing countries as a condition of lending by the World Bank and International Monetary Fund (IMF). Such lending, which is required to relieve massive burdens of national debt confronting many developing countries, carries with it the obligation to radically liberalize their economies, to be open for imports, to eliminate tariffs and other restrictions and to float currencies (Jackson, 2004b).

In practice, however, not all developing countries have been in a position to take advantage of expanding world trade, a division forming between 'emerging' and 'marginalized' economies. According to Ghose (2003), a relatively small number of large developing countries, accounting for nearly 75 per cent of the population of the developing world, have emerged as major exporters of manufactured goods and have benefited from capital inflow and technology transfers. On the other hand, a large number of small developing countries, representing around 25 per cent of the population of the developing world, have remained dependent on primary and agricultural commodities while global demand for such commodities has stagnated. Such countries have received little inflow of foreign capital, are particularly saddled with macro-economic imbalances such as inflation and debt, and so remain peripheral to global trading structures. In general, according to Ghose (2003), global trade liberalization has had a positive effect in the Asian emerging economies, but a negative effect on Latin America (with the notable exception of Brazil and arguably Mexico) and on Sub-Saharan Africa (possibly with the exception of South Africa). Explanations for contrasting passages and pacing of reform in the developing world may be derived from theories of comparative advantage. Following Ghose (ibid.), as the major driver for change in the emerging economies has been the growth of manufactured exports, East Asian economies have been in a relatively strong competitive position as they have tended to specialize in labour-intensive manufacturing as well as possessing a track record in exporting and a suitable base of domestic capabilities. These countries have also been able to benefit from a process of upgrading and labour transfer from low productivity 'traditional' activities to more highly efficient and modern engagement in production and services.

The United Nations Conference on Trade and Development (UNCTAD) World Investment Report (2008) reports the following key developments in global FDI flows:

- In South, East and South East Asia and Oceania, both inward and outward flows of FDI rose to their highest levels ever. China, Hong Kong and India remained top destinations for FDI, with sustained economic growth, demographic changes and new investment opportunities contributing to their attractiveness. A highly significant trend is the growing importance of emerging economies as *sources* of FDI in both developed and developing countries.
- West Asia also enjoyed record flows of inward and outward FDI, four-fifths of inflows being concentrated in Saudi Arabia, Turkey and the United Arab Emirates, where a growing number of energy and construction projects have commenced.
- FDI flows to and from south east Europe and the Commonwealth of Independent States (CIS) reached unprecedented levels. Inward flows were attracted to fast-growing consumer markets and natural resources in the CIS, while these were associated with the privatization of state-owned enterprises in south east Europe. FDI from the Russian Federation soared to $46 billion in 2007, with Russian-owned MNEs extending their reach to Africa in order to increase raw material supplies and access to strategic commodities.
- Latin America and the Caribbean enjoyed a rise in FDI inflows by 36 per cent in 2007, although the bulk of investment targeted extractive industries and natural resource-based manufacturing in South America.
- In Africa, FDI inflows grew to $53 billion in 2007, although the continent's share in global FDI remained at approximately 3 per cent. A large proportion of FDI projects in the region in 2007 was linked to the extraction of natural resources.

While increased flows of capital into Latin America and Africa may be regarded as encouraging by neo-liberal commentators, it should be borne in mind that they continue to represent a relatively small proportion of the global flow of FDI (less than 10 per cent combined for Latin America and Africa) and that they are targeted primarily towards natural resources. In these circumstances, there are serious concerns over the extent to which trade liberalization has the potential to promote sustained and thoroughgoing upgrading of national capacities, including infrastructure and human resources (ibid.). Jackson (2002) provides an exposition of the African 'legacy' that helps to explain its continuing disjuncture from global economic structures, with particular reference to South Africa:

- The economic orientation of African countries as primary producers under colonial administration, with the majority of export earnings being accounted for by agriculture or extraction. The focus on export-led production was associated with an absence of a consumer-based economy and the underdevelopment of processing and service industries and a related skill base. A concentration of labour in heavy industry and mining was reinforced through the system of apartheid that segregated black workers into these areas of industrial activity.
- Although South Africa resides in the upper-middle income group of semi-industrialized economies, it displays many features of 'poverty' in common with its African neighbours, including low life expectancy, low quality of life, high unemployment and illiteracy.
- Separate education systems established under apartheid, with rudimentary education for the majority of the population, have resulted in the under-education and under-skilling of people who are now ill-equipped for jobs in the competitive global market.
- African countries possess growing populations and a high proportion of children and youths, which contributes to a high level of dependence on active earners. The economically active population is adversely affected not only by low life expectancy but also the AIDS epidemic.

Critical to the economic fortunes of developing countries is the extent to which inward investment has a 'trickle down' effect, or 'backward linkages' are established between operations superimposed from foreign sources and indigenous organizations and utilities. Indeed, Bird (2004) criticizes the neo-liberal agenda for encouraging a cost-minimizing mentality on the part of inward investors, at the expense of sustained development based on the establishment and maintenance of social, physical and economic infrastructures. Alternatively, and from an ethically informed position, Bird argues that international businesses may seek to develop their own assets but neglect those of local stakeholders. In order to illustrate this perspective, it is worth quoting Bird's analysis of the Shell Nigeria case in full:

> Shell has extracted billions of dollars worth of oil from the Niger Delta since it began operations there in the late 1950s. Throughout its operation, Shell for the most part followed responsible business guidelines, paid reasonable wages, offered thousands of Nigerians opportunities for advancement, paid generous royalties to the central government and invested in local community programmes. Yet the people of the Delta remain almost as impoverished today. For most of the period, Shell burned 85% of the associated natural gas produced by extracting oil. From an asset-development perspective, how might Shell have acted differently? ... As it was, significant portions of natural capital were wasted and potential social capital, which might have developed these collaborations, was not developed. Likewise, investment in local businesses, which Shell could have helped to initiate, might have fostered a number of economically valuable developments – constructing and maintain-

ing roads, pumping and distributing fresh water, establishing and expanding local systems of credit – all of which would have provided services required for Shell's operations and at the same time benefited the larger local community. If Shell had made these investments, its earnings might have been somewhat lower; it might have paid somewhat smaller royalties to the central government. However, Shell would probably have significantly augmented its social capital, reduced its security threats at least marginally and added at least minimally to the economic well-being of its neighbours'.

(Bird, 2004: 23–24) 🙶

In Sub-Saharan Africa, a number of US corporations have sought to abide by the spirit of social responsibility by acknowledging the principles of the 'Sullivan Code'. The principles aim to support economic, social and political justice, human rights, equal opportunities, to train and advance disadvantaged workers for technical, supervisory and management opportunities and to assist with greater tolerance and understanding among people. For example, Colgate-Palmolive in its African subsidiary has funded educational projects at schools and universities, various community projects including water purification and sanitation, and a number of health and dental projects. Despite the apparent good intentions of the corporation, Jackson (2004b) argues that Colgate-Palmolive's social responsibility programme foundered on its failure to involve local stakeholders in its formulation and implementation, and may be criticized for merely furthering enlightened self-interest through a scheme primarily designed to market its own products.

As the feature below demonstrates, a 'neo-liberal'-inspired approach to reform in the emergent post-communist Russian economy has also been associated with potentially dysfunctional social and economic effects as a privileged cadre of 'winners', mainly comprising energy sector magnates, has been separated profoundly in status from an impoverished majority. As Stiglitz (2002) contends, the 'shock therapy' approach to privatization, incepted by the Yeltsin government at the behest of the IMF and the World Bank in the early 1980s, failed to produce a 'trickle down' effect in the standard of living for the Russian population at large.

---

### The effects of privatization on the distribution of pay in the 'emergent' Russian economy

The rapid programme of privatization incepted in 1991 was associated with the radical overhaul of the national system of income distribution in Russia, exposing previously egalitarian conditions associated with communism to the forces of market liberalism. Mirroring 'shock therapy' treatment of the former state-owned enterprises, the liberalization of pay has played out in an extreme fashion in Russia, creating an elite cadre of 'winners', but also a sizeable proportion of economic 'losers', including the emergence of a new 'underclass'.

According to statistics published by the International Labour Organization (2005) and the World Bank (2004), approximately 27% of the Russian population live below the subsistence level, which has been calculated at standing at 2500 roubles a month (70 Euro or $85) (Tyuryukanova, (2005). Furthermore, it has been estimated that approximately one-third of the poor live in 'extreme poverty' with an average income, of less than half the subsistence minimum (*Financial Times*, 1999). As White (2000)

▶

points out, the 'new poor' includes large families disadvantaged by the rising cost of bringing up children, inhabitants of towns where the factory providing a single source of employment had closed, or the new ranks of the unemployed. (ibid.: 154). Although many in this category are close to starvation, an even more deprived category has emerged, constituting around 10% of the population, including beggars, the homeless, orphans, alcoholics, drug addicts and prostitutes. The position of the new poor in Russia has been exacerbated in 2004 by an array of governmental measures serving to liquidate state provided social benefits that were a prominent feature of the Soviet era. Particularly affected groups include pensioners, war veterans and Chernobyl clean up workers. Established social benefits, including the free use of public transportation, discounts on residential utilities, a free local telephone service, free medication, free annual treatment at sanatoriums and health resorts, free artificial limbs and wheelchairs for invalids and guaranteed employment for the disabled have been 'monetarized', now being replaced by a monthly compensation ranging from 300 (8 Euro) to 1550 (42 Euro) roubles.

By way of stark contrast, subsequent World Development Reports published by the World Bank (ibid.) have suggested that a fifteen-fold income gap has emerged between the richest and poorest 10% of earners. Such polarization is unprecedented in the western experience and equates only with Latin American and African countries. A recent article in the *International Herald Tribune* reveals that Russia now has 27 billionaires, exceeded only by 57 in Germany and 341 in the USA (Arvedlund, 2005). The majority of the Russian 'super rich' cadre control raw materials and associated industries, whilst others represent new business fields such as telecommunications, construction, food production and retail. Indeed the greatest part of shareholdings in the largest Russian enterprises is in the hands of this small social grouping, the 23 largest business groups accounting for 57% of all Russia's industrial production (World Bank, 2003). In terms of personal incomes, the President of Lukoil receives $1.5 million per annum, with the possibility of a $2.2 million bonus. In large scale enterprises, such as the United Mechanical Engineering Works and the Tyumen oil company, basic executive salaries amount to approximately $500,000 per annum (Volkov and Denenberg, 2005). According to World Socialist Web, the President of Basis Element Aluminium, Oleg Deripaska, paid taxes of $294 million on his income in the Siberian Republic of Khakassia, this constituting 105% of total annual revenue for the Republic. Senior state officials may also be counted amongst the more modest beneficiaries of radical economic reform.

Following privatization, the social differentiation of income has also occurred according to region and industrial sector. Recent statistics produced by the State Statistical Committee of Russia and CE Research (2004), reporting average monthly gross earnings for 2002, reveal that in Moscow City, and the Ural Federal District, this figure is approximately 6500 roubles a month, or 220 Euro, compared with an equivalent of around 4300 roubles in Siberia (140 Euro) or 3,400 roubles (110 Euro) in Privolzhsky. As Blasi, Kroumova and Kruse (1997) point out, figures on average earnings need to be treated with some care as they do not take account of wages in the substantial informal economy, estimated to constitute around one-quarter of total economic activity, or the under-reporting of wages by employers in order to escape taxes. Kim (1997) reveals that the same occupation could attract quite different benefits Moscow, St. Petersburg and Vladivostock. So, for example, a secretary with good

English, PC experience, good typing in Russian and English and some prior work experience could expect to earn $400–600 a month in Moscow, $200–400 in St. Petersburg and $400–800 in Vladivostock. Disparities in pay on the basis of region are well illustrated by a recent hunger strike undertaken by air traffic controllers in Rostov-na-Donu in southern Russia. The controllers are employed by Aeronavigatsiya Yugo, which is the subsidiary of a larger state corporation, and are responsible for an area comparable to some of the larger states in Europe. The grievance of staff relates to average monthly earnings of approximately 2,000 roubles a month (55 Euro), which controllers claim is only half comparable rates for the same employer in Moscow. Due to its state-owned status, however, company managers are unable to resolve the dispute at local level and need to refer the issue to a higher authority (BBC Monitoring, 2005).

Liberalization of pay has also been associated with the emergence of a 'topsy turvy' hierarchy of occupations from a western perspective. According to Blasi et. al. (1997), in late 1995, workers in industry earned 111% of the average wage, workers in construction earned 131%, and workers in transportation earned 152%. This compared with those employed in the state controlled education and health sectors, who earned 80% of the average, and agricultural workers who earned 47%. Underlying these statistics is the question of how changing ownership structures have affected earnings in the wake of privatization. Statistics produced by State Statistical Committee of Russia and CE Research (2002) reveal that average earnings in foreign owned enterprises, at 9,348 roubles (or 315 Euro a month) are approximately twice those paid by state-owned or local private enterprises. Whilst those working in foreign-owned enterprises have benefited in a relative sense from recent economic reforms, public sector workers have experienced real decline in their standard of living, including teachers, physicians, nurses and low ranking civil servants (Volkov and Denenberg, 2005). Even more badly affected have been those in rural communes, which have been a focal point of Russian national life and folklore. Villages have suffered through the migration of more highly skilled workers (for example machinery specialists) to urban locations, and through the dismantling of former state benefits such as medical care, job training and entertainment.

Thus, over the past ten to fifteen years the emergence of income differentiation across the economic face of Russia has, from a western perspective, occurred in an irrational and unsystematic fashion. It is only in recent years that very modest signs of mitigating the income gulf between rich and poor have emerged, with the rate of statutory minimum pay being hitched in successive years since 2000 to its current level at around 1700 roubles, or 50 Euro a month. In June 2005, the Minister of Economic Development and Trade was predicting a rise in real disposable incomes by 39% between 2005 and 2008 and wage rises of 44% over the same period in real terms (BBC Monitoring International Reports, 2005). A critical factor in separating status between occupation groupings has been the economic might of enterprise ownership in a volatile and immature market environment. Although the extreme gap between rich and poor in the new Russia undoubtedly represents a threat to social stability, it has been argued, on the more positive side (Blasi et al., 1997) that differences in wages are actually an indication that the free market is beginning to work, as the wages of employees begin to follow what people are willing to pay for the goods they produce.

## HR issues in developing countries

The business environment for HRM in developing countries is one of considerable complexity, having been subject to: (1) post-colonial influences of imperial or occupying powers – for example, the institutional and cultural legacy of English rule in India, or Spanish in Latin America; (2) indigenous and traditional value systems and organizational norms as manifested by the 'native' community; and (3) the agenda for change and reform along 'western lines' as asserted by MNCs and structural adjustment programmes as orchestrated by the World Bank and other powerful international agencies. As discussed above, certain emerging countries are most integral to the 'loop' of global trade, and therefore particularly subject to the transfer of ideas and technology from the developed world.

In the African context, Jackson (2004a) argues that the post- or neo-colonial legacy is perceived to exert a potent effect on management and organization. Thus, a top-down, directive managerial style has been in evidence, associated with bureaucracy, hierarchy and strong task orientation. The autocratic and 'over-led' approach to management has also been associated with discriminatory policies and alienation of employees (ibid.). In her analysis of culture in developing countries with reference to Hofstede's (1991) dimensions, Punnett (2006) discovers indigenous value systems that are reflective of post-colonialism, but which also embody more traditional native world-views. Accordingly, people in developing countries, and particularly the poorer ones, accept differences in status and power. In the richer developing countries, individualistic tendencies are becoming more pronounced, while the group remains the primary focus of loyalty in poorer countries. Other tendencies are towards high uncertainty avoidance, risk aversion possibly being associated with low entrepreneurial capacity, and high masculinity reflecting patriarchal traditions.

Punnett (ibid.) suggests two further cultural predilections of developing countries. First, it is argued that people in the less advanced countries demonstrate a low need for achievement, this has been associated with limited economic resources in these countries, and perhaps a prioritizing of lifestyle factors associated with social/spiritual, as opposed to economic, values. Second, this author asserts that people in developing countries may be more likely to display an external, rather than internal, locus of control. Accordingly, happenings and developments, whether positive or negative, may be attributed to the actions of gods, luck or ancestors rather than to personal action or volition. These values may be traced in the managerial mindset in developing countries, which have been described as fatalistic, resistant to change, reactive, short term, authoritarian, risk-reducing, context-dependent and guided by relationship-based rather than universal criteria (Jackson, 2004b; Kanungo and Jaeger, 1990).

Turning now to appropriate styles of HRM in developing countries, it may be argued that western conceptions of HRM are predicated on a type of 'psychological contract' between management and employees within the enterprise (Rousseau, 1996). Such a contract establishes the 'rules of engagement' within industrial and commercial enterprises, implies reciprocity in professional relationships, and creates mutual obligations to bind managers and managed. It follows that much 'best practice' in the discourse of HRM in developed countries rests on a fundamental notion of actively engaging employees in the goals and values of the organization, frequently through establishing systems for employee involvement and participation.

In developing countries it cannot, however, be taken as read that the 'psychological contract' will be applicable to enterprises, or indeed meaningful to managers or employees. As Jackson (2004b) explains, in Africa going to work may mean 'stepping outside' of people's cultures (p. 452), primary life focal points relating instead to extended family, community or religion. In consequence, familiar western managerial notions and practices may not be readily transferable to organizational settings in which work is not a central concern of participants, and in which work orientation is highly instrumental and gainful employment primarily 'a means to an end' rather than an end in itself. In order for western corporations to gain legitimacy in highly collectivistic societies, it may be incumbent on them to broaden concepts of organization and work to involve stakeholders from the community in the life of the enterprise (ibid.).

Similarly, as Jackson (2004b) argues, in developing countries, an absolutist view of the dignity and value of the human being persists. Jackson uses the African concept of *Ubuntu* in order to explain this principle, which is derived from the proverb 'people are people through other people'. A humanistic view of the orientation and worth of men and women, as embedded in developing societies, tends to conflict with western organization notions of people as a *resource* amenable to deployment in an instrumental fashion in the realization of transcendent economic and competitive priorities. Taking a sympathetic view of societal and work values in developing countries, Jackson argues that western management can learn from the cultural predisposition that places 'an intrinsic value on people for themselves rather than a means to an end of the organization' (p. 455).

Such a view is consistent with the formulation of 'hybridized' conceptions of HRM in developing countries, which combine western-inspired and market-oriented discourses with a holistic view of human capabilities, thus emphasizing the *human*, rather than the *resource*.

Such a philosophy is epitomized in the emerging paradigm for the management of people in India, which is termed 'human resource development', in order to capture the potential for human growth and creativity as an end in itself, rather than inevitably tying human potential to corporate goals. The following are key ingredients of the 'hybridized' Indian HR paradigm (Jackson, 2002):

- HRD is a 'humanistic' concept and a subsuming norm that guides Indian management approaches to employees and a guide to Indian management thought and practice.
- HRD emphasizes that people should not be treated as mere cogs in the 'wheel of production' but with respect as human beings.
- HRD involves a powerful 'culture-building' agenda that combines western managerial concepts with belief in human dignity and potential.

While humanistic values and beliefs emanate from indigenous cultures, and manifest 'soft' tendencies in HRM (Storey, 1992), in practice the integration of emerging economies into global economic structures has rested on their ability to accommodate low-cost and highly intensive productive operations. Thus, a paradoxical picture of HRM is apparent, with benign views of human capacity being tempered by the reality of exploitative employment practices. The following are examples of the more negative features of employment in developing economies.

*Child labour:* according to statistics produced by the ILO (2002), almost 250 million children between the ages of 5 and 17 (one child in six) are workers, with 179 million (one child in eight) doing jobs that are classed as difficult, dangerous and unsuitable. Only around

1 per cent of working children come from the wealthy countries of North America, Western Europe, Japan and Australasia and a further 1 per cent from the Soviet Union. The remaining 98 per cent are found in Asia, Africa, Latin America and the Middle East, with a majority coming from the highly populated South Asian countries of India, Pakistan and Bangladesh. Sub-Saharan Africa has around 23 per cent of the world total, with one child in three working. Around 8 per cent of the world's working children are from Latin America and the Caribbean. Although around 90 per cent of children work in agriculture or related activities in family units, in many cases young children are employed in factories or as outworkers in industries such as garments, footwear, toys, sports goods, artificial flowers and plastic products (Dicken, 2003). Undoubtedly, the exploitation of child labour is directly linked to the issue of poverty in developing countries (ILO, 2002), yet a conviction exists in such countries that the ethical stance taken by western countries against child labour, as embodied in ILO conventions and other codes, merely represents another form of protectionism against their exports and ability to compete on the grounds of low labour costs (Dicken, 2003).

In a well-publicized case, US celebrity Kathy Lee Gifford's women's clothing brand came under attack in 1995 when investigators from the US National Labor Committee found teenage women sewing at her Global Fashion plant in Honduras. It was alleged that the workforce predominantly comprising young women between the ages of 13 and 15, was being employed under 'sweatshop' conditions including: compulsory overtime and 12-hour shifts to meet deadlines, limitations on bathroom visits to twice a day, subjection to physical searches, using unsafe equipment and forceful exclusion from employment and legal rights. In general, wages for child workers in developing countries have been described as 'a pittance' (ibid.) and working conditions often abysmal.

*Export processing zones*: the export processing zone (EPZ) is a measure used by developing countries to stimulate their export industries and to attract FDI (ibid.). An EPZ can be defined as, 'a clearly delineated industrial estate which constitutes a free trade enclave in the customs and trade regime of a country and where foreign manufacturing firms producing mainly for export benefit from a certain number of fiscal and financial incentives' (ILO, 1988). According to Dicken (2003), EPZs are, in effect, export enclaves within which special conditions apply:

- special investment incentives and trade concessions;
- exemption from certain kinds of legislation;
- provision of all physical infrastructure and services necessary for manufacturing activity – roads, power supplies, transportation facilities, low-cost buildings;
- waiving of the restrictions on foreign ownership, allowing 100 per cent ownership of export-processing ventures.

Around 90 per cent of all EPZs in developing countries are located in Latin America, the Caribbean, Mexico and Asia. Although EPZs may vary considerably in size, all tend to concentrate in the production of textiles and the assembly of electronics and employ predominantly a young, unskilled or semi-skilled, female, labour force (ibid.). Ahmadu (1998) identifies the following features commonly associated with EPZs:

- Governments hosting EPZs are often not signatories to international labour conventions, and transgression of minimum labour standards is apparent in the zones. Employment conditions are characterized by low pay, little job security, poor health and safety conditions, very intensive work, long shifts including night work, and high labour turnover. Frequently the right to strike and unionize is prohibited.

■ EPZs tend to be located in urban areas near established air or sea routes. However, they are frequently isolated from the local economy and therefore depend on migrant labour to satisfy intensive labour requirements.

■ The preference to employ young, unskilled and unmarried females is associated with their preparedness to accept lower rates of pay than men, and the absence of alternative employment. Employers may believe that the 'naturally endowed' characteristics of women, such as better eyesight, agility and nimble fingers, qualify them for required semi-skilled activity.

A critical question impacting on the broader role of EPZs in catalysing economic progress in their host environments is the extent to which the zones establish forward or backward linkages with local suppliers, clients and customers – which facilitates transfer of knowledge and technology. Unfortunately, according to Ahmadu (1998), such linkages are not apparent for three main reasons. First, as the zones are primarily export-oriented, they tend to have minimal industrial, technological and commercial interaction with the host country economy. Second, there is a heavy reliance on imported, rather than local, inputs. Third, the aim is typically to produce high-technology products that are disembodied from the traditional skills of the indigenous labour force and pre-existing industrial experience and technical capacities.

The final section of this chapter is devoted to a country study of India, a vanguard emerging economy, which nevertheless is confronted with the need to reconcile past cultural and institutional traditions with rapid modernization and reform.

## India

### Population and demographics

With 1.8 billion inhabitants, India is the world's largest democracy and has the second-largest population. The literacy rate, defined as people over the age of 15 who are capable of reading and writing, is approximately 60 per cent (Budhwar and Saini, 2004). India has a young population, with 64 per cent of its people being between 15 and 64 years of age (Index Munid, 2005). Hindi is the national language, and is the primary tongue of 30 per cent of the population. English is also an official language and is important for industry and commerce. Fourteen other languages are recognized under the Indian constitution (Budhwar and Saini, 2004).

Eighty-three per cent of Indians are Hindu. Hinduism, however, is far from a homogenous religion. It consists of a multiplicity of creeds and faiths, which are further divided among many castes, sects and sub-sects. The caste system in Hindu society is hierarchical in nature and has a deep influence on people's lives. The other major religions represented in Indian society are Muslim (11 per cent), Christians (2 per cent), Sikhs (2 per cent), Buddhists, Jains and Parsis (ibid.).

## Culture

Referring to Hofstede's (1991) dimensions

### Power distance

With a PDI of 77, India ranks very high, culture is explored below. (in comparison to a world average PDI of 56.5). This indicates high inequality of power and wealth. Less powerful individuals accept that power is unequally distributed and expect superiors to lead (Khan-Panni and Swallow, 2003). There is a strong hierarchy in organizations and those in esteemed positions (e.g. teachers or managers) are highly respected. Although barriers between castes are shrinking and 'untouchability' was declared illegal in 1949, the caste system of Hinduism is largely accepted in India. Hindus are born into a caste and cannot change their status. Their position is thought to be the result of behaviour in former lives and is therefore accepted as fate. This affects the entire life of Indians, including their social status and profession.

### Uncertainty avoidance

India's lowest ranking dimension is uncertainty avoidance, which, at 40, compares to the world average of 65. This means that Indians are, in general, open to unstructured ideas and situations. However, Indians respect traditions, caste and heritage that determine their role in society (Khan-Panni and Swallow, 2003).

### Individualism

With an individualism index at 48, India is close to the world average. Collectivistic values are nevertheless highly important in Indian society and the extended family is sacrosanct. Privacy and solitude are not required to the extent that they are in individualistic countries. Establishing personal relations is an absolute necessity, especially in business (Khan-Panni and Swallow, 2003).

### Masculinity

India's masculinity index ranks at 56, which is slightly above the world average at 51 (ITIM). India's average ranking indicates that it may be transitioning between a patriarchal society and one that is more gender-neutral.

### Long-term orientation

India has a long-term orientation rank of 61, that is, higher than the world's average score of 48. Time is perceived very differently in India than in western cultures. Schedules and deadlines do not play as an important a role as relationships and trust (Khan-Panni and Swallow, 2003) (see Table 10.1).

**Table 10.1 Major Indian national cultural characteristics and management practices (Tayeb, 2005)**

| National culture |
| --- |
| ■ Collectivism, clannish, community conscious, large in-group includes extended family and friends |
| ■ Low concern for privacy |
| ■ Large power distance, obedience to seniors and respect for people in positions of power, all wisdom comes from elders |
| ■ Resourcefulness, hard work, tenacity, ability to cope with adversity |
| ■ Emotional dependence |
| ■ Rigid social stratification, caste system |
| ■ Acceptance of status quo, preference for conformity |
| ■ Disciplined, self-restraint, yet emotional and display emotions in public |
| ■ Honest, trustworthy, yet considerable corruption in public service |
| ■ Law-abiding but prepared to bend the rules for friends and relatives |
| ■ Ambitious and materialistic |
| ■ High rate of illiteracy, especially among lower caste people in rural areas |
| **HRM and other related values and practices** |
| ■ Entrepreneurial |
| ■ Preference for paternalistic and authoritarian leadership |
| ■ Prefer to work under supervision |
| ■ Contractual relations with the workplace, in-group does not include the workplace, low level of commitment to organizational interests and objectives |
| ■ Manual workers tend to be unskilled and uneducated |
| ■ Well-educated and highly skilled managers and high-ranking staff |
| ■ National and plant-based trade unions, confrontational industrial relations |
| ■ Pro-worker labour legislation |
| ■ Strong sense of responsibility |
| ■ Centralized decision making, little or no job autonomy for middle- or low-ranking staff and shop floor workers |
| ■ Low level of formalization and use of written instructions and rules and regulations especially at the shop floor, mainly because of workers' illiteracy |
| ■ Differentiated reward systems and control systems for white-collar and manual workers |

## Political background

India's political history has been characterized by corruption, war and civil unrest. Tensions in India centre on the disputed area of Kashmir, the religious warring between Hindus and Muslims, and political corruption and discontent culminating in the assassination of a number of prime ministers.

### Government

India claimed independence from British rule on 15 August 1947. British influence is still in evidence in India as the country is the largest English-speaking country in Asia and its government closely resembles the British Parliament. However, India maintains a federal form of government, with a president and vice-president, who are elected for five-year terms. The role of the President is largely ceremonial, with real governmental power being centred within the Council of Ministers, led by the Prime Minister. The Prime Minister is selected by a majority vote in Parliament.

India's Parliament is bicameral, comprising the Council of States and the Council of Ministers. The Council of States resides over seven territories that are further divided into 28 states. These states and territories elect 238 members to the Council of States, with a further 12 being selected 'in the name of' the President. Members of Council of States serve six-year terms, with one-third of members being elected every two years. The Council of Ministers consists of 545 members who serve five-year terms.

### 2004 elections

In May 2004, the Indian National Congress Party scored a surprise victory over the ruling Bharatiya Janata Party. The Indian National Congress was led by Sonia Ghandi, who was elected as Prime Minister yet declined the position on the grounds that her appointment would cause division. She offered the Prime Ministerial position to Dr Manhohan Singh, a highly respected economist and the former Finance Minister of India and, as a Sikh, the first non-Hindu Prime Minister. Singh is also recognized as the mastermind behind the economic plan in 1991 that helped India avoid financial crisis and achieve economic liberalization for the first time. Shortly after independence, the Indian Government established the Indian Institute of Personnel Management in Calcutta and the National Institute of Labour Management in Bombay. In the 1980s, the two organizations merged into the National Institute of Personnel Management (Budhwar and Saini, 2004).

## The Indian economy

In the early 1990s, following an economic crisis, the Indian economy was fundamentally restructured and liberalized. Despite significant economic growth in recent years, a quarter of the population still live below the poverty line, with the unemployment rate approaching 10 per cent. India has sought to provide a welcoming environment for FDI. Foreign investors can now employ foreign nationals in their domestic operations in India, as well as make financial investments in Indian companies. Advances in sectors such as telecommunications and finance, coupled with changes in industrial policy and tax structure, have catalysed economic growth and integration into the global economy. While economic liberalization has spurred competition between businesses, the country still confronts the task of replacing archaic technology and gaining active commitment of sections of the labour force to their organizations and their goals.

## Human resources

HRM is in a state of transition as traditional practices gradually give way to more westernized management forms and approaches.

## Recruitment

Recruitment practices vary between the deregulated private sector and the more legislated public sector. Common recruitment practices in private sector Indian firms have reflected collectivistic and high context orientations (Hall and Hall, 1990; Hofstede, 1991). Companies tend to promote management from within, and use internal advertisements and word of mouth to recruit new employees (Budhwar and Khatri, 2001). The public sector utilizes a more western system of recruitment. Public companies are legally required to advertise externally and to follow a formal recruitment procedure, including interviews and assessments (ibid.). India's outsourcing and skilled industries operate in a unique labour market environment. From the 1960s to the 1980s, India was confronted with a 'brain drain' as large numbers of educated Indians migrated to developed countries to find better jobs. As opportunities in skilled industries have multiplied in India, this trend has not only stopped, but reversed. Indians who have previously left the country are being lured back (ibid.). Even this return of skilled labour, however, has not been enough to quench demand in the outsourcing industry. Recruitment of skilled labour is increasingly based on attractive pay and benefits packages (Sender, 2000). However, a number of companies are turning to more creative solutions to fill skilled labour vacancies. Technovate, for example, is leading the industry in attracting call centre personnel from Europe. The company targets university students and recent graduates and offers them attractive rates of pay with benefits such as accommodation and time off for travel (Overdorf, 2005). Such employees are attractive to the company as they have the required educational and language skills, and the jobs are attractive to young people who are interested in travel.

## Training

Since the liberalization of the Indian economy in 1991, Indian firms have begun to appreciate the important role of training and development in gaining competitive advantage (Wagner, 1999). Indian training has traditionally focused on technical skills. While skills such as 'accent neutralization', industry and sales training and information technology (IT) skills remain significant, companies are seeing an increasing need to provide employees with soft skills such as communication, cross-cultural understanding and customer orientation (Holloway, 2005; Huff, 2005; Wagner, 1999).

Some of the most successful firms in India are using 'boot camps' to prepare their employees. For example, Progeon, a business process outsourcing firm, recruits highly educated employees (around 90 per cent of whom have a university degree), and then subjects them to rigorous training programmes. This includes six weeks of accent neutralization training for employees who will interact with customers over the phone (Huff, 2005). Thought Works, an IT company with locations worldwide, sends all new recruits to India for four months to participate in their training boot camp. This consists of three weeks in a classroom followed by 13 weeks working in project groups. The company developed this approach because customers in all regions, including India, were dissatisfied with the service provided by new graduates (Holloway, 2005).

While Indian firms recognize the need for employee training, many barriers prevent the Indian economy from procuring the workforce it desires. These barriers include financial constraints, lack of available programmes and classes, limited space in educational institutions and lack of Asian-based teaching materials (Budhwar and Khatri, 2001; Guyer, 2005; Montgomery, 2005). Moreover, training is lacking in general in the unorganized sector as well as in the rural areas (Bowonder and Boddu, 2005). Vocational training institutions are not producing a sufficient number of graduates each year. There are 4,000 training institutions in India, but they have a total capacity of only 750,000 students (Budhwar and Saini, 2004). Currently, the Indian government is working with the GTZ, the German assistance agency, to develop legislation that will speed vocational training. A modular approach to vocational training has resulted from this initiative, as well as a competence-based training system that will allow assessment and certification of trainees (ibid.).

The Indian government is also working to close the technology gap between rural and urban populations. Seventy per cent of Indians still live in rural villages, and, in the past, it has been difficult and costly to expand telecommunications networks to these communities (Narayanan et al., 2005). However, information and communications technology (ICT) platforms, using wireless technology, have significantly lessened the expense of providing digital infrastructure to rural India (Bowonder and Boddu, 2005). This infrastructure is being used in the form of Internet kiosks in rural communities and in improving traditional and agricultural technologies used in industries such as dairy farming and carpet weaving (ibid.).

### Pay and reward

Compensation philosophy in India varies according to the type of organization. Unionized and public sector firms tend to base pay on seniority and work experience while in the private sector, skills or competences of workers are afforded greater significance. Some firms are beginning to relate pay to performance, but this is not currently the norm (Budhwar and Khatri, 2001). The Indian economy is divided between employment in outsourced or offshored industry and the unorganized sector. In outsourced industry, skilled workers are in demand and wages are soaring. In the unorganized sector, however, jobs are scarce and wages are low. The unorganized sector comprises companies with fewer than ten employees and supplies 92 per cent of Indian jobs (Slater, 2004). The sector includes farmers, street vendors, truck drivers, traders and migrant labourers. As one-quarter of the population lives below the poverty line, and around 40 million people are unemployed, all paid employment is in demand. When Indian Railways advertised 2,700 vacancies recently, 600,000 applicants presented themselves and a riot ensued (ibid.).

As a result of India's history of high taxation rates, which are now lifted but whose legacy remains, employees receive an extensive array of perks that may total up to 50 per cent of their compensation package. Middle management perks include housing subsidies, transportation allowances, mobile phones, clothing allowances, company credit cards and paid trips abroad (ACN, 2003; Cox, 1996). Such perks were allowed free of tax for many years, but the government is gradually introducing taxation for these items. Indian companies use large performance bonuses to increase productivity and 'golden handcuffs' to enhance employee retention, that is, long-term loans whose repayment terms increase if the employee leaves the company (Cox, 1996).

### Severance

Since India liberated its economy in 1991, companies have rationalized their operations in order to remain competitive. For example, the Tata group, India's oldest conglomerate, reduced its workforce from 320,000 to 220,000 in the decade from 1993 to 2003 (Slater, 2004). Although legislation restricts employers' ability to lay off workers, in practice job security provisions are rarely enforced (Budhwar and Khatri, 2001).

## Conclusion

India is a nation in a state of flux, as Hinduism gives way to western ideals, and traditional business practices are subject to modernization. Following economic liberalization, HRM is emerging as a strategically important element in business activity. Today, Indian companies are focusing on increasing productivity, targeting recruitment, lowering labour turnover, paying competitive wages and keeping staff levels lean. The issues and opportunities facing India include reducing poverty rates, increasing the capacities of universities and vocational educational institutions and expanding education in rural communities while the population continues to expand.

## Acknowledgement

Thanks to Carla Botteselle, Susanne Piringer, Charlie Rodrigues, Jerod Shellenberger and Simon Wolfmayr, students at the International Summer Programme, Copenhagen Business School, Summer 2005, for researching HRM in India.

### Activity

You are on the management team of a well-known (western) high street cosmetics store sourcing products in developing countries. Formulate an action plan to optimize 'backward' integration into the local economy and suggest reasons as to how this would benefit your organization.

## Summary

In this chapter a distinction has been drawn between emerging economies, which are integrating into global trading structures, such as China and India, and those which are at a lesser state of development, and are contributing to global trade almost entirely on the basis of extractive industries, including Latin American and African countries. It is argued that real progress in developing countries may only occur through inward investors establishing tangible 'backward' linkages into the local economy and society. HRM is in a state of flux in many developing countries, combining traditional and modernizing tendencies. Yet the maintenance of 'humanism' in the organizational and social fabric of developing economies perhaps provides a valuable reference and learning point for western corporations seeking to maximize human potential.

## Further reading

**Budhwar, P.W. and Debrah, Y.W.** (**eds**) (2001) *Human Resource Management in Developing Countries*, London and New York: Routledge.

In this edited book, contributors examine the influence of core national factors, including national culture, national institutions, the business environment and industrial sectors on the determination of HRM policies and practices. Countries under consideration include China, South Korea, Taiwan, India, Nepal, Pakistan, Iran, Saudi Arabia, Algeria, Nigeria, Ghana, Kenya and South Africa. The country-by-country chapters are prefaced by a framework for examining HRM in developing countries.

**Bird, F. and Herman, S.W.** (2004) *International Businesses and the Challenges of Poverty in the Developing World: Case Studies on Global Responsibilities and Practices*, Basingstoke: Palgrave Macmillan.

This essay-based book examines the practices of international companies operating in developing countries and, with reference to case studies, considers the extent to which these companies have aided economic growth and helped to reduce poverty.

**Hoogvelt, A.** (2001) *globalization and the Postcolonial World: The New Political Economy of Development*, Basingstoke: Palgrave Macmillan.

This book argues that globalization has rendered a 'new architecture' of core periphery relations in the world economy. Taking a historical view, the author argues that globalization has been primarily associated with the management of social exclusion. A regional analysis is undertaken of the globalization process, involving an examination of its effects in Sub-Saharan Africa, the Middle East, East Asia and Latin America. The volatility of global financial markets, the emergence of the new 'digital economy' and the resurgent global influence of the USA are prevalent themes.

## Useful websites

The following are the home sites of key global institutional actors in world trade:

The World Trade Organization (WTO)
www.wto.org
The International Monetary Fund (IMF)
www.imf.org
The United Nations Conference on Trade and Development (UNCTAD)
www.unctad.org
The International Labour Organization (ILO)
www.ilo.org

Other website
www.thesullivanfoundation.org/gsp/principles/gsp/default.asp

# References

**ACN** (2005) Perking up the compensation package, *Asian Chemical News*, 9(15): 389.

**Ahmadu, M.** (1998) Labour and employment conditions in export processing zones: a socio-legal analysis of South Asia and South Pacific, *Journal of South Pacific Law Working Papers*, 3(2).

**Arvedlund, E.** (2005) In Russia's boom, riches and rags, *New York Times*, 15 April.

**BBC Monitoring International Reports** (2005) Russian minister forecasts sharp rise in disposable incomes, 16 June.

**BBC Monitoring** (2005) Air traffic controllers' hunger strike widens in Southern Russia, Russian HTV, 10 June.

**Bird, F.** (2004) Ethical reflections on the challenges facing international businesses in developing areas, in F. Bird and S.W. Herman (eds) *International Businesses and the Challenges of Poverty in the Developing World: Case Studies on Global Responsibilities and Practices*, Basingstoke: Palgrave Macmillan.

**Blasi, J.R., Kroumova, M. and Kruse, D.** (1997) *Kremlin Capitalism: Privatizing the Russian Economy*, Ithaca and London: Cornell University Press.

**Bowonder, B. and Boddu, G.** (2005) Internet kiosks for rural communities: using ICT platforms for reducing the digital divide, *International Journal of Service Technology and Management*, 6(3): 1.

**Budhwar, P.S. and Khatri, N.** (2001) A comparative study of HR practices in Britain and India, *International Journal of Human Resource Management*, 12(5): 800–26.

**Budhwar, P.S. and Saini, D.S.** (2004) HRM in India, in Y.A. Debrah (ed.) *HRM in India*, London: Routledge.

**Cox, K.** (1996) Corporate India introduces the ol' compensation ploy, *World Business*, 2(6): 7.

**Dicken, P.** (2003) *Global Shift: Reshaping the Global Economic Map in the 21st Century*, London: Sage Publications.

*Financial Times* (1999) *Russia, 30 April*.

**Ghose, A.J.** (2003) *Jobs and Incomes in a Globalizing World*, Geneva: ILO.

**Guyer, L.** (2005) There's quantity, not always quality, in Chinese, and Indian, engineering ranks, *Automotive News*, 9 May.

**Hall, E.T. and Hall, M.R.** (1990) *Understanding Cultural Differences*, Yarmouth, MA: Intercultural Press.

**Hofstede, G.** (1991) *Cultures and Organizations: Software of the Mind*, London: McGraw-Hill.

**Hollinshead, G.** (2007) Pay in Russia, in M.E. Domsch and T. Likokhoven (eds) *Human Resource Management*, Farnham: Ashgate.

**Holloway, A.** (2005) Camp Bangalore, *Canadian Business*, 78(13): 69–72.

**Hoogvelt, A.** (2001) *Globalization and the Postcolonial World: The New Political Economy of Development* (2nd edn.), Basingstoke: Palgrave Macmillan.

**Huff, C.** (2005) Accent on training, *Workforce Management*, 84(3): 54.

**Index Munid** (2005) *Indian Age Structure*, www.indaz.com/index.html.

**International Labour Organization** (2002) *A Future Without Child Labour*, Geneva: ILO.

**International Labour Organization** (2005) What wage policy for Russia? Budapest Bulletin Newsletter, 2–94.

**International Labour Organization** (2008) *Economic and Social Effects of Multinational Enterprises in Export Processing Zones*, Geneva: ILO.

**Jackson, T.** (2002) *International HRM: A Cross-cultural Approach*, London: Sage Publications.

**Jackson, T.** (2004a) HRM in developing countries, in A.W. Harzing and J.V. Ruysseveldt (eds) *International Human Resource Management*, London: Sage Publications.

**Jackson, T.** (2004b) Management in action in developing countries, in H.W. Lane, M.L. Maznevski, M.E. Mendenhall and J. McNett (eds) *The Blackwell Handbook of Global Management: A Guide to Managing Complexity*, Malden MA, Oxford and Victoria: Blackwell.

**Kanungo, R.N. and Jaeger, A.M.** (1990) Introduction: the need for indigenous management in developing countries, in A.M. Jaeger and R.N. Kanungo (eds) *Management in Developing Countries*, London: Routledge.

**Kennedy, P** (1996) The global gales ahead, *New Statesman/Society*, 3 May, pp. 28–29.

**Khan-Panni, P. and Swallow, D.** (2003) *Communicating Across Cultures*, Oxford: Oxford How to Books.

**Kim, A.** (1997) *Employment Practices in Russia*, St. Petersburg: Bisnis.

**Montgomery, D.B.** (2005) Asian management education: some twenty-first-century issues, *Journal of Public Policy*, 24(1): 150–154.

**Narayanan, A., Jain, A. and Bowonder, B.** (2005) Providing rural connectivity infrastructure: ICT diffusion through private sector participation, *International Journal of Services Technology and Management*, 6(3): 1.

**Overdorf, J.** (2005) Outsourcing jobs to ... Europeans?, *Business*, 6(1): 32.

**Punnett, B.J.** (2004) Introduction to management in developing countries, in H. Lane, M. Maznevski, M. Mendenhall and J. McNett (eds) *The Blackwell Handbook to Global Management: A Guide to Managing Complexity*, Oxford: Blackwell.

**Reich R.B.** (1991) *The Work of Nations, Preparing Ourselves for 21st Century Capitalism*, New York: Alfred A. Knopf.

**Rousseau, D.M.** (1996) *Psychological Contracts in Organizations: Understanding Written and Unwritten Agreements*, Newbury Park, CA: Sage Publications.

**Sender, H.** (2000) Soaring Indian tech salaries reflect the country's brain drain, *Wall Street Journal*, 25 July.

**Slater, J.** (2004) India, a job paradox; despite economic surge, many workers still lack steady pay, *Wall Street Journal* (*Eastern Edition*), 5 May.

**State Statistical Committee of Russia and CE Research** (2004) *Labour Costs Russia*, Moscow.

**Stiglitz, J.E.** (2002) *Globalization and its Discontents*, London: Penguin Books.

**Storey, J.** (1992) *Developments in the Management of Human Resources*, Oxford: Blackwell.

**Tayeb, M.** (2005) *International Human Resource Management: A Multinational Company Perspective*, Oxford: Oxford University Press.

**Tyuryukanova, E.** (2005) *Forced Labour in the Russian Federation Today*, Geneva: ILD.

**United Nations Conference on Trade and Development** (**UNCTAD**) (2008) *World Investment Report: Transnational Corporations and the Infrastructure Challenge*, New York and Geneva, United Nations.

**Verbeke, A.** (2009) *International Business Strategy*, Cambridge: Cambridge University Press.

**Volkov, V. and Denenberg, J.** (2005) *Wealth and Poverty in Modern Russia*, World Socialist Web.

**Wagner, S.** (1999) Oh Calcutta, *Training and Development*, 53(8): 57.

**White, S.** (2000) *Russia's New Politics: The Management of a Postcommunist Society*, Cambridge: Cambridge University Press.

**World Bank** (2003) *World Development Indicators*, Washington, DC: World Bank.

**World Bank** (2004) *World Development Indicators*, Washington, DC: World Bank.

# CHAPTER

# 11

# Conclusion and summary

## Introduction

This chapter aims to provide the reader with a brief recap of the issues covered within the text, to enable a review of the concepts that have been discussed. It also attempts to address two important questions central to the study and practice of international human resource management (IHRM), namely:

- *What is the connection between IHRM and economic performance?*
- *Are business and human resource systems converging across global regions?*

## Summary of key themes

To conclude this text, a summary of key themes is first provided:

- The disciplinary area of IHRM remains at a formative stage of development, although trends in the internationalization of business, and life in general, are bringing the complex issues associated with managing and working across borders to the fore. While IHRM covers similar functional areas to more standard and domestic formulations of HRM, including HR planning, recruitment, training, pay, performance management, employment relations and staff severance, in the context of the multinational operation, these functions become complicated by factors such as the need to manage the strategic relationship between home and host operations and the associated cross-cultural interactions of actors. In Chapter 1, a key distinction was drawn between *international* HRM, which refers to strategic considerations in formulating HR and employment policies affecting the staffing of the MNCs (multinational companies) and *comparative* HRM, which relates to the investigation of embedded contexts, policies and practices in specific national and regional domains. Both trajectories of study have been pursued, a major constituent element of the international dimension relating to international staffing and expatriation, while comparative analysis comprised a review of various national and regional systems of HRM.
- In order to comprehend diversity in observed international practice in HRM, Chapter 2 explored the significance of institutional 'hardware' and cultural 'software'. While various

institutional forms and interrelationships are evident across nations, a broad distinction was drawn between *neo-liberal* and *neo-corporatist* institutional arrangements. In the former, the state purports to abstain from economic regulation, preferring to allow market forces to flow in an unmitigated fashion. In those countries most complying with neo-liberal economic orthodoxy (notably, the USA, Canada, Australia, New Zealand, the UK and arguably a number of eastern European countries), management retains a high degree of autonomy in managing HR, experiencing few external constraints on its ability to recruit, pay, train, discharge staff, and so on, according to its own strategic imperatives. On the other hand, in the *neo-corporatist* institutional milieu, the state demonstrates a more heavily interventionist role in economic management, circumscribing through regulation and legislation managerial latitude in respect of staff engagement, severance and other HR policies. Cultural theories seek to explain, typically through stereotyping predispositions and mindsets across nations, how human value systems serve to mould diverse organizational typologies. Cultural theory can therefore be a powerful tool in helping to understand the complications of international communication and team working.

- In Chapter 3, we find that MNCs represent critical organizational actors in the field of IHRM, and a critical strategic dilemma they face is whether to centralize decision-making authority in the head office/home country (ethnocentricity) or to devolve some or all functional activities to subsidiaries (polycentricity). Running operations from the centre provides advantages of coordination and control, yet forgoes the benefits of capitalizing on local knowledge and responding flexibly to local market and other circumstances. Where an ethnocentric orientation is adopted, an emphasis is likely to be placed on expatriation as a key staffing mechanism – expatriates embodying corporate authority and values in overseas locations. Where MNCs devolve managerial responsibilities to subsidiaries, IHRM policies and decisions become more complex as international and local managers need to engage in international team working, and will exchange respective categories of international and locally-based knowledge. Consequently, where strategic devolution occurs, the MNC is confronted with the challenges of reconciling or harmonizing international HR policies on reward, training, performance management, and so on, as well as resolving the complexities of inter-cultural communication. Typically, MNCs are seeking to reap the strategic benefits of centralized control and coordination through *integration*, most notably international economies of scale, while simultaneously engendering strategic *differentiation*, or semi-autonomous responsiveness of subsidiaries to local markets and productive environments.

- The expatriation process may be depicted as a cycle, as elaborated in Chapters 4 and 5, commencing with the recruitment and training of international assignees, and concluding with the return of the expatriate and his or her spouse and family to the home base. The possibility of expatriate failure, that is, premature return of international assignees due to failure to adjust to the new working and living environment, is being taken seriously by many organizations, due to the high financial and personal costs of managerial underperformance overseas. Consequently, increasing attention is being devoted by companies to training expatriates in 'softer' cross-cultural skills as well as 'harder' technical skills to facilitate higher levels of personal adjustment to the host country, although in many cases such training may still be regarded as minimal. The management of expatriation demands sensitive and sophisticated administration of pay and reward packages, as home and host country relativities may be subject to direct comparison through information-sharing across borders and international team working. Similarly, effective management by companies of the performance of international assignees demands the 'raising of international antennae' to appreciate, and be sensitive towards, unforeseen and perhaps unfamiliar challenges facing compatriots in distant locales.

■ The characteristics of employment relations actors and institutions vary considerably across international regions, as exemplified by the comparative analysis of the EU, the USA and Japan in Chapter 6. Thus, variations are apparent in trade union membership, structures and objectives, in the significance and functions of employers' associations, and in systems of collective bargaining and pay determination. Of particular significance to MNCs are varying international structures and systems in employee participation and involvement. As Chapters 6 and 8 demonstrate, in much of continental Europe, a common statutory obligation is for companies to establish works councils. Such bodies seek to engender a spirit of social partnership at the workplace and typically oblige management to gain employee acquiescence to important decisions affecting their employment. By way of contrast, in the USA, initiatives to involve employees in corporate decision making tend to be employer-led, and designed to obtain 'buy in' to strategic initiatives formulated by management in order to gain competitive advantage. Taking, therefore, the example of a US corporation operating in Europe, significant employment relations issues to be resolved are likely to relate to trade union recognition, employers' association membership, commitment to collective bargaining over pay and other conditions, and purpose and form of employee involvement and participation. Also of concern to MNCs operating across national borders, and particularly in developing countries, are the international codes of labour standards recommended by the International Labour Organization (ILO) and Organization for Economic Co-operation and Development (OECD). Although the resolutions of these organizations do not have mandatory force, they may influence the actions of international companies that are conscious of their corporate social responsibilities.

■ In Chapter 7, we turned to a regional study of the USA and Mexico. The USA may be regarded as the global exemplar of 'neo-liberal' ideology (although this may now be questioned in the light of governmental takeovers of major financial concerns in the context of the economic downturn in 2008/2009) and, in general, HR policies reflect the doctrine of 'freedom to manage'. Consequently, in the context of a relatively flexible and mobile labour market, employers have a high degree of discretion concerning recruitment, reward, training and severance of staff. The USA has a predominance of non-union enterprises, and consequently schemes for employee involvement and communication tend to be direct between management and employees (and not via third parties). The 'United States of Mexico' has now become a major trading partner of the USA and Canada under the auspices of the North American Free Trade Agreement (NAFTA), and it has a ruptured industrial complexion, possessing economic strength and buoyancy in the northern region, while displaying the features of a developing economy in the centre and south. There has been considerable concern about low pay and working conditions in Mexican factories as international companies have relocated productive facilities to take advantage of low-cost and flexible labour as well as tax incentives. However, recent evidence has suggested that working conditions have improved with general economic advancement. HRM in Mexico demonstrates a 'Latin' orientation, with an emphasis being placed on strong personal relations building on family traditions.

■ In Chapter 8, the distinctive features of 'HRM in Europe' were considered, with particular reference to the 'Rhineland' model that embodies the notion of 'social partnership'. Although considerable variations exist in the practice of HRM and employment relations across Europe, and established 'paradigms' in employment are subject to challenge and change, the Rhineland model exemplifies European traditions through placing an emphasis on support for trade union and other forms of employee representation, a sense of managerial responsibility towards employees and involvement of statutory bodies (both national and EU-wide) and employment regulation. In this chapter we also considered the particular HR challenges confronting managers in the post-socialist transitional economies as they seek to respond to international market forces. There is evidence that western-inspired HR practices are now being transposed to the East, while some eastern European countries are now providing international benchmarks for cost-effectiveness and labour flexibility.

■ Chapter 9 placed a focus on the leading East Asian economies of Japan and China. While the former might be characterized as a 'capitalist market economy' and the latter a 'socialist market economy', each has been powerfully moulded by Confucian teachings, epitomized in principles of family, harmony, hierarchy and reciprocation. Japanese economy and employment has been subject to modernization and westernization in recent years, tending to moderate principles of security, consensus and organizational loyalty in the drive towards performance orientation as manifested in individualized pay packages and increased staff mobility between enterprises. As China emerges to become a global economic 'super-power', it too is engaging in 'westernization' of employment and HR policies following its extended transition from a planned to a market economy. Currently, China appears to be simultaneously following 'high' and 'low' roads to reform, continuing to capitalize on cheap labour in the manufacture of toys, clothes and so on, while increasingly employing a reservoir of knowledge workers in the provision of highly engineered products and quality services.

■ Chapter 10 examined HRM issues in developing countries. While leading 'emerging' economies are integrating into global economic structures, for example China and India, others are locked into a spiral of poverty and marginalization. Where international companies have invested in or set up sites in developing economies, the extent of their real integration into local economies remains open to question for many. In such countries, hybridized forms and paradigms of HRM are emerging, combining western, modernizing tendencies with indigenous orientations towards humanism and the importance of community.

We now turn to two key issues emerging from the study of IHRM.

## What is the connection between IHRM and economic performance?

In Chapter 1, a number of questions were raised relating to the connection between various types of HR policy (e.g. relating to employment security, job flexibility, training provision, performance-related pay, trade unionism) and corporate and national performance. While these issues have been addressed directly or implicitly throughout the text, they essentially refer to the notion of regulation considered in Chapter 2. More specifically, much current economic and management orthodoxy is predicated on the *neo-liberal* assertion that excessive regulation to protect and upgrade the position of labour in enterprises is counterproductive as it places a 'burden on business', stifling the leanness of its response to competitive product markets. Accordingly, training will be regarded as an 'overhead' to be trimmed in difficult economic circumstances, employees may be 'hired and fired' according to the exigencies of the marketplace, and collectivistic mobilization of employees, through trade unionism, to enhance pay and other conditions, may be viewed as a dysfunctional incursion into management's ability to control labour costs. The USA may be regarded as the global exemplar of neo-liberalism, while Germanic and Scandinavian countries continue to demonstrate relatively high degrees of regulation/legislation into employment. In these countries, labour costs tend to be relatively high, considerable investment is made in training, and trade unions enjoy a pivotal position in economic management. If managerial 'recipe books' based on neo-liberal principles were to have true predictive value, the reader may expect the US economy to outperform systematically its more highly regulated rivals, but scrutiny of national economic performance, in reality, presents a more complex and ambiguous picture.

Despite the recent slowdown in economic performance, Denmark and other Nordic countries provide solid examples of how relatively regulated economies, based on concepts of social partnership, may match or even outperform their more deregulated rivals. In the latest Global Competitiveness Report (2008–2009), produced by the World Economic Forum, the following rankings are provided of national economic competitiveness:

1  USA
2  Switzerland
3  Denmark
4  Sweden
5  Singapore
6  Finland
7  Germany
8  Netherlands
9  Japan
10  Canada

In seeking to explain what may be regarded as a remarkable performance by Denmark, it is instructive to cite Lindholm (2006: 27), as follows:

> " the in-built security that exists in Danish society resulting from – seen from an international perspective – a generous, tax-financed social security net does not make the people any less motivated or willing to take risks. On the contrary, the combination of broadly qualified skills and a finely meshed safety net appears to encourage more people to take the risk.
>
> The same sense of security is built into the Danish labour market – the so-called flexicurity model – which combines employment flexibility with a high degree of financial security. The Danes have entered into a collective contract in a negotiation-based rather than legislation-based labour market, where employers can be easily hired and fired by employers in return for high unemployment benefits and upgrading of qualifications, financed by the employees themselves, the employers and the state. This provides for an

amazingly adaptable workforce that is used to changing jobs and adjusting to changing requirements and opportunities. It is a model that the OECD calls 'the best in the world' and one that is worth copying.

**"**

## Are business and HR systems converging across global regions?

As talk of the 'global village' abounds, it is tempting to assume that manifestations of HRM, as with other business practices, are destined to become homogenous across developed and developing regions. Convergence may be thought to be spurred by factors such as MNCs, the Internet, the consolidation of trade blocs and international labour mobility. Indeed, the convergence thesis has been postulated for some time; an influential work by Kerr et al. (1960) posits that the process of industrialization would be all-embracing and would lead to the replication of organizational forms and structures at a global level. According to these authors, as technology expands and reproduces, so the world becomes divided into those who are industrialized and those who are becoming so. Indeed, it is asserted that technology creates a 'logic of industrialization' and that the drive for efficiency ensures that the most effective ways of dealing with problems of efficient production, including the management of people, would be adopted worldwide. Convergence theory also holds that, when organizations reach a certain size in terms of the number of employees, it becomes necessary to introduce functional specialisms. Controlling these functions leads to replication of formalized systems, involving rules, norms, regulations and hierarchies.

In an extensive research project covering nine European automobile manufacturing engine plants, belonging to four different companies, and located in four different countries, Mueller (1992) found that moves towards broadening the jobs of operatives and multi-skilling had occurred to a greater or lesser extent in all companies. Explanations for these developments included the international system of production technology, product development and manufacturing operations to meet competitive pressures, as well as Japanese principles of production and organization. This author also asserts that the social action programme instigated by the European Commission may have exerted some common legalistic and collectively agreed terms across plants. Thus, the following causes of convergence are suggested:

- internationalization of product markets;
- technological restraints;
- the increasingly competitive industry environment;
- the examples set by Japanese transplant operations in the USA and the UK;
- the European action programme and European legislation.

Indeed, movements towards convergence in observed corporate practice may be viewed against a broader backcloth of changes in the 'production paradigm' over the past 50 years or so, these changes arguably impacting on the logic of production at a global level. These paradigms relate to dominant principles of organization and production in relation to the nature of surrounding product markets. 'Fordism' equates division of labour, standardization of production, and collective labour relations with the existence of mass markets, while 'post-Fordism' connects the development of 'niche' and volatile markets with flexibility in the design of work (Hollinshead and Leat, 1995). Ferner and Hyman (1992) locate Fordist and post-Fordist typologies in a broader political/economic and historical context by providing the following elaborations:

*Fordism (thought to prevail in the middle decades of the twentieth century)*

- Based on mass production with largely semi-skilled labour.
- Standardized products for price-competitive mass markets.
- Macro-level state economic regulation, public welfare provision, standardization of employment relations.
- Associated growth in public services, legitimization of trade unionism and spread of collective bargaining.

*Post-Fordism*

- Quality – competitive products.
- Shifting and differentiated markets.
- Greater need for qualified labour.
- Less state intervention in the labour market.
- Greater personal or corporate responsibility for welfare provision.
- A more flexible and differentiated management of employment relations.

In Chapter 2, we addressed the significance of Marxist and socialist perspectives. Critical views on the labour process may be regarded as having universalistic appeal in explaining the endemic struggle between capital and labour; the owners of the means of production profiting and competing by exploiting labour and extracting its surplus value, that is, paying wages that are lower than the value of the goods. For Marxists, management–labour relationships throughout the world will reflect the phase of capitalism through which economies are passing, and convergence will be apparent in the experience of work across nations due to the international reproduction of the dominant form of capitalist accumulation.

In a more recent departure in convergence theory, the 'market forces model' (Brewster et al., 2004) contends that 'neo-liberal' developments in the USA represent a precursor of universal developments. Taking a retrospective view of the comparative section of this text, the pervasiveness and potency of neo-liberal forces should clearly not be underestimated at a global level. As we have seen, reforms in developing countries have been guided by the prescriptions of the 'Washington Consensus'. Japan's system of *keiretsu*, or network organization, has become diluted in favour of a more 'shareholder-oriented' model, and debate between the 'regulationists' and 'deregulationists' in Europe continues to be heated, although unequivocal moves have been witnessed towards 'flexibility'.

Our study has also demonstrated, however, the strength of the 'status quo' in various national and regional business system settings. So, for example, the human bonds established by ubuntu (people are people through other people) has remained intact in Africa in the face of the inward investment activities of international firms. In Russia and central and eastern Europe, some nostalgia remains harboured for the security and comfort offered by former communist regimes. And in China, moves towards market reform continue to be guided by protective yet authoritarian state machinery. Indeed, at a time of global economic crisis, it would seem that guiding ideologies are 'up for grabs' as the USA, the global exemplar of 'neo-liberalism', pumps billions of dollars from the coffers of the state into the faltering financial and automobile manufacturing sectors.

As a counter, then, to convergence perspectives, cultural and institutional theorists (referred to in Chapter 2) argue that business and organizational forms are embedded in particular social contexts. Organizational change is therefore constrained by a range of institutional pressures, including the state, regulatory structures and public opinion (DiMaggio and Powell, 1983; Hollingsworth and Boyer, 1997; Meyer and Scott, 1983; Oliver, 1991). Accordingly, it is suggested that global or convergent stimuli for change will be impeded by 'path-dependent' institutional constraints, which are conditioned by the 'pull' of history. As Brewster et. al. (2004) argue, national and regional contexts are slow to change as they derive from deep-seated beliefs and because significant redistributions of power are involved.

Organizational and institutional change may therefore be depicted in essentially dualistic terms, juxtaposing endogenous and exogenous factors of influence (Hollinshead and Maclean, 2007). Transition in both developed and developing societies may therefore be characterized as a form of institutional and cultural transplantation from abroad, mingling 'with the soil of the prevailing informal constraints of human behaviour and thought' (Zweynert and Goldschmidt, 2005: 2). In this context, the process of globalization is likely to spawn various 'hybridized' models of HRM as universalized concepts and policies, particularly as channelled through MNCs and other conduits, merge with indigenous customs and practices.

In conclusion, therefore, it may be argued that, notwithstanding the terminological distinction drawn between 'international' and 'comparative' HRM adopted at the outset of this text, the social reality of international employment practices is blurred, indefinite and dynamic. The new global environment for doing business is indeed complex and ambiguous, and may be visualized as a mosaic displaying organizational and managerial colourations from international and local sources.

## Further reading

Scholarly investigation into many of the comparative and international issues raised in this text can be pursued in leading journals, notably the *International Journal of Human Resource Management*, published by Routledge, and the *Human Resource Management Journal*, published by Wiley-Blackwell.

## References

**Brewster, C., Mayrhofer, W. and Morley, M.** (2004) *Human Resource Management in Europe: Evidence of Convergence?*, Oxford: Butterworth-Heinemann.

**DiMaggio, P.J. and Powell, W.W.** (1983) The iron cage revisited: institutional isomorphism and collective rationality in organizational fields, *American Sociological Review*, 48: 147–160.

**Ferner, A. and Hyman, R.** (1992) *Industrial Relations in the New Europe*, Oxford: Blackwell.

**Hollingsworth, J.R. and Boyer, R.** (1997) Co-ordination of economic actors and social systems of production, in J.R. Hollingsworth and R. Boyer (eds) *Contemporary Capitalism*, Cambridge: Cambridge University Press.

**Hollinshead, G. and Leat, M.** (1995) *Human Resource Management: An International and Comparative Perspective*, London: Pitman Publishing.

**Hollinshead, G. and Maclean, M.** (2007) Transition and organizational dissonance in Serbia, *Human Relations*, 60(10): 1551–1574.

**Kerr, C., Dunlop, J.T., Harbison, F.H. and Myers, C.A.** (1960) *Industrialisation and Industrial Man*, Cambridge, MA: Harvard University Press.

**Lindholm, M.R.** (2006) The Danish model, in C. MacCarthy and W. Schmidt (eds) *Denmark Limited: Global by Design*, Copenhagen: Gads-Forlag.

**Meyer, J. and Scott, W.** (1983) *Organizational Environments: Ritual and Reality*, Beverly Hills, CA: Sage Publications.

**Mueller, F.** (1992) Flexible working practices in engine plants: evidence from the European automobile industry, *Industrial Relations Journal*, 23(3): 191–204.

**Oliver, C.** (1991) Strategic responses to institutional processes, *Academy of Management Review*, 16(1): 145–179.

**World Economic Forum** (2008–2009) Global Competitiveness Report, www.weforum.org/en/initiatives.gcp.

**Zweynert, J. and Goldschmidt, N.** (2005) The two transitions in central and eastern Europe and the relation between path dependent and politically implemented institutional change, HWSA discussion paper, March.

# Index